1997
YEARBOOK OF
ASTRONOMY

1997 YEARBOOK of ASTRONOMY

edited by
Patrick Moore

MACMILLAN

First published 1996 by Macmillan

an imprint of Macmillan Publishers Limited
25 Eccleston Place, London SW1W 9NF
and Basingstoke

Associated companies throughout the world

ISBN 0 333 65892 2

9 8 7 6 5 4 3 2 1

A CIP catalogue record for this book is available from
the British Library.

Photoset by Rowland Phototypesetting Limited
Bury St Edmunds, Suffolk
Printed and bound in Great Britain by
Mackays of Chatham plc, Chatham, Kent

Contents

Editor's Foreword

The latest *Yearbook* follows the traditional pattern; as usual, Gordon Taylor has provided the data for the monthly charts, and we have articles both from our regular contributors, notably Drs Paul Murdin and Ron Maddison, and from some very welcome newcomers.

Comets have been very much to the fore! In the *1996 Yearbook* we could do no more than give a summary of the collision between Comet Shoemaker–Levy 9 and Jupiter; in the current issue Dr Steven Miller, one of the principal investigators, gives us a detailed account. Once again we have a 'stop press' item. Comet Hyakutake became brilliant in April, just as this *Yearbook* had to go to press, and the only course was to provide an introduction to it. Yet another comet, Hale–Bopp, is on the way, and should be conspicuous during the early part of 1997.

PATRICK MOORE
Selsey, April 1996

Preface

New readers will find that all the information in this *Yearbook* is given in diagrammatic or descriptive form; the positions of the planets may easily be found from the specially designed star charts, while the monthly notes describe the movements of the planets and give details of other astronomical phenomena visible in both the northern and southern hemispheres. Two sets of star charts are provided. The **Northern Charts** (pp. 14 to 39) are designed for use at latitude 52°N, but may be used without alteration throughout the British Isles, and (except in the case of eclipses and occultations) in other countries of similar northerly latitude. The **Southern Charts** (pp. 40 to 65) are drawn for latitude 35°S, and are suitable for use in South Africa, Australia and New Zealand, and other locations in approximately the same southerly latitude. The reader who needs more detailed information will find *Norton's Star Atlas* an invaluable guide, while more precise positions of the planets and their satellites, together with predictions of occultations, meteor showers and periodic comets, may be found in the *Handbook* of the British Astronomical Association. Readers will also find details of forthcoming events given in the American *Sky & Telescope*.

Important Note
The times given on the star charts and in the Monthly Notes are generally given as local times, using the 24-hour clock, the day beginning at midnight. All the dates, and the times of a few events (e.g. eclipses), are given in Greenwich Mean Time (GMT), which is related to local time by the formula

Local Mean Time = GMT − west longitude

In practice, small differences in longitude are ignored, and the observer will use local clock time, which will be the appropriate Standard (or Zone) Time. As the formula indicates, places in west longitude will have a Standard Time slow on GMT, while places in east longitude will have a Standard Time fast on GMT. As examples we have:

Standard Time in

New Zealand	GMT	+	12 hours
Victoria; NSW	GMT	+	10 hours
Western Australia	GMT	+	8 hours
South Africa	GMT	+	2 hours
British Isles	GMT		
Eastern ST	GMT	−	5 hours
Central ST	GMT	−	6 hours, etc.

If Summer Time is in use, the clocks will have been advanced by one hour, and this hour must be subtracted from the clock time to give Standard Time.

In Great Britain and Northern Ireland, Summer Time will be in force in 1997 from March 30 until October 26.

Notes on the Star Charts

The stars, together with the Sun, Moon and planets, seem to be set on the surface of the celestial sphere, which appears to rotate about the Earth from east to west. Since it is impossible to represent a curved surface accurately on a plane, any kind of star map is bound to contain some form of distortion. But it is well known that the eye can endure some kinds of distortion better than others, and it is particularly true that the eye is most sensitive to deviations from the vertical and horizontal. For this reason the star charts given in this volume have been designed to give a true representation of vertical and horizontal lines, whatever may be the resulting distortion in the shape of a constellation figure. It will be found that the amount of distortion is, in general, quite small, and is only obvious in the case of large constellations such as Leo and Pegasus, when these appear at the top of a chart and so are elongated sideways.

The charts show all stars down to the fourth magnitude, together with a number of fainter stars which are necessary to define the shapes of constellations. There is no standard system for representing the outlines of the constellations, and triangles and other simple figures have been used to give outlines which are easy to follow with the naked eye. The names of the constellations are given, together with the proper names of the brighter stars. The apparent magnitudes of the stars are indicated roughly by using four different sizes of dots, the larger dots representing the brighter stars.

The two sets of star charts are similar in design. At each opening there is a group of four charts which give a complete coverage of the sky up to an altitude of 62½°; there are twelve such groups to cover the entire year. In the **Northern Charts** (for 52°N) the upper two charts show the southern sky, south being at the centre and east on the left. The coverage is from 10° north of east (top left) to 10° north of west (top right). The two lower charts show the northern sky from 10° south of west (lower left) to 10° south of east (lower right). There is thus an overlap east and west.

Conversely, in the **Southern Charts** (for 35°S) the upper two charts show the northern sky, with north at the centre and east on the right. The two lower charts show the southern sky, with south at the centre and east on the left. The coverage and overlap is the same on both sets of charts.

Because the sidereal day is shorter than the solar day, the stars appear to rise and set about four minutes earlier each day, and this amounts to two hours in a month. Hence the twelve groups of charts in each set are sufficient to give the appearance of the sky throughout the day at intervals of two hours, or at the same time of night at monthly intervals throughout the year. The actual range of dates and times when the stars on the charts are visible is indicated at the top of each page. Each group is numbered in bold type, and the number to be used for any given month and time may be found from the following table:

Local Time	18ʰ	20ʰ	22ʰ	0ʰ	2ʰ	4ʰ	6ʰ
January	11	12	1	2	3	4	5
February	12	1	2	3	4	5	6
March	1	2	3	4	5	6	7
April	2	3	4	5	6	7	8
May	3	4	5	6	7	8	9
June	4	5	6	7	8	9	10
July	5	6	7	8	9	10	11
August	6	7	8	9	10	11	12
September	7	8	9	10	11	12	1
October	8	9	10	11	12	1	2
November	9	10	11	12	1	2	3
December	10	11	12	1	2	3	4

The charts are drawn to scale, the horizontal measurements, marked at every 10°, giving the azimuths (or true bearings) measured from the north round through east (90°), south (180°) and west (270°). The vertical measurements, similarly marked, give the altitudes of the stars up to 62½°. Estimates of altitude and azimuth made from these charts will necessarily be mere approximations, since no observer will be exactly at the particular latitude, or at the stated time, but they will serve for the identification of stars and planets.

The ecliptic is drawn as a broken line on which longitude is marked every 10°; the positions of the planets are then easily found by reference to the table on p. 71. It will be noticed that on the Southern Charts the **ecliptic** may reach an altitude in excess of 62½°

on star charts 5 to 9. The continuations of the broken line will be found on the charts of overhead stars.

There is a curious illusion that stars at an altitude of 60° or more are actually overhead, and beginners may often feel that they are leaning over backwards in trying to see them. These overhead stars are given separately on the pages immediately following the main star charts. The entire year is covered at one opening, each of the four maps showing the overhead stars at times which correspond to those for three of the main star charts. The position of the zenith is indicated by a cross, and this cross marks the centre of a circle which is 35° from the zenith; there is thus a small overlap with the main charts.

The broken line leading from the north (on the Northern Charts) or from the south (on the Southern Charts) is numbered to indicate the corresponding main chart. Thus on p. 38 the N–S line numbered 6 is to be regarded as an extension of the centre (south) line of chart 6 on pp. 24 and 25, and at the top of these pages are printed the dates and times which are appropriate. Similarly, on p. 65, the S–N line numbered 10 connects with the north line of the upper charts on pp. 58 and 59.

The overhead stars are plotted as maps on a conical projection, and the scale is rather smaller than that of the main charts.

1L

October 6 at 5ʰ	October 21 at 4ʰ
November 6 at 3ʰ	November 21 at 2ʰ
December 6 at 1ʰ	December 21 at midnight
January 6 at 23ʰ	January 21 at 22ʰ
February 6 at 21ʰ	February 21 at 20ʰ

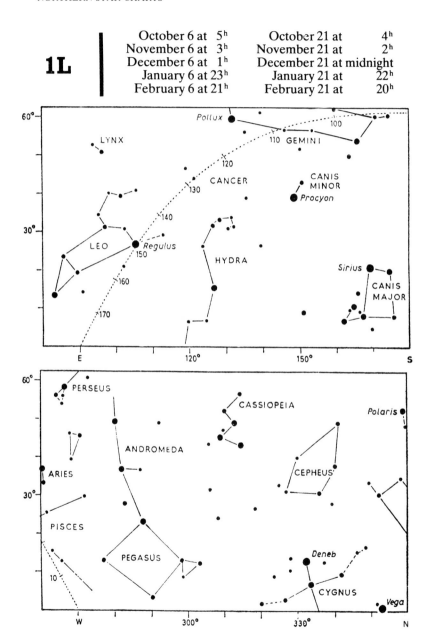

October 6 at 5^h October 21 at 4^h
November 6 at 3^h November 21 at 2^h
December 6 at 1^h December 21 at midnight
January 6 at 23^h January 21 at 22^h
February 6 at 21^h February 21 at 20^h

1R

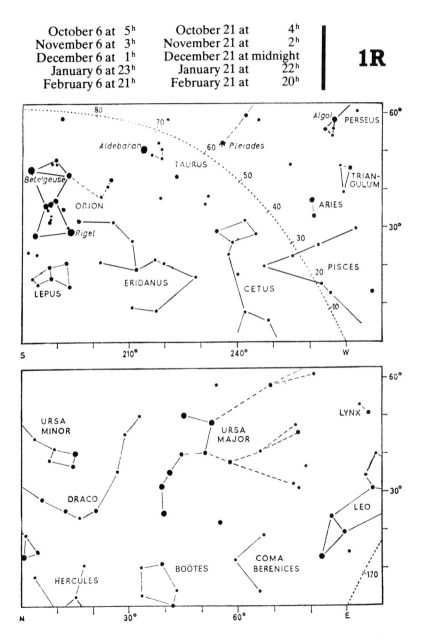

2L

November 6 at 5ʰ	November 21 at 4ʰ
December 6 at 3ʰ	December 21 at 2ʰ
January 6 at 1ʰ	January 21 at midnight
February 6 at 23ʰ	February 21 at 22ʰ
March 6 at 21ʰ	March 21 at 20ʰ

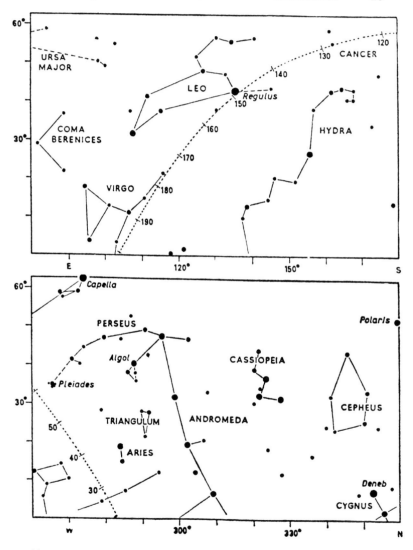

November 6 at 5^h   November 21 at   4^h
December 6 at 3^h   December 21 at   2^h
January 6 at   1^h   January 21 at midnight
February 6 at 23^h February 21 at   22^h
March 6 at   21^h March 21 at   20^h

2R

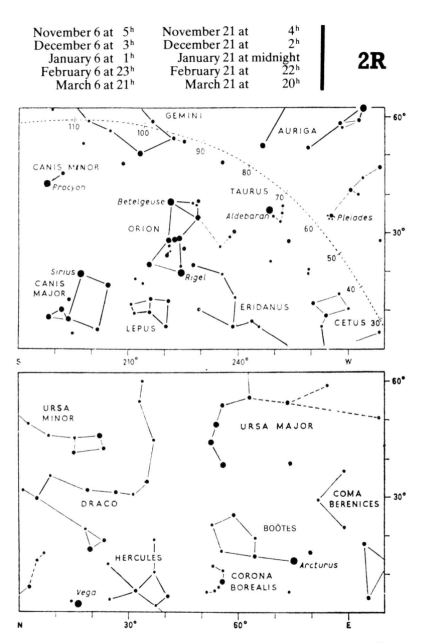

3L

December 6 at 5^h	December 21 at 4^h
January 6 at 3^h	January 21 at 2^h
February 6 at 1^h	February 21 at midnight
March 6 at 23^h	March 21 at 22^h
April 6 at 21^h	April 21 at 20^h

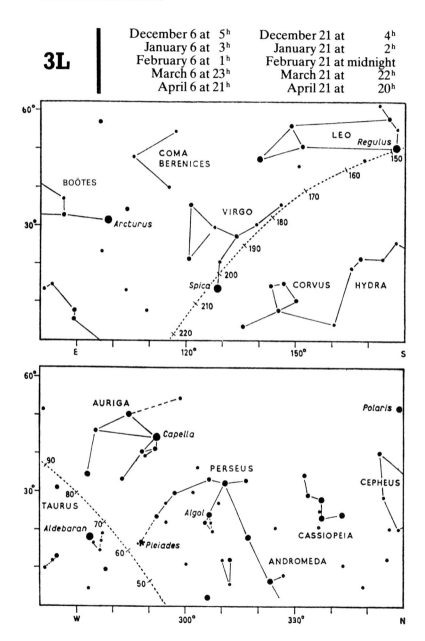

December 6 at 5ʰ	December 21 at 4ʰ
January 6 at 3ʰ	January 21 at 2ʰ
February 6 at 1ʰ	February 21 at midnight
March 6 at 23ʰ	March 21 at 22ʰ
April 6 at 21ʰ	April 21 at 20ʰ

3R

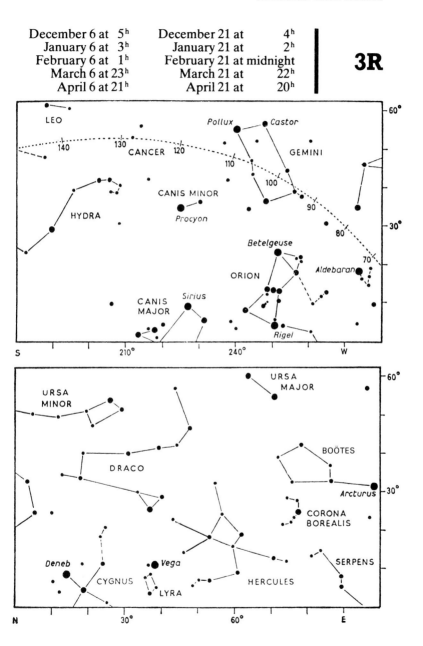

4L

January 6 at 5^h January 21 at   4^h
February 6 at 3^h February 21 at   2^h
March 6 at 1^h March 21 at midnight
April 6 at 23^h April 21 at   22^h
May 6 at 21^h May 21 at   20^h

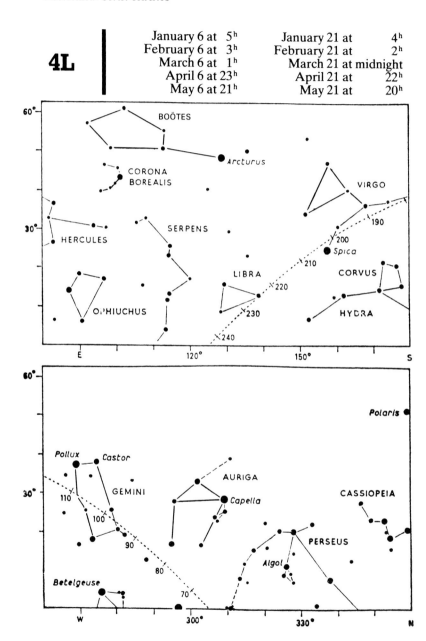

January 6 at 5ʰ   January 21 at   4ʰ
February 6 at 3ʰ   February 21 at   2ʰ
March 6 at 1ʰ   March 21 at midnight
April 6 at 23ʰ   April 21 at   22ʰ
May 6 at 21ʰ   May 21 at   20ʰ

4R

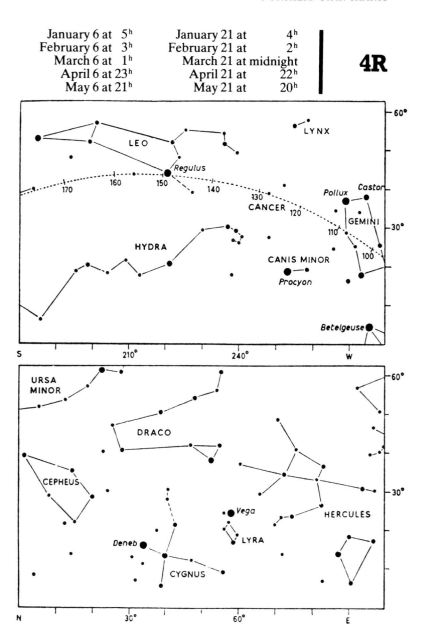

21

5L

January 6 at 7ʰ	January 21 at 6ʰ
February 6 at 5ʰ	February 21 at 4ʰ
March 6 at 3ʰ	March 21 at 2ʰ
April 6 at 1ʰ	April 21 at midnight
May 6 at 23ʰ	May 21 at 22ʰ

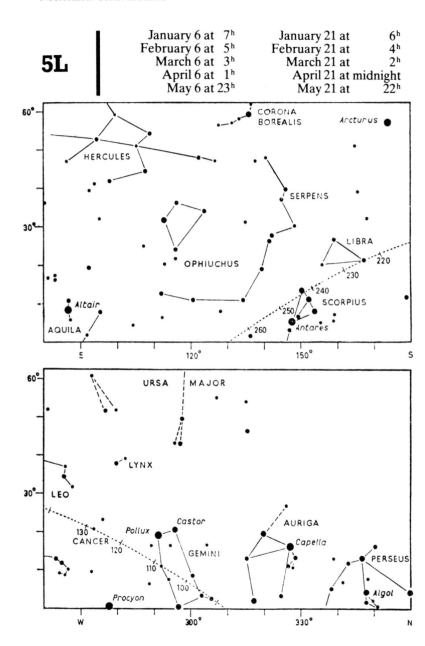

January 6 at 7ʰ	January 21 at 6ʰ	
February 6 at 5ʰ	February 21 at 4ʰ	**5R**
March 6 at 3ʰ	March 21 at 2ʰ	
April 6 at 1ʰ	April 21 at midnight	
May 6 at 23ʰ	May 21 at 22ʰ	

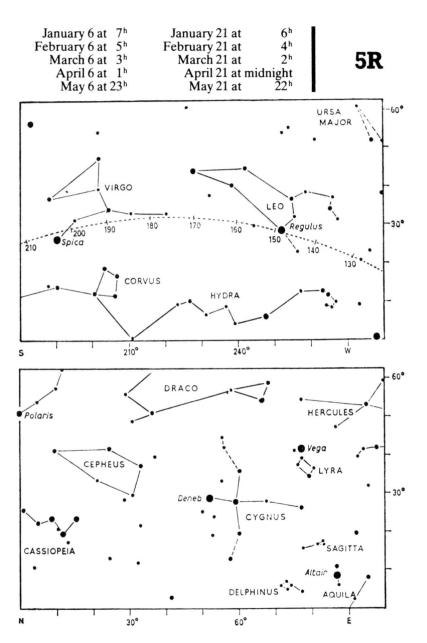

6L

March 6 at 5ʰ	March 21 at 4ʰ
April 6 at 3ʰ	April 21 at 2ʰ
May 6 at 1ʰ	May 21 at midnight
June 6 at 23ʰ	June 21 at 22ʰ
July 6 at 21ʰ	July 21 at 20ʰ

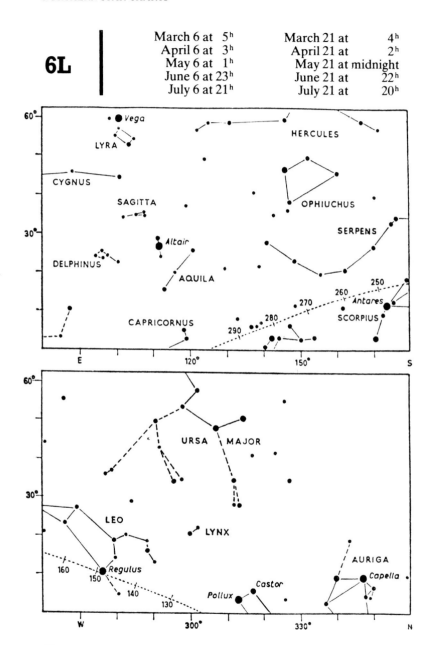

March 6 at 5ʰ   March 21 at   4ʰ
April 6 at 3ʰ   April 21 at   2ʰ
May 6 at 1ʰ   May 21 at midnight
June 6 at 23ʰ   June 21 at   22ʰ
July 6 at 21ʰ   July 21 at   20ʰ

6R

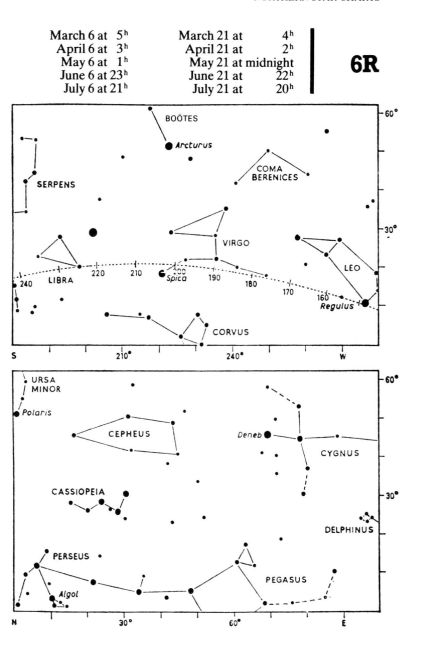

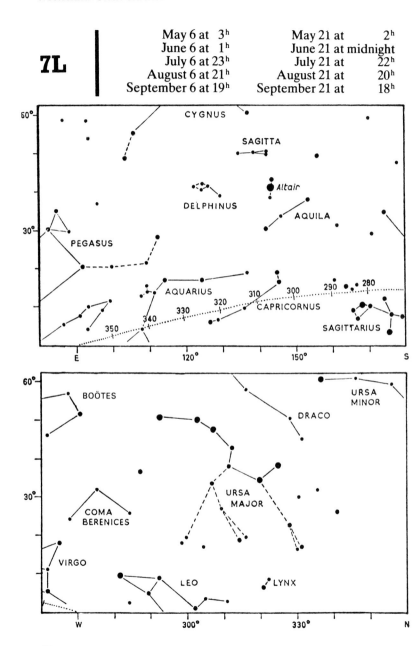

7L

May 6 at 3ʰ
June 6 at 1ʰ
July 6 at 23ʰ
August 6 at 21ʰ
September 6 at 19ʰ

May 21 at 2ʰ
June 21 at midnight
July 21 at 22ʰ
August 21 at 20ʰ
September 21 at 18ʰ

May 6 at 3^h May 21 at 2^h
June 6 at 1^h June 21 at midnight
July 6 at 23^h July 21 at 22^h **7R**
August 6 at 21^h August 21 at 20^h
September 6 at 19^h September 21 at 18^h

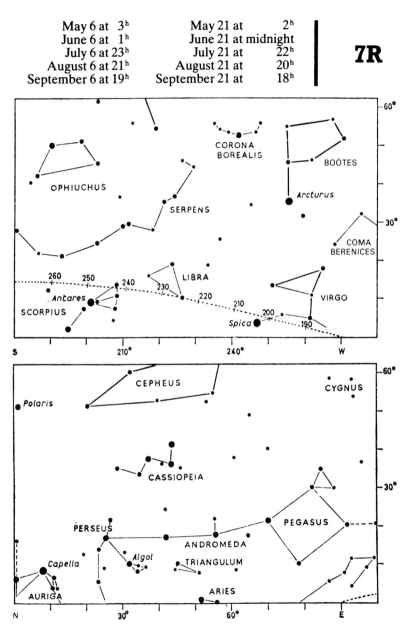

27

8L

July 6 at 1ʰ	July 21 at midnight
August 6 at 23ʰ	August 21 at 22ʰ
September 6 at 21ʰ	September 21 at 20ʰ
October 6 at 19ʰ	October 21 at 18ʰ
November 6 at 17ʰ	November 21 at 16ʰ

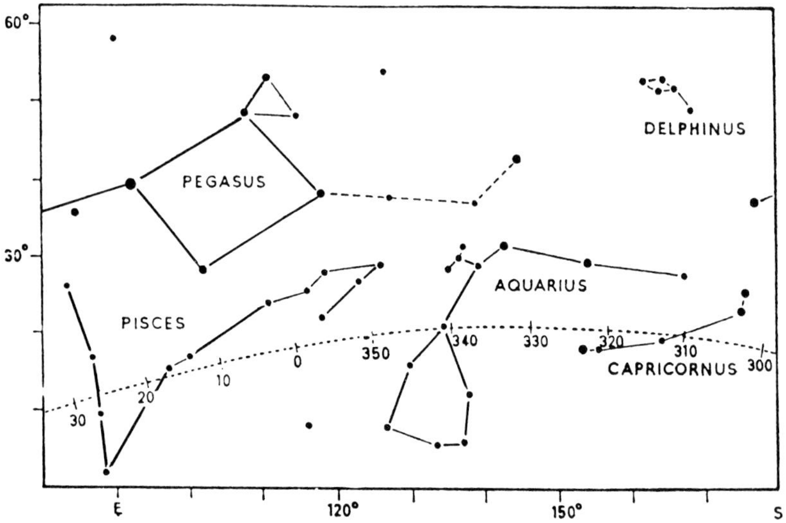

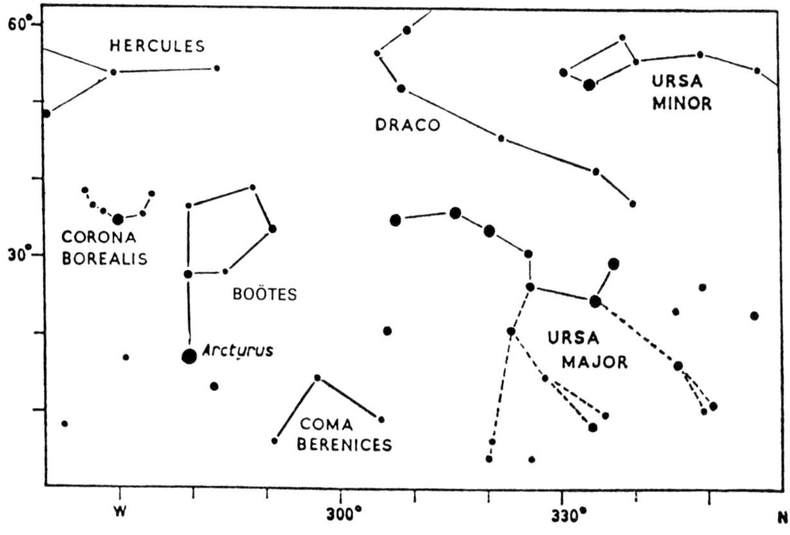

DELPHINUS

PEGASUS

AQUARIUS

PISCES

340 330 320 310 300

350 0

340

CAPRICORNUS

10

20

30

E 120° 150° S

HERCULES

DRACO

URSA MINOR

CORONA BOREALIS

BOÖTES

Arcturus

URSA MAJOR

COMA BERENICES

W 300° 330° N

July 6 at 1^h	July 21 at midnight	
August 6 at 23^h	August 21 at 22^h	**8R**
September 6 at 21^h	September 21 at 20^h	
October 6 at 19^h	October 21 at 18^h	
November 6 at 17^h	November 21 at 16^h	

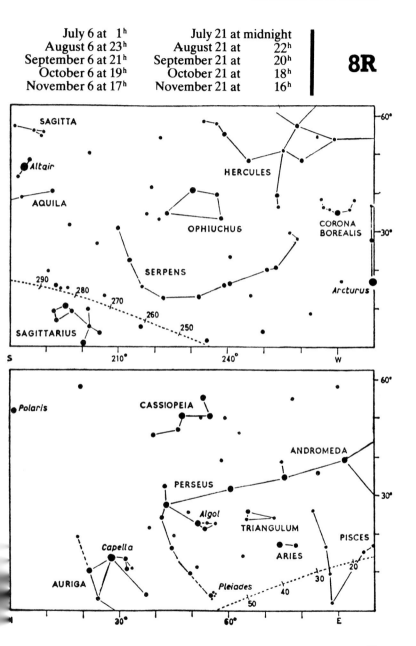

9L

August 6 at 1ʰ	August 21 at midnight
September 6 at 23ʰ	September 21 at 22ʰ
October 6 at 21ʰ	October 21 at 20ʰ
November 6 at 19ʰ	November 21 at 18ʰ
December 6 at 17ʰ	December 21 at 16ʰ

August 6 at 1ʰ	August 21 at midnight	
September 6 at 23ʰ	September 21 at 22ʰ	**9R**
October 6 at 21ʰ	October 21 at 20ʰ	
November 6 at 19ʰ	November 21 at 18ʰ	
December 6 at 17ʰ	December 21 at 16ʰ	

10L

August 6 at 3^h	August 21 at 2^h
September 6 at 1^h	September 21 at midnight
October 6 at 23^h	October 21 at 22^h
November 6 at 21^h	November 21 at 20^h
December 6 at 19^h	December 21 at 18^h

August 6 at 3ʰ	August 21 at 2ʰ
September 6 at 1ʰ	September 21 at midnight
October 6 at 23ʰ	October 21 at 22ʰ
November 6 at 21ʰ	November 21 at 20ʰ
December 6 at 19ʰ	December 21 at 18ʰ

10R

33

11L

September 6 at   3ʰ   September 21 at   2ʰ
October 6 at   1ʰ   October 21 at midnight
November 6 at 23ʰ   November 21 at   22ʰ
December 6 at 21ʰ   December 21 at   20ʰ
January 6 at 19ʰ   January 21 at   18ʰ

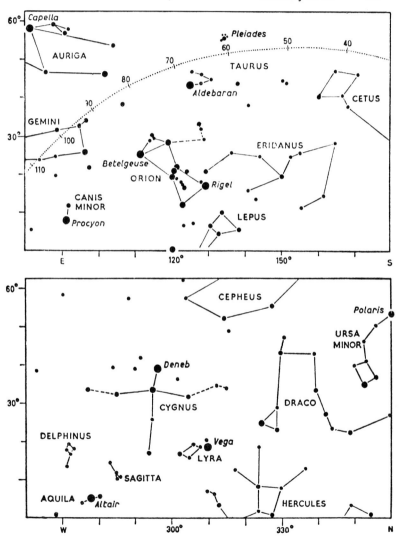

September 6 at 3ʰ   September 21 at   2ʰ
October 6 at 1ʰ   October 21 at midnight
November 6 at 23ʰ   November 21 at   22ʰ
December 6 at 21ʰ   December 21 at   20ʰ
January 6 at 19ʰ   January 21 at   18ʰ

11R

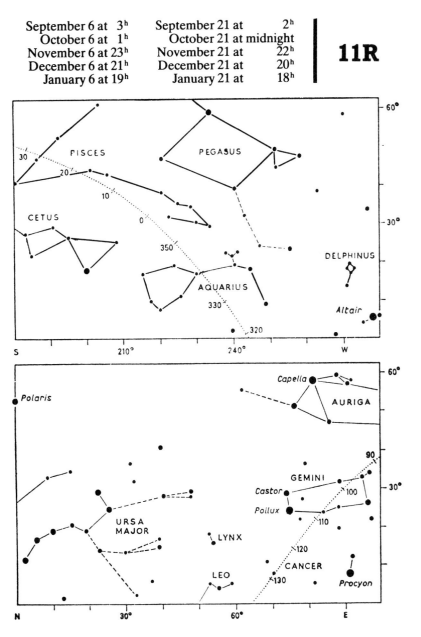

12L

October 6 at 3ʰ October 21 at 2ʰ
November 6 at 1ʰ November 21 at midnight
December 6 at 23ʰ December 21 at 22ʰ
January 6 at 21ʰ January 21 at 20ʰ
February 6 at 19ʰ February 21 at 18ʰ

October 6 at 3ʰ   October 21 at   2ʰ
November 6 at 1ʰ   November 21 at midnight
December 6 at 23ʰ   December 21 at   22ʰ   **12R**
January 6 at 21ʰ   January 21 at   20ʰ
February 6 at 19ʰ   February 21 at   18ʰ

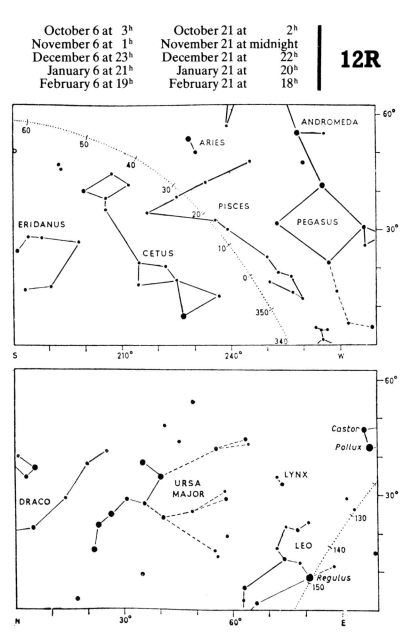

37

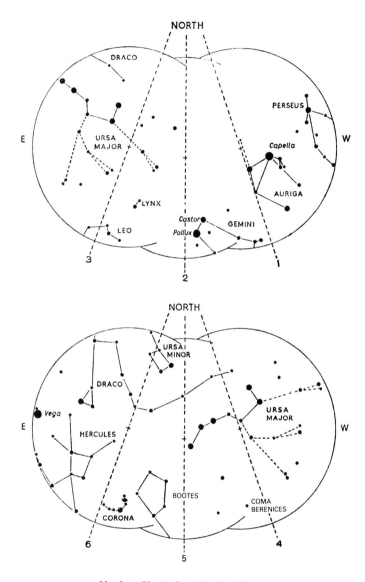

Northern Hemisphere Overhead Stars

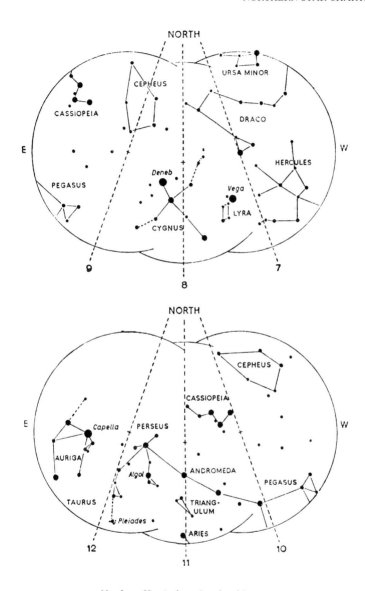

Northern Hemisphere Overhead Stars

1L

October 6 at 5ʰ	October 21 at 4ʰ
November 6 at 3ʰ	November 21 at 2ʰ
December 6 at 1ʰ	December 21 at midnight
January 6 at 23ʰ	January 21 at 22ʰ
February 6 at 21ʰ	February 21 at 20ʰ

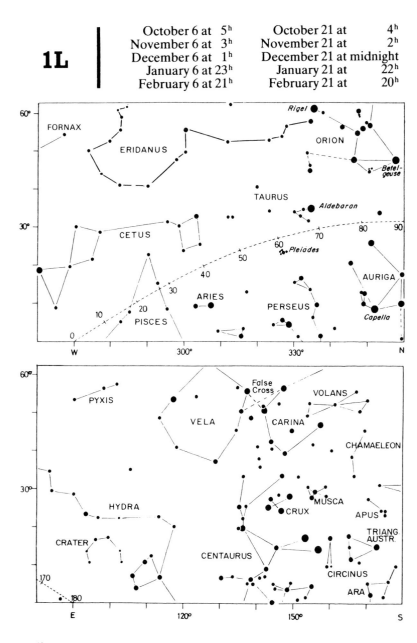

October 6 at 5^h October 21 at   4^h
November 6 at 3^h November 21 at   2^h
December 6 at 1^h December 21 at midnight
January 6 at 23^h January 21 at   22^h
February 6 at 21^h February 21 at   20^h

1R

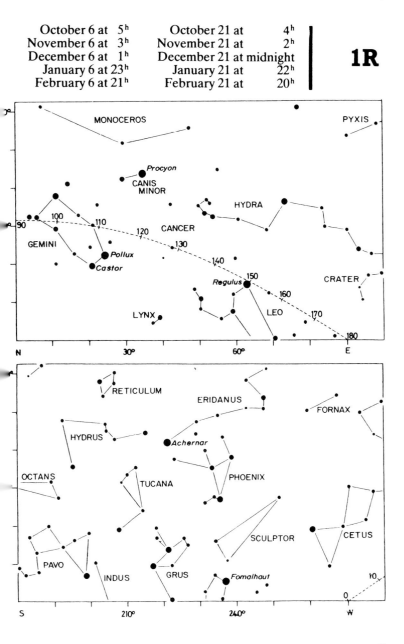

2L

November 6 at 5ʰ	November 21 at 4ʰ
December 6 at 3ʰ	December 21 at 2ʰ
January 6 at 1ʰ	January 21 at midnight
February 6 at 23ʰ	February 21 at 22ʰ
March 6 at 21ʰ	March 21 at 20ʰ

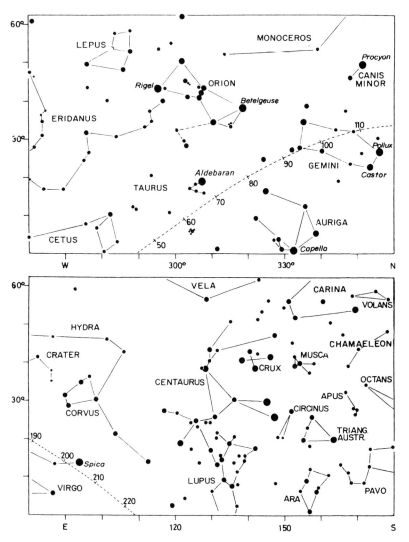

November 6 at 5ʰ   November 21 at   4ʰ
December 6 at 3ʰ   December 21 at   2ʰ
January 6 at 1ʰ   January 21 at midnight
February 6 at 23ʰ   February 21 at   22ʰ
March 6 at 21ʰ   March 21 at   20ʰ

2R

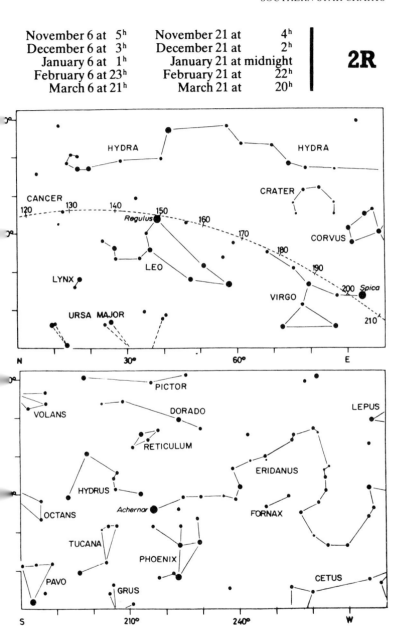

3L

January 6 at 3ʰ	January 21 at 2ʰ
February 6 at 1ʰ	February 21 at midnight
March 6 at 23ʰ	March 21 at 22ʰ
April 6 at 21ʰ	April 21 at 20ʰ
May 6 at 19ʰ	May 21 at 18ʰ

January 6 at 3ʰ	January 21 at 2ʰ
February 6 at 1ʰ	February 21 at midnight
March 6 at 23ʰ	March 21 at 22ʰ
April 6 at 21ʰ	April 21 at 20ʰ
May 6 at 19ʰ	May 21 at 18ʰ

3R

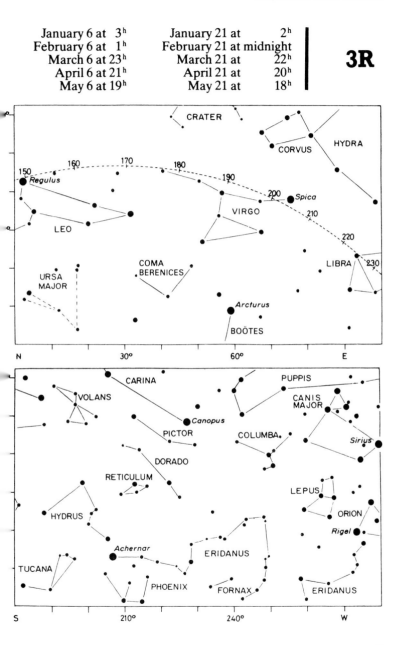

4L

February 6 at 3ʰ	February 21 at 2ʰ
March 6 at 1ʰ	March 21 at midnight
April 6 at 23ʰ	April 21 at 22ʰ
May 6 at 21ʰ	May 21 at 20ʰ
June 6 at 19ʰ	June 21 at 18ʰ

February 6 at 3ʰ   February 21 at   2ʰ
March 6 at 1ʰ   March 21 at midnight
April 6 at 23ʰ   April 21 at   22ʰ
May 6 at 21ʰ   May 21 at   20ʰ
June 6 at 19ʰ   June 21 at   18ʰ

4R

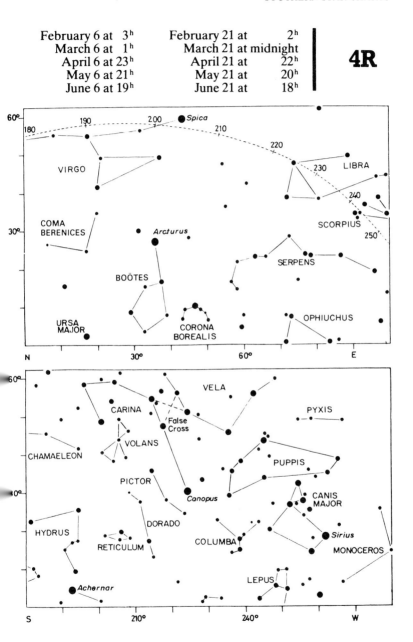

5L

March 6 at 3ʰ	March 21 at 2ʰ
April 6 at 1ʰ	April 21 at midnight
May 6 at 23ʰ	May 21 at 22ʰ
June 6 at 21ʰ	June 21 at 20ʰ
July 6 at 19ʰ	July 21 at 18ʰ

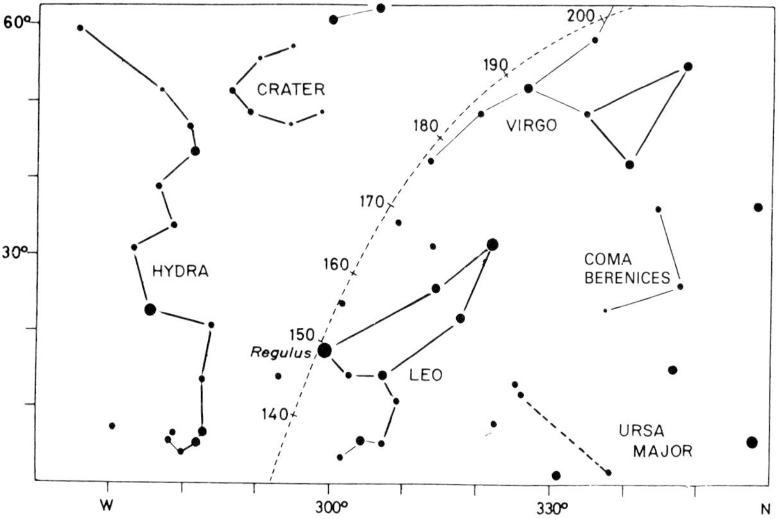

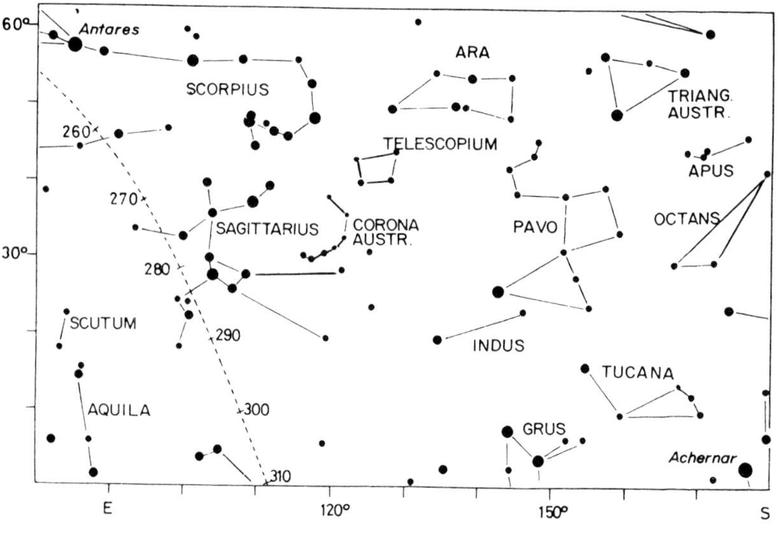

60°
200
190
CRATER
180
VIRGO
170
30°
COMA
BERENICES
HYDRA
160
150
Regulus
LEO
140
URSA
MAJOR
W   300°   330°   N

60°
Antares
ARA
SCORPIUS
TRIANG.
AUSTR.
260
TELESCOPIUM
APUS
270
OCTANS
SAGITTARIUS   CORONA
AUSTR.   PAVO
30°
280
SCUTUM
290
INDUS
TUCANA
AQUILA
300
GRUS
310
Achernar
E   120°   150°   S

March 6 at 3ʰ   March 21 at   2ʰ
April 6 at 1ʰ   April 21 at midnight
May 6 at 23ʰ   May 21 at   22ʰ   **5R**
June 6 at 21ʰ   June 21 at   20ʰ
July 6 at 19ʰ   July 21 at   18ʰ

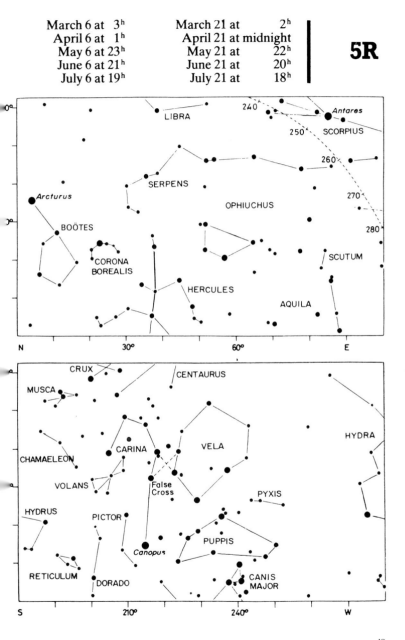

6L

March 6 at 5ʰ	March 21 at 4ʰ
April 6 at 3ʰ	April 21 at 2ʰ
May 6 at 1ʰ	May 21 at midnight
June 6 at 23ʰ	June 21 at 22ʰ
July 6 at 21ʰ	July 21 at 20ʰ

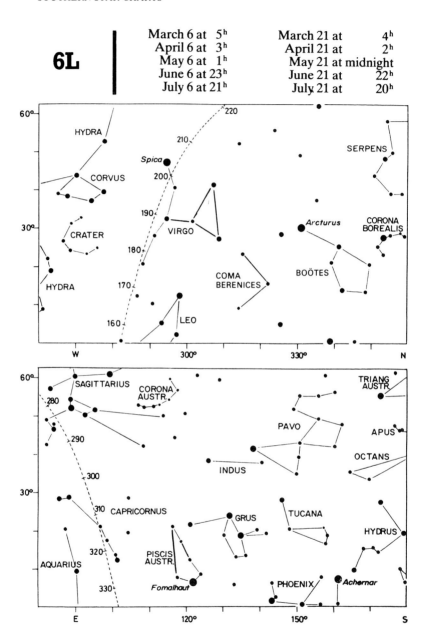

March 6 at 5ʰ   March 21 at 4ʰ
April 6 at 3ʰ   April 21 at 2ʰ
May 6 at 1ʰ   May 21 at midnight
June 6 at 23ʰ   June 21 at 22ʰ
July 6 at 21ʰ   July 21 at 20ʰ

6R

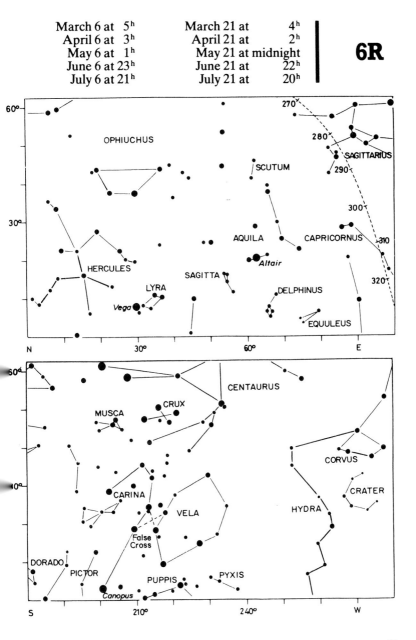

7L

April 6 at 5ʰ	April 21 at 4ʰ
May 6 at 3ʰ	May 21 at 2ʰ
June 6 at 1ʰ	June 21 at midnight
July 6 at 23ʰ	July 21 at 22ʰ
August 6 at 21ʰ	August 21 at 20ʰ

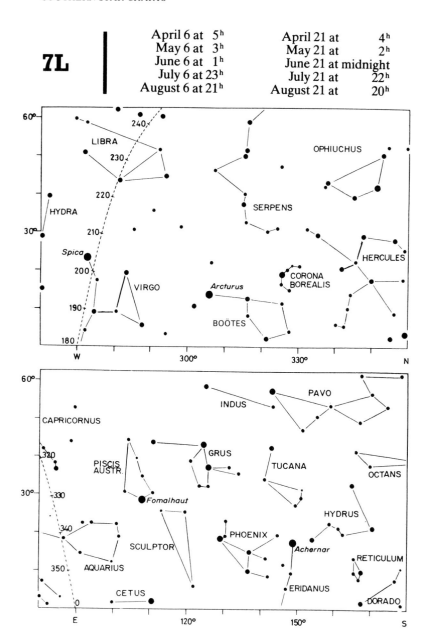

April 6 at	5ʰ	April 21 at	4ʰ	
May 6 at	3ʰ	May 21 at	2ʰ	**7R**
June 6 at	1ʰ	June 21 at midnight		
July 6 at	23ʰ	July 21 at	22ʰ	
August 6 at	21ʰ	August 21 at	20ʰ	

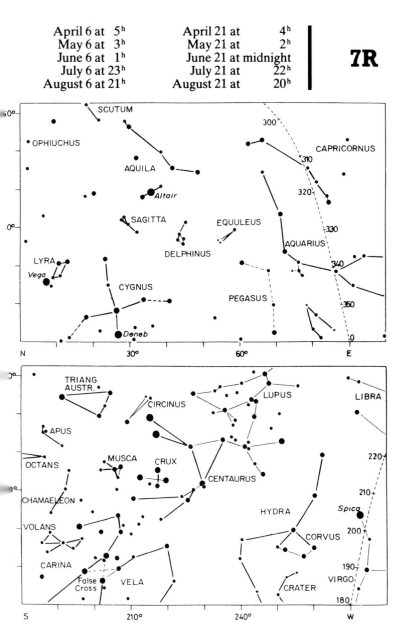

8L

May 6 at 5ʰ	May 21 at 4ʰ
June 6 at 3ʰ	June 21 at 2ʰ
July 6 at 1ʰ	July 21 at midnight
August 6 at 23ʰ	August 21 at 22ʰ
September 6 at 21ʰ	September 21 at 20ʰ

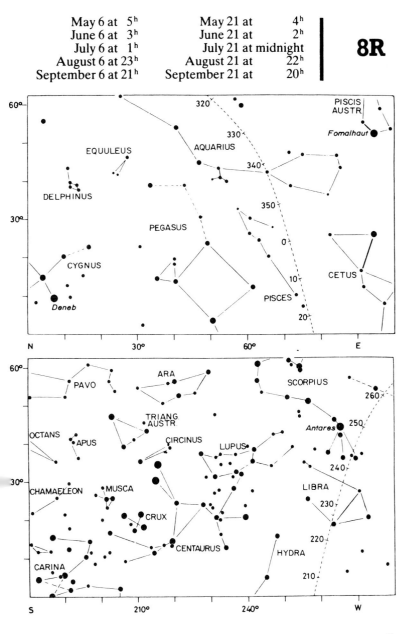

May 6 at 5ʰ   May 21 at 4ʰ
June 6 at 3ʰ   June 21 at 2ʰ
July 6 at 1ʰ   July 21 at midnight
August 6 at 23ʰ   August 21 at 22ʰ
September 6 at 21ʰ   September 21 at 20ʰ

8R

PISCIS AUSTR.
Fomalhaut
EQUULEUS
AQUARIUS
DELPHINUS
PEGASUS
CYGNUS
CETUS
Deneb
PISCES
N   30°   60°   E

ARA
PAVO
SCORPIUS
Antares
TRIANG. AUSTR.
OCTANS
APUS
CIRCINUS
LUPUS
LIBRA
CHAMAELEON
MUSCA
CRUX
CENTAURUS
HYDRA
CARINA
S   210°   240°   W

9L

June 6 at 5ʰ	June 21 at 4ʰ
July 6 at 3ʰ	July 21 at 2ʰ
August 6 at 1ʰ	August 21 at midnight
September 6 at 23ʰ	September 21 at 22ʰ
October 6 at 21ʰ	October 21 at 20ʰ

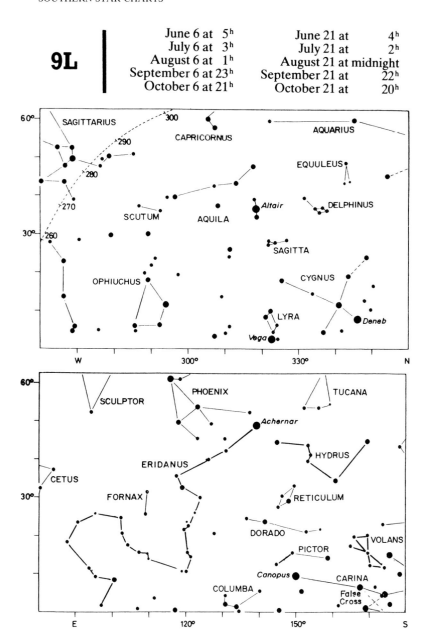

June 6 at 5ʰ   June 21 at   4ʰ
July 6 at 3ʰ   July 21 at   2ʰ
August 6 at 1ʰ   August 21 at midnight
September 6 at 23ʰ September 21 at 22ʰ
October 6 at 21ʰ   October 21 at   20ʰ

9R

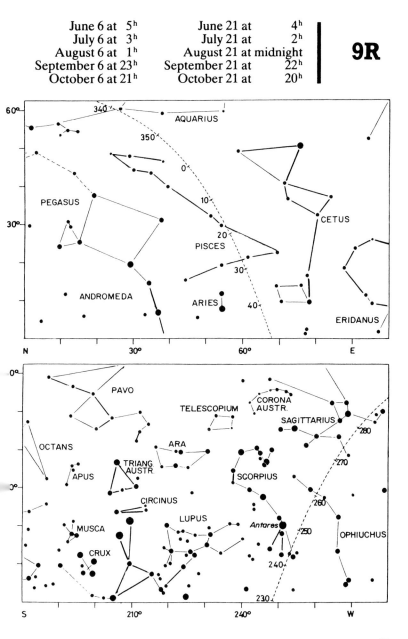

10L

July 6 at 5ʰ	July 21 at 4ʰ
August 6 at 3ʰ	August 21 at 2ʰ
September 6 at 1ʰ	September 21 at midnight
October 6 at 23ʰ	October 21 at 22ʰ
November 6 at 21ʰ	November 21 at 20ʰ

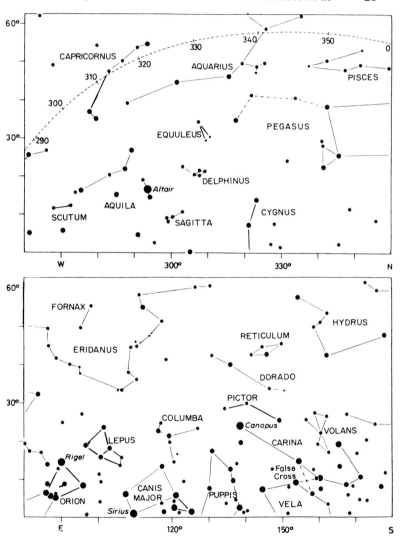

July 6 at	5^h	July 21 at	4^h	
August 6 at	3^h	August 21 at	2^h	
September 6 at	1^h	September 21 at midnight		**10R**
October 6 at	23^h	October 21 at	22^h	
November 6 at	21^h	November 21 at	20^h	

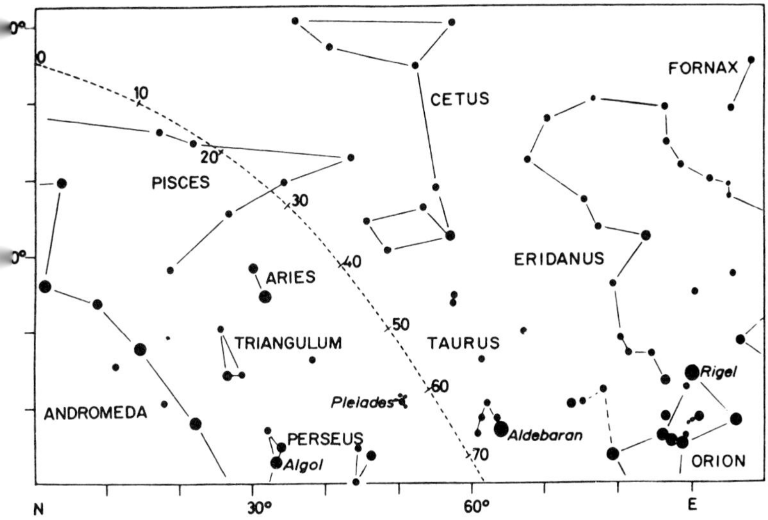

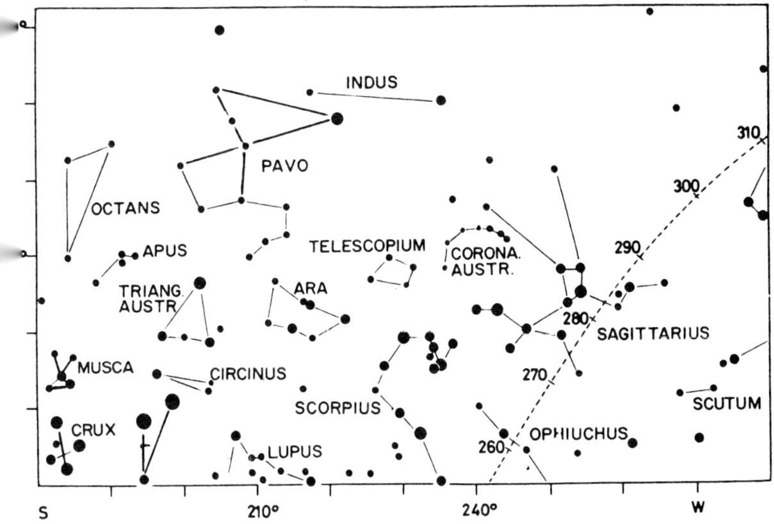

FORNAX

CETUS

PISCES

0

10

20

30

ARIES

40

ERIDANUS

TRIANGULUM

50

TAURUS

60

Pleiades

Rigel

ANDROMEDA

PERSEUS

Aldebaran

Algol

70

ORION

N   30°   60°   E

INDUS

PAVO

OCTANS

310

APUS

TELESCOPIUM

CORONA AUSTR.

300

290

TRIANG AUSTR

ARA

280

SAGITTARIUS

MUSCA

CIRCINUS

270

CRUX

SCORPIUS

SCUTUM

LUPUS

260

OPHIUCHUS

S   210°   240°   W

11L

August 6 at 5ʰ   August 21 at 4ʰ
September 6 at 3ʰ   September 21 at 2ʰ
October 6 at 1ʰ   October 21 at midnight
November 6 at 23ʰ   November 21 at 22ʰ
December 6 at 21ʰ   December 21 at 20ʰ

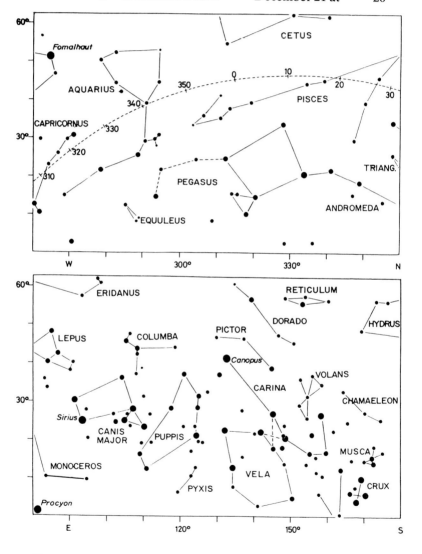

August 6 at 5^h	August 21 at 4^h	
September 6 at 3^h	September 21 at 2^h	**11R**
October 6 at 1^h	October 21 at midnight	
November 6 at 23^h	November 21 at 22^h	
December 6 at 21^h	December 21 at 20^h	

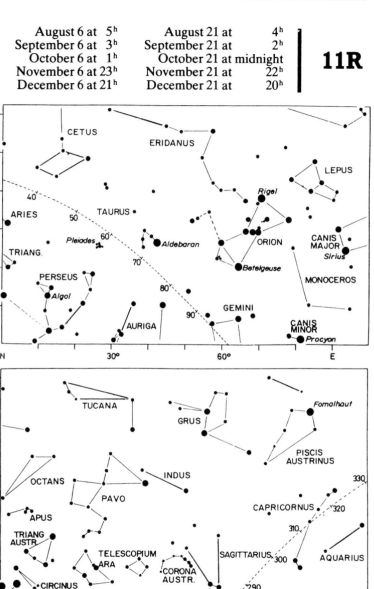

12L

September 6 at 5^h	September 21 at 4^h
October 6 at 3^h	October 21 at 2^h
November 6 at 1^h	November 21 at midnight
December 6 at 23^h	December 21 at 22^h
January 6 at 21^h	January 21 at 20^h

September 6 at 5ʰ	September 21 at 4ʰ	
October 6 at 3ʰ	October 21 at 2ʰ	
November 6 at 1ʰ	November 21 at midnight	**12R**
December 6 at 23ʰ	December 21 at 22ʰ	
January 6 at 21ʰ	January 21 at 20ʰ	

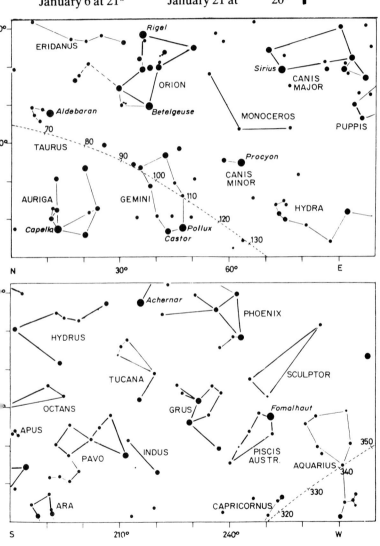

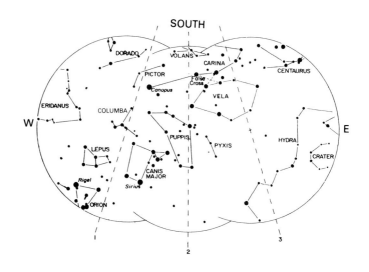

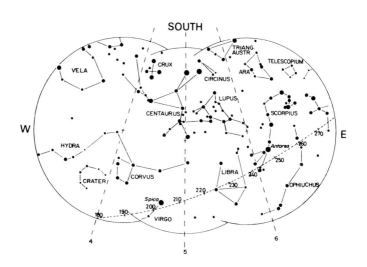

Southern Hemisphere Overhead Stars

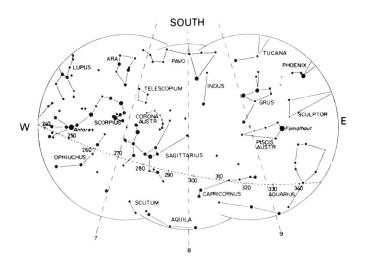

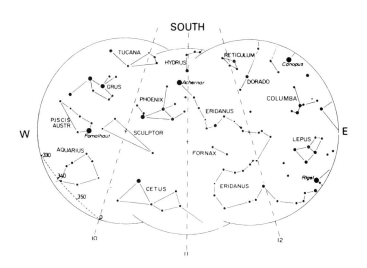

Southern Hemisphere Overhead Stars

The Planets and the Ecliptic

The paths of the planets about the Sun all lie close to the plane of the ecliptic, which is marked for us in the sky by the apparent path of the Sun among the stars, and is shown on the star charts by a broken line. The Moon and planets will always be found close to this line, never departing from it by more than about 7°. Thus the planets are most favourably placed for observation when the ecliptic is well displayed, and this means that it should be as high in the sky as possible. This avoids the difficulty of finding a clear horizon, and also overcomes the problem of atmospheric absorption, which greatly reduces the light of the stars. Thus a star at an altitude of 10° suffers a loss of 60 per cent of its light, which corresponds to a whole magnitude; at an altitude of only 4°, the loss may amount to two magnitudes.

The position of the ecliptic in the sky is therefore of great importance, and since it is tilted at about 23½° to the Equator, it is only at certain times of the day or year that it is displayed to the best advantage. It will be realized that the Sun (and therefore the ecliptic) is at its highest in the sky at noon in midsummer, and at its lowest at noon in midwinter. Allowing for the daily motion of the sky, it follows that the ecliptic is highest at midnight in winter, at sunset in the spring, at noon in summer and at sunrise in the autumn. Hence these are the best times to see the planets. Thus, if Venus is an evening object in the western sky after sunset, it will be seen to best advantage if this occurs in the spring, when the ecliptic is high in the sky and slopes down steeply to the horizon. This means that the planet is not only higher in the sky, but will remain for a much longer period above the horizon. For similar reasons, a morning object will be seen at its best on autumn mornings before sunrise, when the ecliptic is high in the east. The outer planets, which can come to opposition (i.e. opposite the Sun), are best seen when opposition occurs in the winter months, when the ecliptic is high in the sky at midnight.

The seasons are reversed in the Southern Hemisphere, spring beginning at the September Equinox, when the Sun crosses the Equator on its way south, summer beginning at the December Solstice, when the Sun is highest in the southern sky, and so on.

Thus, the times when the ecliptic is highest in the sky, and therefore best placed for observing the planets, may be summarized as follows:

	Midnight	*Sunrise*	*Noon*	*Sunset*
Northern lats.	December	September	June	March
Southern lats.	June	March	December	September

In addition to the daily rotation of the celestial sphere from east to west, the planets have a motion of their own among the stars. The apparent movement is generally *direct*, i.e. to the east, in the direction of increasing longitude, but for a certain period (which depends on the distance of the planet) this apparent motion is reversed. With the outer planets this *retrograde* motion occurs about the time of opposition. Owing to the different inclination of the orbits of these planets, the actual effect is to cause the apparent path to form a loop, or sometimes an S-shaped curve. The same effect is present in the motion of the inferior planets, Mercury and Venus, but it is not so obvious, since it always occurs at the time of inferior conjunction.

The *inferior planets*, Mercury and Venus, move in smaller orbits than that of the Earth, and so are always seen near the Sun. They are most obvious at the times of greatest angular distance from the Sun (greatest elongation), which may reach 28° for Mercury, and 47° for Venus. They are seen as evening objects in the western sky after sunset (at eastern elongations) or as morning objects in the eastern sky before sunrise (at western elongations). The succession of phenomena, conjunctions and elongations, always follows the same order, but the intervals between them are not equal. Thus, if either planet is moving round the far side of its orbit its motion will be to the east, in the same direction in which the Sun appears to be moving. It therefore takes much longer for the planet to overtake the Sun – that is, to come to superior conjunction – than it does when moving round to inferior conjunction, between Sun and Earth. The intervals given in the following table are average values; they remain fairly constant in the case of Venus, which travels in an almost circular orbit. In the case of Mercury, however, conditions vary widely because of the great eccentricity and inclination of the planet's orbit.

		Mercury	*Venus*
Inferior Conjunction	to Elongation West	22 days	72 days
Elongation West	to Superior Conjunction	36 days	220 days
Superior Conjunction	to Elongation East	36 days	220 days
Elongation East	to Inferior Conjunction	22 days	72 days

The greatest brilliancy of Venus always occurs about 36 days before or after inferior conjunction. This will be about a month *after* greatest eastern elongation (as an evening object), or a month *before* greatest western elongation (as a morning object). No such rule can be given for Mercury, because its distance from the Earth and the Sun can vary over a wide range.

Mercury is not likely to be seen unless a clear horizon is available. It is seldom as much as 10° above the horizon in the twilight sky in northern latitudes, but this figure is often exceeded in the Southern Hemisphere. This favourable condition arises because the maximum elongation of 28° can occur only when the planet is at aphelion (farthest from the Sun), and it then lies well south of the Equator. Northern observers must be content with smaller elongations, which may be as little as 18° at perihelion. In general, it may be said that the most favourable times for seeing Mercury as an evening object will be in spring, some days before greatest eastern elongation; in autumn, it may be seen as a morning object some days after greatest western elongation.

Venus is the brightest of the planets and may be seen on occasions in broad daylight. Like Mercury, it is alternately a morning and an evening object, and it will be highest in the sky when it is a morning object in autumn, or an evening object in spring. The phenomena of Venus given in the table on p. 67 can occur only in the months of January, April, June, August and November, and it will be realized that they do not all lead to favourable apparitions of the planet. In fact, Venus is to be seen at its best as an evening object in northern latitudes when eastern elongation occurs in June. The planet is then well north of the Sun in the preceding spring months, and is a brilliant object in the evening sky over a long period. In the Southern Hemisphere a November elongation is best. For similar reasons, Venus gives a prolonged display as a morning object in the months following western elongation in November (in northern latitudes) or in June (in the Southern Hemisphere).

The *superior planets*, which travel in orbits larger than that of the Earth, differ from Mercury and Venus in that they can be seen opposite the Sun in the sky. The superior planets are morning objects after conjunction with the Sun, rising earlier each day until they come to opposition. They will then be nearest to the Earth (and therefore at their brightest), and will be on the meridian at midnight, due south in northern latitudes, but due north in the Southern Hemisphere. After opposition they are evening objects, setting earlier each evening until they set in the west with the Sun at the next conjunction. The difference in brightness from one opposition to another is most noticeable in the case of Mars, whose distance from Earth can vary considerably and rapidly. The other superior planets are at such great distances that there is very little change in brightness from one opposition to the next. The effect of altitude is, however, of some importance, for at a December opposition in northern latitudes the planets will be among the stars of Taurus or Gemini, and can then be at an altitude of more than 60° in southern England. At a summer opposition, when the planet is in Sagittarius, it may only rise to about 15° above the southern horizon, and so makes a less impressive appearance. In the Southern Hemisphere the reverse conditions apply, a June opposition being the best, with the planet in Sagittarius at an altitude which can reach 80° above the northern horizon for observers in South Africa.

Mars, whose orbit is appreciably eccentric, comes nearest to the Earth at oppositions at the end of August. It may then be brighter even than Jupiter, but rather low in the sky in Aquarius for northern observers, though very well placed for those in southern latitudes. These favourable oppositions occur every fifteen or seventeen years (1988, 2003, 2018), but in the Northern Hemisphere the planet is probably better seen at oppositions in the autumn or winter months, when it is higher in the sky. Oppositions of Mars occur at an average interval of 780 days, and during this time the planet makes a complete circuit of the sky.

Jupiter is always a bright planet, and comes to opposition a month later each year, having moved, roughly speaking, from one Zodiacal constellation to the next.

Saturn moves much more slowly than Jupiter, and may remain in the same constellation for several years. The brightness of Saturn depends on the aspects of its rings, as well as on the distance from Earth and Sun. The Earth passed through the plane of Saturn's rings in 1995 and 1996, when they appeared edge-on; we shall next see them at maximum opening, and Saturn at its brightest, around 2002. The rings will next appear edge-on in 2009.

Uranus, *Neptune* and *Pluto* are hardly likely to attract the attention of observers without adequate instruments.

Phases of the Moon, 1997

	New Moon			First Quarter			Full Moon			Last Quarter		
	d	*h*	*m*		*d*	*h*	*m*		*d*	*h*	*m*		*d*	*h*	*m*
												Jan.	2	01	45
Jan.	9	04	26	Jan.	15	20	02	Jan.	23	15	11	Jan.	31	19	40
Feb.	7	15	06	Feb.	14	08	58	Feb.	22	10	27	Mar.	2	09	38
Mar.	9	01	15	Mar.	16	00	06	Mar.	24	04	45	Mar.	31	19	38
Apr.	7	11	02	Apr.	14	17	00	Apr.	22	20	33	Apr.	30	02	37
May	6	20	47	May	14	10	55	May	22	09	13	May	29	07	51
June	5	07	04	June	13	04	51	June	20	19	09	June	27	12	42
July	4	18	40	July	12	21	44	July	20	03	20	July	26	18	28
Aug.	3	08	14	Aug.	11	12	42	Aug.	18	10	55	Aug.	25	02	24
Sept.	1	23	52	Sept.	10	01	31	Sept.	16	18	50	Sept.	23	13	35
Oct.	1	16	52	Oct.	9	12	22	Oct.	16	03	46	Oct.	23	04	48
Oct.	31	10	01	Nov.	7	21	43	Nov.	14	14	12	Nov.	21	23	58
Nov.	30	02	14	Dec.	7	06	09	Dec.	14	02	37	Dec.	21	21	43
Dec.	29	16	57												

All times are GMT.

Longitudes of the Sun, Moon and Planets in 1997

		Sun	Moon	Venus	Mars	Jupiter	Saturn
		°	°	°	°	°	°
January	6	286	243	265	181	296	2
	21	301	92	283	184	300	3
February	6	317	294	304	186	304	4
	21	332	137	322	185	307	6
March	6	345	303	339	181	310	7
	21	0	146	357	176	313	9
April	6	16	356	17	170	316	11
	21	31	190	35	167	318	13
May	6	46	34	54	167	320	15
	21	60	223	72	170	321	16
June	6	75	84	92	175	322	18
	21	90	272	110	181	322	19
July	6	104	118	129	188	321	20
	21	118	310	146	195	319	20
August	6	134	163	166	205	317	20
	21	148	4	183	214	316	20
September	6	163	207	203	224	314	19
	21	178	56	220	234	313	18
October	6	193	241	237	245	312	17
	21	208	92	253	255	312	16
November	6	224	290	271	268	313	15
	21	239	138	284	279	315	14
December	6	254	328	296	290	317	14
	21	269	169	303	302	320	14

Longitude of *Uranus* 306°
Neptune 298°

Moon: Longitude of ascending node
Jan. 1: 183°   Dec. 31: 164°

Mercury moves so quickly among the stars that it is not possible to indicate its position on the star charts at convenient intervals. The monthly notes must be consulted for the best times at which the planet may be seen.

The positions of the other planets are given in the table on p. 71. This gives the apparent longitudes on dates which correspond to those of the star charts, and the position of the planet may at once be found near the ecliptic at the given longitude.

Examples
In the Southern Hemisphere two planets are seen in the western evening sky in early November. Identify them.

> The Southern Star Chart 10R shows the western sky at November 6^{d} 21^{h} for longitudes 260° to 310°. Reference to the table on p. 71 gives the longitude of Venus as 271° and that of Mars as 268°. Thus these are the planets to be found in the western sky, and the lower one is Mars.

The positions of the Sun and Moon can be plotted on the star maps in the same manner as for the planets. The average daily motion of the Sun is 1°, and of the Moon 13°. For the Moon an indication of its position relative to the ecliptic may be obtained from a consideration of its longitude relative to that of the ascending node. The latter changes only slowly during the year, as will be seen from the values given on p. 71. Let us call the difference in longitude of Moon-node, d. Then if $d = 0°$, 180° or 360° the Moon is on the ecliptic. If $d = 90°$ the Moon is 5° north of the ecliptic, and if $d = 270°$ the Moon is 5° south of the ecliptic.

On June 6 the Moon's longitude is given as 84°, and the longitude of the node is found by interpolation to be about 175°. Thus $d = 269°$, and the Moon is about 5° south of the ecliptic. Its position may be plotted on Northern Star Charts 2R, 3L, 3R, 4L, 9R, 10R, 11L and 12L, and on Southern Star Charts 1L, 2L, 3L, 11R and 12R.

Events in 1997

ECLIPSES

There will be four eclipses, two of the Sun and two of the Moon.

March 8–9: total eclipse of the Sun – E Asia, NW of North America.
March 24: partial eclipse of the Moon – Africa, Europe, the Americas.
September 1–2: partial eclipse of the Sun – Australasia.
September 16: total eclipse of the Moon – Australasia, Asia, Africa, Europe.

THE PLANETS

Mercury may be seen more easily from northern latitudes in the evenings about the time of greatest eastern elongation (April 6) and in the mornings around greatest western elongation (September 16). In the Southern Hemisphere the corresponding most favourable dates are around January 24 (mornings) and August 4 (evenings).

Venus is visible in the mornings until the end of February and in the evenings from May to December.

Mars is at opposition on March 17.

Jupiter is at opposition on August 9.

Saturn is at opposition on October 10.

Uranus is at opposition on July 29.

Neptune is at opposition on July 21.

Pluto is at opposition on May 25.

JANUARY

New Moon: January 9   *Full Moon*: January 23

EARTH is at perihelion (nearest to the Sun) on January 2, at a distance of 147 million kilometres (91.4 million miles).

MERCURY attains its greatest western elongation (25°) on January 24. It is slightly further south than the Sun and thus poorly placed for observation by those in northern temperate latitudes, from where it may be seen only during the ten days before greatest elongation, low above the south-east horizon about the time of beginning of morning civil twilight. However, Mercury is much better situated for observation by those nearer the Equator and in the Southern Hemisphere, from where the planet will best be seen above the east-south-eastern horizon about half an hour before sunrise, after the 10th of the month. Mercury increases in brightness quite markedly during this period, its magnitude increasing from +0.9 to −0.1.

VENUS, magnitude −3.9, is a brilliant object in the east-south-eastern sky before sunrise. However, for observers in the latitudes of the British Isles, it is unlikely to be seen during the last week of the month because of its very low altitude as it moves closer to the Sun.

MARS is visible as a conspicuous object low in the eastern sky shortly before midnight. Mars is in Virgo, and by the end of January its magnitude has brightened to −0.2.

JUPITER is too close to the Sun for observation, superior conjunction occurring on January 19.

SATURN, magnitude +1.0, is visible in the south-western sky in the evenings. Saturn is in Pisces, and its path among the stars is shown in Figure 12, given with the notes for October. The rings will be quite difficult to detect in smaller telescopes since the minor axis is only 3 arcseconds.

THE EARTH'S ORBIT. It is always said that the orbit of the Earth round the Sun is not a circle, but an ellipse. Of course this is quite true – as was demonstrated originally by Kepler; before his time, it had been tacitly assumed that all celestial orbits must be circular, since the circle is the 'perfect' form, and nothing short of perfection can be allowed in the heavens!

On the other hand, in the case of the Earth the departure from circularity is not great. The eccentricity is only 0.017, so that if the orbit were drawn on a scale to fit this page it would be hard to detect any ellipticity. Moreover, it must be remembered that a circle is simply an ellipse with eccentricity zero.

Of the principal planets, only Venus and Neptune have orbits which are less elliptical than that of the Earth. The values are:

Mercury	0.206
Venus	0.007
Earth	0.017
Mars	0.093
Jupiter	0.048
Saturn	0.056
Uranus	0.047
Neptune	0.009

Pluto's orbit is of eccentricity 0.248, but it now seems quite certain that Pluto is not a normal planet; more probably it is what is termed a Kuiper Belt object.

The Earth's changing distance from the Sun makes very little difference to the seasons, particularly since the greater amount of sea in the Southern Hemisphere tends to stabilize the temperature there. However, the difference is much more important for Mars, where the distance from the Sun ranges between 249 million km (154 million miles) and only 207 million km (128 million miles) (these figures are 'rounded off'). Since Mars, like Earth, has its southern summer when at perihelion, the southern hemisphere temperatures on Mars have a much greater range than those in the north.

THOMAS GWYN ELGER. Elger was one of the early British lunar observers; his map of the Moon is still used by some observers.

Elger was never a professional astronomer: he was a civil engineer, and was concerned largely with railroad construction. He was born in 1838, and his interest in astronomy dated from 1864, when he built his first observatory in the garden of his house at Bedford and equipped it with a reflecting telescope. The Moon was his main interest, and he began systematic observation. In 1871 he joined the Royal Astronomical Society, and in 1878 the energetic though short-lived Selenographical Society. In 1890 the British Astronomical Association was founded, and soon established a Lunar Section. Elger became Director, and built up the Section into an active and skilled organization.

In 1895 he completed his book, *The Moon*, with a small but clear

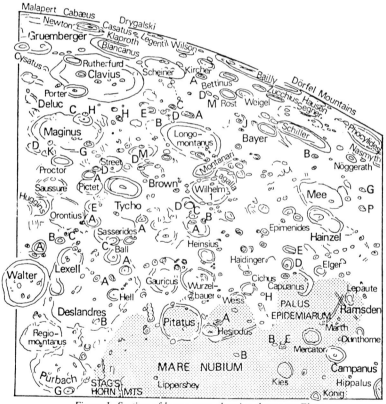

Figure 1. Section of lunar map, showing the crater Elger.

and accurate map. Sadly, he died only two years later. As Director of the BAA's Lunar Section he was succeeded by Walter Goodacre, who held the office for many years (he retired only in 1937); later Directors have included T. L. Macdonald, E. A. Whitaker, Gilbert Fielder and the present Editor of this *Yearbook*. Elger's outline map is still in print.

FEBRUARY

New Moon: February 7   *Full Moon*: February 22

MERCURY continues to be well placed for observation by those in tropical and southern latitudes for all except the last week of the month. It is still best seen above the east-south-east horizon about half an hour before sunrise. By the end of this period of visibility, Mercury has increased slightly in brightness to magnitude -0.7. Mercury passes 1° south of Jupiter on the 12th. Since Jupiter is over a magnitude brighter than Mercury, it could prove to be a useful guide to locating Mercury around that date. For observers in northern temperate latitudes the planet remains unsuitably placed for observation.

VENUS, magnitude -3.9, continues to move closer to the Sun, though observers in tropical and southern latitudes will still be able to see it for a short while low in the eastern sky before dawn. Venus is moving rapidly eastwards relative to Jupiter, and at 02^h on February 6 passes only 0°.3 south of it.

MARS is clearly visible in the eastern sky in the late evenings, and becoming increasingly noticeable as its magnitude brightens from -0.2 to -0.9 during the month. Mars reaches its first stationary point in Virgo on February 6, and its path among the stars during the year is shown in Figure 2.

JUPITER, magnitude -1.9, becomes visible as a morning object by the middle of the month, low in the south-eastern sky before dawn. However, observers in the British Isles will have to wait until next month as the planet is so far south of the Equator.

SATURN, magnitude $+1.0$, continues to be visible as an evening object in the south-western sky in the evenings. By the end of February it becomes a difficult object to detect in the evening twilight.

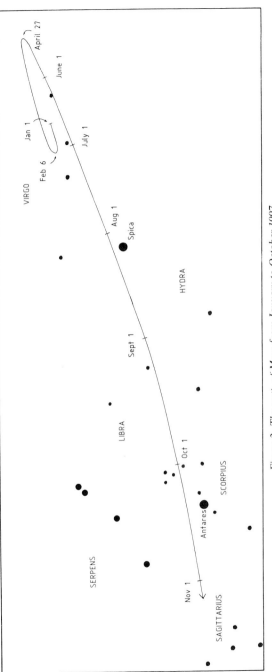

Figure 2. The path of Mars from January to October 1997.

THE GREAT DOG. A Hunter must have his dogs; Orion has two – Canis Major and Canis Minor. Both are visible in the evening sky during February, and both are easy to locate. Canis Minor has one first-magnitude star – Procyon – if little else. Canis Major is a large and important constellation, covering 380 square degrees of the sky, and is distinguished by the inclusion of Sirius, much the most brilliant of all the stars.

Yet its eminence is due solely to the fact that at a distance of less than 9 light-years, it is one of our nearest neighbours in the Galaxy. It is 'only' 26 times as powerful as the Sun, and this is puny indeed compared with some of the other stars of Canis Major. According to the authoritative Cambridge catalogue, *Sky Catalogue 2000.0*, the details of the leading stars are:

Star	Proper name	Distance, light-years	Luminosity, Sun = 1
Delta	Wezea	3060	132,000
Eta	Aludra	2500	52,500
Beta	Mirzam	720	7200
Epsilon	Adhara	490	5000
Zeta	Phurad	290	450
Alpha	Sirius	8.6	26

If Wezea were as close to us as Sirius, it would cast very strong shadows! Adhara is an important star to astronomers, because it is exceptionally powerful as an emitter of extreme ultraviolet radiation.

Sirius is a pure-white star, though the fact that as seen from Britain it is always rather low down means that it seems to twinkle strongly; from more southerly latitudes the twinkling is less. Strangely, some of the old star-gazers recorded it as being red. Certainly it is not red today, and any permanent change is most unlikely, but it is an interesting little problem – no doubt an error in interpretation.

Sirius is not alone. It has a white dwarf companion, as massive as the Sun but smaller than the planet Neptune; it is of amazing density, and has long since used up its store of nuclear 'fuel'. The orbital period is 50 years. In fact it is not particularly faint, but it is not easy to see telescopically because of the glare from its primary. Procyon, leader of Canis Minor, also has a white dwarf companion which is even more elusive.

Another feature of Canis Major is the open cluster Messier 41, which is on the fringe of naked-eye visibility and is easy to see with binoculars.

The area between Canis Major and Orion is occupied mainly by Monoceros (the Unicorn). There are no bright stars here, but there are some rich fields.

BERNARD FERDINAND LYOT. Lyot, one of the greatest of modern French astronomers, was born on 27 February 1897 in Paris, and was educated at Paris University. He became an assistant at Meudon Observatory in 1920, and specialized in studies of the Sun; he invented the coronagraph, and with it obtained the first views of the solar corona at times of non-eclipse. He was also an eminent spectroscopist. He died suddenly in 1952 while returning from an eclipse expedition to Africa.

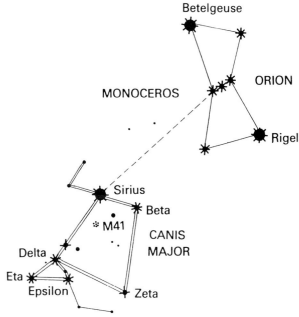

Figure 3. The constellations Canis Major and Orion.

MARCH

New Moon: March 9   *Full Moon*: March 24

Equinox: March 20

Summer Time in Great Britain and Northern Ireland commences on March 30.

MERCURY passes through superior conjunction on March 11 and about a fortnight later becomes visible as an evening object, reaching greatest eastern elongation (19°) on April 6. Being well north of the Sun, it offers observers in the Northern Hemisphere the best view. For observers in northern temperate latitudes this will be the most favourable evening apparition of the year. Figure 4 shows, for observers at latitude 52°N, the changes in the azimuth (the true bearing from the north through east, south and west) and altitude of Mercury on successive evenings when the Sun is 6° below the horizon. This position of the Sun marks the end of evening civil twilight, and at this latitude and time of year it occurs about 35 minutes after sunset. The changes in the brightness of the planet are indicated by the relative sizes of the circles, which mark Mercury's position at five-day intervals. It will be noticed that Mercury is at its brightest before it reaches greatest eastern elongation (19°) on April 6. Its magnitude on March 25 is −1.2, but this has fallen to +0.9 by April 10. It is not suitably placed for observation by Southern Hemisphere observers.

VENUS remains too close to the Sun throughout the month for observation to be possible.

MARS is visible throughout the night as it reaches opposition on March 17, with a magnitude of −1.3. Even inexperienced observers should have little difficulty in identifying it, especially as it has a slightly reddish colour. At its closest approach, three days after opposition, Mars is 99 million kilometres (61 million miles) from the Earth.

JUPITER, already visible from equatorial and southern latitudes, becomes visible to observers in the latitudes of the British Isles soon after the middle of March. Jupiter is a morning object in the south-eastern sky before dawn, at magnitude −2.0.

SATURN, magnitude +0.8, becomes increasingly difficult to detect low in the west-south-western sky in the early evenings at the beginning of the month. Thereafter it is lost in the gathering twilight as it passes through conjunction on March 30.

THIS MONTH'S ECLIPSES. Two eclipses take place this month: one of the Sun and one of the Moon. Unfortunately, the solar eclipse, on March 9, is not going to be very accessible as the track of totality is confined to Siberia and the Arctic region. The maximum length of totality will be 2 minutes 10 seconds, but the climatic conditions over most of the track are not expected to be really good – though

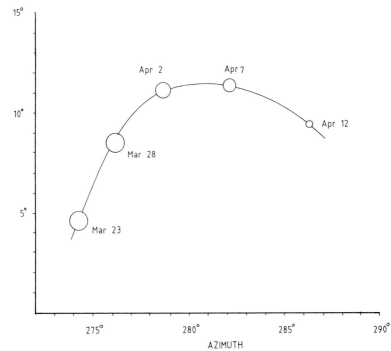

Figure 4. Evening apparition of Mercury, from latitude 52°N.

this will certainly not deter avid eclipse-chasers from making the journey! (There is another solar eclipse, on September 2, but it is not total; at maximum obscuration 90 per cent of the Sun will be hidden. The track is confined to the Antarctic.)

The lunar eclipse is due on March 24; the time of mid-eclipse is 4^h 41^m GMT. The eclipse is partial, but 92 per cent of the Moon's disk will be in shadow, so that the eclipse will be well worth watching – and photographing. It cannot honestly be said that eclipses of the Moon are astronomically important, but they can be very lovely. The eclipse of September 16 will be total, and on this occasion totality will last for over an hour.

THE FIRST EUROPEAN LIQUID-FUELLED ROCKET. March 14, 1931, was an important day in the story of space research, though few people can have realized it at the time. This was the day when the first 'modern-type' rocket was fired, by the German engineer Johannes Winkler.

Winkler was born a hundred years ago, in 1897, and worked for the German aircraft firm of Junkers. He was an early spaceflight enthusiast, and joined the first major German society, the VfR (Society for Space Travel), in 1927, becoming its President; another early member was Wernher von Braun. Practical experiments began at the Rocket Flying Field outside Berlin, but for a while Winkler preferred to work independently, and his first successful rocket with liquid-fuel propellant soared to a height of several hundred feet. It was described as looking like 'a prism placed on end', and had three tanks, containing respectively liquid oxygen, liquid methane and compressed nitrogen.

In fact, the American rocket engineer Robert Hutchings Goddard had successfully launched a liquid-fuelled rocket some years earlier, in 1926; but Goddard was always disinclined to publish his results, and since the Germans knew nothing about them they naturally assumed that Winkler's rocket was the first of its kind. Subsequently the workers at the Rocket Flying Field managed to launch various small rockets. Winkler himself never had much more success, but at least he had shown the way. He died in 1947.

APRIL

MERCURY continues to be visible in the evenings for the first ten days of the month, though not to observers in southern latitudes. Observers in northern temperate latitudes should refer to Figure 4, given with the notes for March.

VENUS passes slowly through superior conjunction on April 2, and therefore remains unsuitably placed for observation throughout the month.

MARS is in the eastern part of Leo and is still visible for most of the night, appearing well above the eastern horizon as soon as the sky is dark enough. During April its magnitude fades from -1.1 to -0.5. Mars reaches its second stationary point on April 27.

JUPITER, magnitude -2.1, is a brilliant object in the south-eastern sky before dawn.

SATURN remains too close to the Sun for observation.

CALLING UP THE MARTIANS! Mars is now prominent in Leo, and telescopes all over the world will be trained upon it. Mars has always been regarded as the one world in the Solar System, apart from Earth, which might harbour life, and certainly there is strong evidence of liquid water having existed on the surface in the past, in which case the climate was then friendlier than it is today. Not so many decades ago, Percival Lowell was still claiming that the famed 'canals' were artificial waterways. Only when the Mariner and Viking probes showed that the canals did not exist did this attractive idea finally die.

Yet Mars is also the planet beloved of the eccentrics – and even today there are weird theories which some people continue to take seriously! The best known of these concerns the 'face'. In one of the Viking orbiter pictures, a rock does bear an uncanny resemblance to a face. Of course it is simply a chance arrangement of light and shadow, but the 'fringe' writers – astrologers, flying saucer enthusiasts and the like – fastened on to it; books were written, and we had the usual 'conspiracy' theories, claiming that the truth was being deliberately concealed by the authorities. (Conspiracy theories are, of course, characteristic of the pseudo-scientific crackpot.) Next, it was suggested that there were artificial pyramid structures, and finally a claim that in the remote past a Martian expedition landed in Wiltshire and set up the arrangement of stones now marking the village of Avebury!

Earlier, no less a person than the great mathematician C. F. Gauss suggested drawing vast geometrical patterns in the Siberian tundra, to alert the Martians; this was in 1802. In 1874 a French engineer, Charles Cros, proposed to focus the Sun's heat on to the Martian deserts by means of a huge burning glass, swinging the glass around and writing words (though he never said what words he proposed to inscribe). In 1924, when Mars was at opposition, radio transmitters over parts of America were temporarily shut down so that signals from Mars could be picked up; and in 1926 a Dr Robinson went to the Central Telegraph Office in London and dispatched a telegram to Mars – for which he was charged the standard 18 pence per word (the postal authorities noted it as 'Reply not guaranteed'). And there was, of course, the Guzman Prize, offered in 1900 by a wealthy French widow. The prize – 100,000 francs – was to be given to the first scientist to establish communication with another civilization; but contact with Mars was specifically excluded, as being too easy!

What can one make of all this? Of course, there is no possibility of advanced life on Mars, and it seems that conditions there have never been suited to it; but we cannot rule out past life of a more primitive form, and indeed this may survive even now, possibly underground. Further probes to the planet are to be launched in 1997, and before long we may well be able to obtain samples of Martian material. Whether any 'fossils' will be found remains to be seen; most astronomers are sceptical, but we cannot be sure. One can only regret that there seems no possibility of finding a truly ancient Martian civilization!

This year's opposition is not, in fact, a close one. Data for the present and future oppositions are as follows:

| Year and date | Closest approach, millions of | | Max. apparent diameter, | Magnitude |
	km	miles	"	
1997 March 17	99	62	14.2	−1.1
1999 April 24	87	54	16.2	−1.5
2001 June 13	67	42	20.8	−2.1
2003 August 28	56	35	25.1	−2.7

MAY

New Moon: May 6   *Full Moon*: May 22

MERCURY attains its greatest western elongation (25°) on May 22 and is therefore visible as a morning object after the first fortnight of the month, though only for observers in tropical and southern latitudes. For observers in southern latitudes this will be the most favourable morning apparition of the year. Figure 5 shows, for observers at latitude 35°S, the changes in the azimuth and altitude of Mercury on successive evenings when the Sun is 6° below the horizon, at the beginning of morning civil twilight, about 30 minutes before sunrise. The changes in the brightness of the planet are indicated by the relative sizes of the circles, which mark Mercury's position at five-day intervals. Mercury is at its brightest after it reaches greatest western elongation (25°) on May 22.

VENUS, magnitude -3.9, emerges out of the evening twilight during the first half of the month, becoming a brilliant object in the western sky for a short while after sunset.

MARS is now about one magnitude fainter than when at opposition, and by the end of the month its magnitude has faded to $+0.2$, though it is still quite a prominent object in the south-west during the evenings.

JUPITER, magnitude -2.3, continues to be visible as a brilliant object in the south-eastern sky in the early mornings. Jupiter is in Capricornus, and its path among the stars during its 1997 apparition is shown in Figure 6, given with the notes for June.

SATURN is still unsuitably placed for observation.

THE SURFACE OF PLUTO. Pluto comes to opposition on May 25. Its magnitude is only 14, and in ordinary telescopes it looks exactly like a faint star. It was discovered by Clyde Tombaugh in 1930, and has proved to be very much of a puzzle. It is smaller than the Moon, and also smaller than Neptune's senior satellite Triton; its diameter is 2324 km (1444 miles), and it is attended by a second body, Charon, with a diameter of 1270 km (790 miles). The two are 'locked': Charon's orbital period is the same as Pluto's rotation period – 6^d 9^h 17^m. There is a tenuous atmosphere, but when Pluto approaches aphelion it seems likely that this atmosphere will condense out on to the surface; remember that the orbit is more eccentric than those of the other planets.

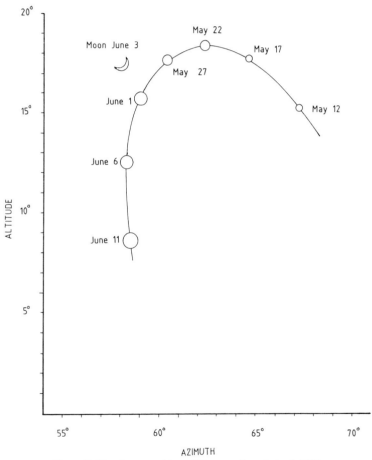

Figure 5. Morning apparition of Mercury, from latitude 35°S.

Pluto's average apparent diameter is only 0.1 of an arc second, so that 18,000 Plutos would have to be lined up to equal the apparent diameter of the full Moon. It is therefore not surprising that surface details are hard to make out – it has been said that the problem is much the same as that of trying to read the maker's name on a golf-ball 53 km (33 miles) away. Ground-based telescopes are unequal to the task, and no space probe has yet been anywhere near Pluto, but the Hubble Space Telescope has at last been able to provide a preliminary map.

The Hubble pictures cover most of the surface of Pluto, and show that the details are very complex. There seems to be a dark equatorial belt, with bright polar caps. (The axial inclination of Pluto was already known; it is 122°.5 to the perpendicular to its orbit, so that in this respect Pluto is more like Uranus than like the Earth.) The northern polar cap has been described as 'ragged', and it is bisected by a dark strip; there are at least twelve albedo features, including a cluster of dark spots and a bright spot which rotates with the planet.

Obviously, the nature of these features is uncertain as yet. There may be basins or craters; it may also be that many of the features are due to the complicated distribution of frosts which migrate across Pluto's surface with its seasonal changes. Whether or not Pluto lacks major surface relief – as Triton does – remains to be seen.

Pluto's nature is very much a matter for debate. It is not a normal planet; it seems too large to be an asteroid; in all probability it comes from the Kuiper Belt, but whether or not it is an exceptional Kuiper Belt object is also unknown (though all the rest so far discovered are much smaller than Pluto or even Charon). When the photograph was taken with the Hubble Space Telescope, in mid-1994, Pluto was approximately 4800 million km (3000 million miles) from the Earth.

EDWARD JAMES STONE. Stone was born in London in 1831, and educated at Cambridge; he became chief assistant at Greenwich in 1860, and in 1870 went to South Africa as HM Astronomer at the Cape. He spent nine years there, after which he returned to England as Radcliffe Observer at Oxford. His great work was the *Cape Catalogue* of 2892 stars. He died a hundred years ago, on May 9, 1897.

JUNE

New Moon: June 5   *Full Moon*: June 20

Solstice: June 21

MERCURY is at superior conjunction on June 25 and is too close to the Sun for observers in northern temperate latitudes. However, for those nearer the Equator or in southern latitudes Mercury may be seen low above the east-north-east horizon in the mornings, about half an hour before sunrise, for about the first fortnight in the month, magnitude 0.0 to −1.0.

VENUS, magnitude −3.9, is a brilliant object in the evening sky, though still only visible low in the western sky for a short while after sunset – in the latitudes of the British Isles, this period is only about half an hour. Venus passes south of Castor and Pollux during the second half of the month.

MARS continues to be visible as a prominent object in the south-west, though by the middle of the month it has sunk below the western horizon before midnight. Its magnitude fades from +0.2 to +0.6 during June.

JUPITER is a brilliant object, magnitude −2.6, in the south-eastern sky in the mornings. Being so far south of the Equator it is always seen at low altitudes from the British Isles. Its path among the stars is shown in Figure 6.

SATURN is now becoming visible as a morning object, magnitude +0.8, low above the east-south-east horizon before the increasing twilight glow inhibits observation.

ANTARES AND BETA LIBRÆ. The constellations of the Zodiac are very unequal in both size and importance. Scorpius is one of the most imposing; Libra, the Balance, one of the most obscure. Both are on view during June evenings.

    Antares is unmistakable, partly because of its brilliance and

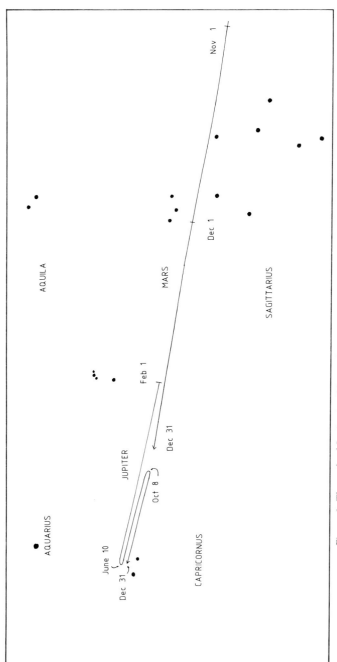

Figure 6. The path of Jupiter in 1997, and the path of Mars for November and December.

partly because of the fiery red hue which has led to its being called the 'Rival of Mars' (Ares). Moreover, it is flanked on either side by a fainter star. (So is Altair in Aquila, but there can be no confusion; Altair is pure white.) Antares is a huge supergiant, well over 7000 times as luminous as the Sun, and with a real diameter of over 300 million km (around 200 million miles). This is greater than the diameter of the Earth's orbit. However, the density is very low, at least in the outer layers, and the mass is probably little more than ten times that of the Sun. There is a fainter companion which is usually described as green in colour, though no doubt this is due partly to contrast with the red primary. The companion is of magnitude 5.4, and is 2.6 seconds of arc from the primary, so that it is not a difficult object.

Other companions of red stars are also said to be green (Alpha Herculis being a good example), but single green stars are almost unknown. The classic case is that of Beta Libræ, which has the little-used proper name of Zubenelchemale, the 'Northern Claw'; Libra used to be included in Scorpius, and indeed the star now listed as Sigma Libræ used to be Gamma Scorpii.

Beta Libræ is of magnitude 2.6; it is 121 light-years away, and 105 times as luminous as the Sun. It is of spectral type B8. Various observers have commented on the greenish hue, but most people will certainly call it white! There is, however, a minor mystery associated with it: a few of the old star-gazers, notably Eratosthenes

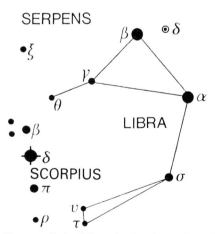

Figure 7. The constellation Libra, showing the star Beta (β) Libræ.

of Cyrene (around 230 BC) ranked it of the first magnitude, and fully the equal of Antares. Today, Antares is the brighter of the two by more than a magnitude and a half.

This is not the only case of alleged secular change: for example, Delta Ursæ Majoris in the Great Bear was sometimes ranked equal to its companions, though it is now obviously fainter. However, it would be very unwise to place too much reliance on naked-eye estimates made many centuries ago, and it is most improbable that Beta Libræ has faded perceptibly since the time of Eratosthenes.

Libra does not contain many objects of immediate interest to the owner of a small telescope, but Delta is an Algol-type eclipsing binary with a period of 2.3 days. As its magnitude range is from 4.9 to 5.9, it is always visible with binoculars. Sigma Libræ – the former Gamma Scorpii – is of spectral type M4, so that its red colour is obvious, though not so striking as that of the much brighter Antares.

JULY

New Moon: July 4   *Full Moon*: July 20

EARTH is at aphelion (furthest from the Sun) on July 4, at a distance of 152 million kilometres (94.5 million miles).

MERCURY remains unsuitably placed for observation by those in northern temperate latitudes. After the first week in July it becomes visible to observers further south, in the west-north-western sky in the evenings, its magnitude fading gradually during this period from −0.8 to +0.3.

VENUS continues to be visible as a magnificent object, magnitude −3.9, in the western sky for a short while after sunset. On July 23 Venus passes 1° north of Regulus.

MARS has now faded to magnitude +0.7, two magnitudes fainter than when it was at opposition. However, it is still visible in the western sky in the evenings.

JUPITER continues to brighten as it moves towards opposition, reaching a magnitude of −2.8. Even for observers in northern temperate latitudes it is visible above the south-eastern horizon before midnight.

SATURN, magnitude +0.6, is a morning object and is visible in the south-eastern sky before the morning twilight gets too bright. Saturn is in Pisces.

GREAT COMETS. During 1996 we were visited by Comet Hyakutake, described elsewhere in this *Yearbook*. The next interesting visitor was Hale–Bopp, which has been on view during the past few months. Obviously the *Yearbook* has to go to press well ahead of time, so that details about Hale–Bopp could not be given here; however, an account will appear in our 1998 edition.

Brilliant comets were quite common during the 19th century, and some of them – notably those of 1811, 1843 and 1882 – were bright enough to cast shadows; all these were visible in broad daylight. However, since 1910 there had been a dearth of them – until 1996. It may be of interest to list the 'great comets' seen during the past few centuries:

1744   De Chéseaux's Comet; six tails. Brilliant, but did not last for long.

1811   Comet discovered by Honoré Flaugergues. It became most imposing, and was in fact the brightest comet of the century with the possible exception of that of 1843; at one time the tail was 70° long. In 1811 the wine harvest in Portugal was particularly good, and the growers attributed this to the comet. Bottles of 'Comet Wine' still turn up occasionally!

1843   Magnificent comet; tail grew to 90°. Its period has been calculated at 517 years.

1858   Donati's Comet, arguably the most beautiful ever seen; it had a straight ion tail and a curved dust tail. Its period seems to be of the order of 2000 years.

1861   Discovered by the Australian amateur J. Tebbutt. It became brilliant, and on June 30 it seems that the Earth actually passed through its tail; the only reports – unconfirmed – were of a slight yellowness of the sky. The period is given as 409 years.

1874   Coggia's Comet; brilliant, with a very active head and a long tail. The period is of the order of 14,000 years.

1882   Wells' Comet, one of the brightest on record. (Often known as the Great September Comet.) It was photographed from the Cape by Sir David Gill; when Gill developed the photograph he realized that many stars were shown – and that the best way to map the sky would be photographically. The nucleus was observed to split. The period amounts to several centuries.

1910   The Daylight Comet, discovered by South African diamond miners. The tail attained a length of 50°, and was visible when close to the Sun. It was at its best in January, and was much brighter than Halley's Comet, which reached perihelion a few months later. The period may be around 4 million years.

1927   Comet Skjellerup–Maristany. This was observed mainly from the Southern Hemisphere; on December 18 it was visible with the naked eye when only 5° from the Sun. The orbit is elliptical, with a period estimated at 36,500 years.

1965   Comet Ikeya–Seki. This was undoubtedly a 'great' comet, but it was never well seen from Britain; the tail extended at one time to 60°. The period has been given as 880 years.

1996   Comet Hyakutake; described in this *Yearbook*.

There have of course been other naked-eye comets, which cannot be classed as 'great' but which caused general interest; notably Comets Arend–Roland (1957), Mrkos (1957), Bennett (1970) and West (1976). Kohoutek's Comet of 1973 was expected to become brilliant, but failed to do so, though it was easily seen without optical aid. Halley's Comet was not so bright in 1986 as it had been in 1910 and in 1835, simply because of its unfavourable position relative to the Earth.

AUGUST

New Moon: August 3   *Full Moon*: August 18

MERCURY is at greatest eastern elongation (27°) on August 4 and continues to be visible in the western sky in the evenings for the first half of the month, though not to observers in northern temperate latitudes. Mercury is fading during this period, from magnitude +0.3 to +1.2, as it moves rapidly towards the Sun, passing through inferior conjunction on the last day of the month.

VENUS, magnitude −4.0, continues to be visible as a brilliant object in the western sky after sunset. Disappointingly for observers in the latitudes of the British Isles, it is still only visible for about half an hour after sunset.

MARS, magnitude +0.9, is still an evening object in the south-western sky, passing 2° north of Spica on the evening of August 2. Mars is moving closer to the Sun, and observers in the latitudes of the British Isles are unlikely to see it after the middle of the month.

JUPITER, magnitude −2.8, is visible throughout the hours of darkness since it reaches opposition on August 9, when its distance from the Earth is 606 million kilometres (377 million miles). Jupiter is in Capricornus. Don't bother to look for the Galilean satellites on August 27 between $21^h 39^m$ and $21^h 59^m$, since none of them will be visible – a rare event!

SATURN continues to be visible as a morning object, magnitude +0.5. It is becoming a more prominent object in the night sky and by the end of the month is visible in the eastern sky as soon as the sky is really dark.

THE GALILEANS. It is indeed a rare event for all four of Jupiter's large satellites to be out of view simultaneously. All four are planet-sized bodies, and all have their own special characteristics (it has been said that 'there is no such thing as an uninteresting Galilean').

Callisto and Ganymede are icy and cratered; Europa icy and smooth; Io orange-red and violently volcanic. The Ionian volcanoes were discovered during the Voyager missions, but they can now be monitored with the Hubble Space Telescope, and it is plain that eruptions are going on all the time. Moreover, Io moves in the midst of Jupiter's radiation zones, so that it must be just about the most lethal world in the entire Solar System.

Their orbital periods in days are: 1.769 (Io), 3.551 (Europa), 7.155 (Ganymede) and 16.689 (Callisto). All four have orbits which are practically circular.

As seen from Jupiter, the apparent average diameter of the Sun would be 6′ 9″, so that all four Galileans could produce total eclipses: from the planet, their apparent average diameters would by 35′ 40″ (Io), 17′ 0″ (Europa), 18′ 6″ (Ganymede) and 9′ 30″ (Callisto). The inner satellite Amalthea, with an apparent diameter of 7′ 24″, could also blot out the Sun.

The Galileo probe is now orbiting Jupiter, and by the time that this *Yearbook* appears in print it is hoped that detailed views of the Galilean satellites will have been received; if so, they will be reported in our 1998 issue. In all, six spacecraft have now encountered Jupiter:

Probe	Launch date	Encounter date
Pioneer 10	1972 March 2	1973 December 3
Pioneer 11	1973 April 5	1974 December 2
Voyager 1	1977 September 5	1979 March 5
Voyager 2	1977 August 20	1979 July 9
Galileo	1989 October 18	1995 December 7
Ulysses	1990 October 6	1992 February 8

Of these, only Ulysses did not have Jupiter as its prime target – its purpose was to survey the poles of the Sun, and the gravitational pull of Jupiter had to be used to throw the spacecraft out of the plane of the ecliptic. However, Ulysses passed Jupiter at 378,000 km (235,000 miles), and the opportunity was taken to make some useful measurements.

CAPRICORNUS. Capricornus, the Sea-Goat, is not a very imposing constellation, and its outline bears no resemblance to a goat, marine or otherwise. Its brightest star, Delta, is only of magnitude 2.9.

Alpha is a wide double; the magnitudes of the two components are 3.6 and 4.2, and the separation is over 6 arc minutes, so the pair can be split with the naked eye. However, they are not genuinely associated: the distance of the brighter member of the pair is 104 light-years, while the companion is much more remote, at 1600 light-years. Both are themselves double, though their resolution is beyond the capability of small telescopes. Beta (magnitude 3.1) has a 6th-magnitude companion at a separation of nearly 2½ arc minutes, so good binoculars will resolve it.

At the moment, of course, Capricornus is completely dominated by the presence of Jupiter.

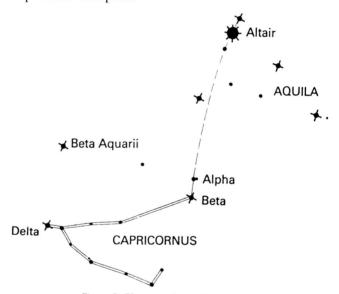

Figure 8. The constellation Capricornus.

SEPTEMBER

New Moon: September 1   *Full Moon*: September 16

Equinox: September 22

MERCURY is emerging from the morning twilight and becomes visible after the first twelve days of the month. For observers in northern temperate latitudes this will be the most favourable morning apparition of the year. Figure 9 shows, for observers at latitude 52°N, the changes in the azimuth and altitude of Mercury on successive mornings when the Sun is 6° below the horizon (at the beginning of morning civil twilight), which at this time of year occurs about 35 minutes before sunrise. The changes in the brightness of the planet are indicated by the relative sizes of the circles, which mark Mercury's position at five-day intervals. Mercury is at its brightest after it reaches greatest western elongation (18°) on

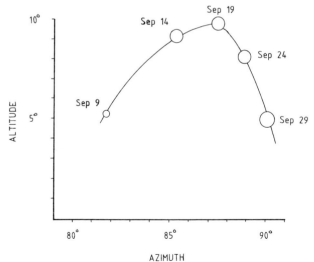

Figure 9. *Morning apparition of Mercury, from latitude 52°N.*

September 16. Its magnitude brightens from +0.8 to −1.2 during this period. It is not suitably placed for observation by Southern Hemisphere observers.

VENUS continues to be visible as a magnificent evening object in the western sky after sunset. Its magnitude is −4.0. Unfortunately for observers in the latitudes of the British Isles, its increasing southerly declination means that it is visible only for about half an hour each evening. On September 5, Venus passes 1°.9 north of Spica.

MARS continues to be visible as an evening object, magnitude +1.1, in the south-western sky, though not for observers in the British Isles.

JUPITER, magnitude −2.7, continues to be visible, but observers in northern temperate latitudes will find that it is no longer visible after midnight, by the end of the month. Observers with a good pair of binoculars, provided that they are steadily supported, should attempt to detect the four Galilean satellites. The main obstacle to observing them is the overpowering brightness of Jupiter itself.

SATURN, magnitude +0.3, is in Pisces and is now visible during the greater part of the night.

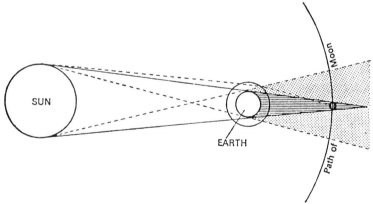

Figure 10. Diagram of a lunar eclipse (not to scale). Sunlight passing through the Earth's atmosphere (indicated by the upper dashed line passing through the outer circle) illuminates the eclipsed Moon.

LUNAR ECLIPSES AND THE DANJON SCALE. The eclipse of the Moon on September 16 is total, but how dark or how bright the eclipsed Moon will be is something which cannot be predicted accurately. All the light reaching the Moon during eclipse must pass through the shell of atmosphere surrounding the Earth (see Figure 10), so that everything depends upon the state of our atmosphere at the time. Volcanic activity, for example, leads to a 'dusty' upper atmosphere and hence a 'dark' eclipse.

An eclipse scale was introduced by the French astronomer André Danjon (1890–1967), for many years Director of the Paris Observatory. He attempted to link the brightness of the eclipsed Moon with the state of the solar cycle, and his scale was as follows:

0   Very dark eclipse, with the Moon almost invisible near totality.
1   Dark eclipse, with greys and browns, and with details on the surface barely identifiable near mid-totality.
2   Deep red or rusty, with the outer edges of the umbra relatively bright.

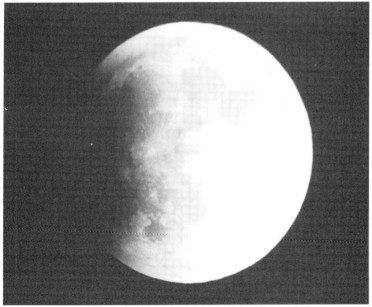

Figure 11. The lunar eclipse of April 4, 1996, photographed by Tim Adams with a Zenith 122 camera on ISO 400 film, exposure ⅓ second.

3   Brick-red, with a bright or yellow rim to the shadow.
4   Very bright; orange or coppery-red, with a bright bluish rim to the shadow.

It is on record that at the eclipse of 1761 the Swedish astronomer Per Wargentin (after whom the famous lunar plateau is named) found that the Moon vanished so completely that it could not be found even with a telescope, while in 1848 the eclipsed Moon remained so bright that it was not easy to tell that an eclipse was happening at all.

THE FIRST POINT OF LIBRA. Originally the equinoxes lay in Aries and Libra; precession has now shifted them into the adjacent constellations of Pisces and Virgo. The nearest naked-eye star to the 'autumnal equinox' is now Beta Virginis, of magnitude 3.6. It has a little-used proper name, Zavijava, and is a normal main-sequence star, 147 light-years away and 120 times as luminous as the Sun.

W. H. M. GREAVES. William Michael Herbert Greaves was born in Barbados (British West Indies) on 10 September 1897, and was educated at Cambridge. In 1924 he became Chief Assistant at the Royal Greenwich Observatory, and in 1938 transferred to Edinburgh as Astronomer Royal for Scotland, an office he held till his death in 1955. He carried out a great deal of important research, notably in connection with the temperatures of the stars. A lunar crater has been named in his honour; its position is latitude 13.2°N, 52.7°E, and its diameter is 8 km (5 miles).

OCTOBER

New Moon: October 1, 31   *Full Moon*: October 16

Summer Time in Great Britain and Northern Ireland ends on October 26.

MERCURY passes through superior conjunction on October 13. As a result it is virtually impossible to observe the planet with the naked eye at all during the month.

VENUS, magnitude −4.2, continues to be visible in the south-western sky in the early evening. Venus passes 2° south of Mars on October 26, having previously passed 2° north of Antares on October 16.

MARS, magnitude +1.1, is an evening object in the south-western sky. Mars is moving eastwards and passes 3° north of Antares on October 11 (see Figure 2, given with the notes for February, for its path among the stars). Mars continues to move towards the Sun, and is no longer observable from northern temperate latitudes.

JUPITER is still visible as a splendid object in the south-western sky in the evenings, magnitude −2.5.

SATURN reaches opposition on October 10, and is therefore visible throughout the hours of darkness. Its magnitude is +0.4. At opposition, Saturn's distance from the Earth is 1255 million km (780 million miles). Figure 12 shows the path of Saturn among the stars during the year. The rings are continuing to open, and now have a minor axis of 8 arc seconds (for comparison, the polar diameter of Saturn itself is 18 arc seconds).

FÉLIX SAVARY AND XI URSÆ MAJORIS. The French astronomer Félix Savary was born in Paris on 4 October 1797, and became assistant at the Paris Observatory, where he spent all his working life (he died on 15 July 1841). He accomplished much good work, but is now

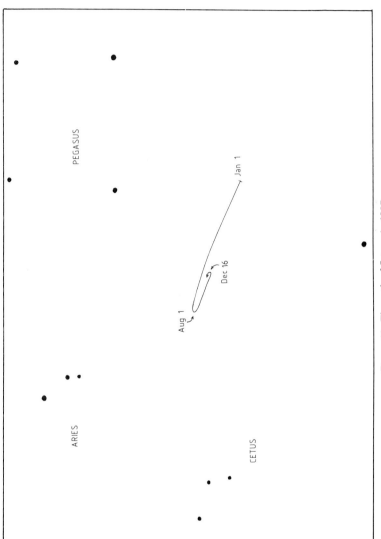

Figure 12. The path of Saturn in 1997.

remembered chiefly as being the first man to compute the orbit of a binary star.

The existence of binary systems had been demonstrated by William Herschel, but no orbits had been worked out, because of course for most pairs the changes in separation and position angle are comparatively slow. Savary concentrated upon Xi Ursæ Majoris, which has very similar components (magnitudes 4.3 and 4.8), and which we now know to be relatively nearby – its distance from us is only 25 light-years (though of course star distances would not be determined until 1838, when Bessel calculated the distance of 61 Cygni). In 1828 Savary announced that the orbital period of Xi Ursæ Majoris was of the order of 60 years, and in this he was correct, since the actual value is 59.8 years.

The present separation is between 1.4 and 1.5 arc seconds, but in 1975 was as much as 3.1 arc seconds, decreasing to less than 1 arc second in 1992–3. It is now known that both components are spectroscopic binaries, so that Xi Ursæ Majoris is in fact a quadruple system.

Xi is easy to find, some way from the famous 'Plough' pattern of Ursa Major; it makes up a neat little pair with Nu Ursæ Majoris, of

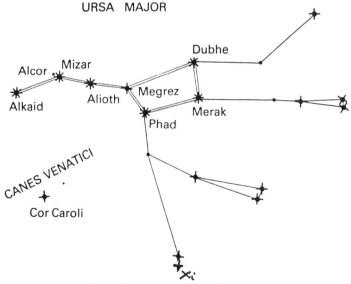

Figure 13. The constellation Ursa Major.

magnitude 3.5. Xi does have an old proper name – Alula Australis – though this is hardly ever used; Nu has been called Alula Borealis.

THE MAGNITUDE OF SATURN. Saturn is at opposition this month; the rings are starting to come back into proper view following the edgewise presentation of 1995. The aspect of the rings affects the overall brightness of the planet, which is naturally least when the rings are edge-on and, to all intents and purposes, out of view. The changing distance also has an effect; Saturn will next be at perihelion in 2003, and at aphelion in 2018.

Recent and future opposition magnitudes are as follows:

1994	+0.7
1995	+0.8
1996	+0.7
1997	+0.4
1998	+0.2
1999	0.0
2000	−0.1
2002	−0.3
2003	−0.3
2005	−0.2

(There is no opposition in 2004. The 2003 opposition falls on December 31, so that the next will be on January 13, 2005.)

This year, Saturn is approximately equal in brightness to Procyon in Canis Minor; at its best, early in the new century, it will outshine every star apart from Sirius and Canopus.

NOVEMBER

New Moon: November 30   *Full Moon*: November 14

MERCURY attains its greatest eastern elongation on November 28, and is thus visible in the evenings to observers in the tropics and the Southern Hemisphere for the whole of the month. For observers in southern latitudes this will be the most favourable evening apparition of the year. Figure 14 shows, for observers at latitude 35°S, the changes in the azimuth and altitude of Mercury on successive evenings when the Sun is 6° below the horizon, at the end of evening civil twilight, at this time of year about 30 minutes after sunset. The changes in the brightness of the planet are indicated by the relative sizes of the circles, which mark Mercury's position at five-day intervals. Mercury is at its brightest before it reaches greatest

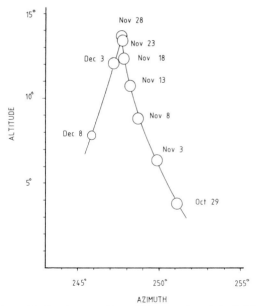

Figure 14. Evening apparition of Mercury, from latitude 35°S.

eastern elongation (22°) on November 28. During November Mercury fades only very slowly in brightness, from −0.5 to −0.3. It is not visible to observers in northern temperate latitudes.

VENUS has slowly been increasing in brightness over the past few months and is now at magnitude −4.5. It reaches its maximum eastern elongation (47°) on November 6. At last, for observers in the British Isles, Venus is gradually becoming visible for a little longer every evening, low on the south-western horizon; by the end of the month it is visible for an hour and a half after sunset.

MARS, now only about 40° from the Sun, can be seen in the south-western sky only by observers in equatorial and southern latitudes. Its magnitude is +1.1.

JUPITER, magnitude −2.3, continues to be visible as a splendid object in the south-western sky in the evenings.

SATURN, magnitude +0.4, is still visible for the greater part of the night, though setting over the western horizon well before dawn.

THE SATELLITE OF VENUS. In size and mass, Venus and the Earth are near-twins, and once it seemed logical to assume that Venus, like our own world, must be attended by a satellite. This problem was taken up in 1686 by G. D. Cassini, the Italian astronomer called to Paris to become Director of the observatory there. Cassini was an expert planetary observer; he discovered the gap in Saturn's rings still named in his honour, and also four of Saturn's satellites: Iapetus (1671), Rhea (1672) and Tethys and Dione (1684). In his journal, he recorded:

> 1686 August 18, at 4.15 in the morning. Looking at Venus with a telescope of 34 feet focal length, I saw at a distance of ⅗ of her diameter, eastward, a luminous appearance of a shape not well defined, that seemed to have the same phase with Venus, which was then gibbous on the western side. The diameter of this object was nearly one-quarter that of Venus . . . I had seen a like phenomenon on 1672 January 25.

It was then recalled that something similar had been seen in 1645 by F. Fontana. Then, on October 23, 1740, the well-known telescope-maker James Short made a very interesting observation:

Directing a reflecting telescope, of 16.5 inches focus, toward Venus, I perceived a small star pretty nigh upon her . . . I put a magnifying power of 240 times, and, to my great surprise, I found this star put on the same phase with Venus.

On May 20, 1759, the German astronomer Tobias Mayer reported the satellite as 'a little globe of inferior brightness, about 1 to 1½ diameters of Venus from herself.' During the transit of 1761, A. Scheuten reported a black spot following Venus across the solar disk, and then, in 1761, came a series of observations by J. L. Montaigne of Limoges which sounded most convincing. On several occasions, Montaigne recorded a small satellite showing the same phase as the planet itself.

In a memoir read to the French Académie des Sciences, A. Baudouin announced that:

The year 1761 will be celebrated in astronomy, in consequence of the discovery that was made on May 3 of a satellite circling round Venus . . . We learn that the new star has a diameter one-quarter that of Venus, is distant from Venus almost as far as the Moon from the Earth, and has a period of 9 days, 7 hours.

In 1773, the German astronomer J. H. Lambert calculated an orbit which gave the mean distance from Venus as 417,000 km (259,000 miles), with a period of 11^d 5^h. Frederick the Great of Prussia proposed to name the satellite 'D'Alembert', in honour of his old friend Jean d'Alembert, but the prudent mathematician declined the honour with thanks! Further observations were made in 1764 by Roedkiaer and C. Horrebow, at Copenhagen, and by Montbaron at Auxerre. And henceforth the satellite disappears from the observation books.

Obviously it never existed, but the idea took a long time to die. It was suggested that it might have a variable surface brightness, or that it had been simply a passing asteroid. But all in all, it seems definite that it was simply a telescopic ghost; a brilliant body such as Venus will show up any imperfections in an optical system. Per Wargentin once commented that he owned a telescope which never failed to show companions to Venus or to any other bright object!

Had the satellite existed, it would surely have been found by now: but Venus, like Mercury, is a solitary traveller in space.

DECEMBER

Solstice: December 21

MERCURY continues to be visible in the south-western sky in the early evening for the first week of the month, though not to observers in northern temperate latitudes. During this period its magnitude fades from −0.3 to +0.5. It passes through inferior conjunction on December 17, and moves rapidly west of the Sun to become visible as a morning object for the last week of the month, its magnitude increasing from +0.9 to 0.0 during this period. Since Mercury remains almost stationary about 10° from Antares (magnitude +1.0) during this period, observers will have a good opportunity of watching the increasing brightness of Mercury relative to Antares.

VENUS attains its greatest brilliancy, magnitude −4.7, on December 11, and as it is still 40° from the Sun it dominates the south-western sky in the early evenings. Observers in the latitudes of the British Isles will find it is visible for about two hours after sunset.

MARS, magnitude +1.2, continues to be visible as an evening object low in the south-western sky, but only for observers in equatorial and southern latitudes. By the end of the year it is only 30° from the Sun.

JUPITER continues to be visible as a splendid object in the south-western sky in the early evenings, magnitude −2.2. It is coming towards the end of its apparition, being only about 40° from the Sun by the end of the year.

SATURN continues to be visible as an evening object, magnitude +0.6, in the south-western sky.

F. A. T. WINNECKE. Our centenary this month is that of Friedrich August Theodor Winnecke, who was born at Hildesheim, in

Germany, on February 5, 1835, and died at Strasbourg on December 2, 1897.

Winnecke's father was a Lutheran minister; the boy was educated at Hanover and Göttingen, and then went to the Bonn Observatory to work with F. G. W. Argelander. He was an expert observer of variable stars, and measured the distance of one of the nearest stars, Lalande 21185. From Bonn he went to Pulkova, working with the Struves; he married Otto Struve's daughter, and worked at Pulkova until 1872, when he was appointed Director of the Strasbourg Observatory.

Winnecke discovered five comets. Four of these were unremarkable, but the fifth was very interesting indeed. He discovered it on March 9, 1858, when it was of around the 7th magnitude. Calculations showed that it was identical with a comet which had been found in 1819 by J. L. Pons, and today the comet is known as Comet Pons–Winnecke. Its period is 6.36 years; its distance from the Sun ranges between 1.2 and 5.6 astronomical units, and its orbital inclination is just over 22°.

Since 1869 the comet has been seen at most returns. In 1927 it reached magnitude 3.5, with a degree-long tail – one of the few short-period comets to attain naked-eye visibility. However, perturbations by Jupiter mean that the comet is now less well placed, and has become a very faint object. The last return was that of 1996.

VISIBILITY OF THE FIRST-MAGNITUDE STARS. To find the limiting declination of visibility, all that has to be done is to subtract one's latitude from 90°. Thus, if you are observing from latitude 50°, your co-latitude is 40°. Any star south of declination −40° will never rise, and any star north of declination +40° will be circumpolar. (In practice, the effects of refraction cause a minor modification to these values.)

The northernmost of the first-magnitude stars is Capella (declination, in round numbers, +46°); the southernmost is Alpha Crucis (−63°). From Britain, only Canopus, Achernar, Agena, Alpha Centauri and Alpha and Beta Crucis are unavailable. From Invercagill in the southernmost part of New Zealand (latitude 46°S) only Capella and Deneb are permanently out of view.

The nearest first-magnitude stars to the celestial equator are Betelgeuse (+7°), Procyon (+2°) and Rigel (−8°).

Eclipses in 1997

During 1997 there will be four eclipses, two of the Sun and two of the Moon.

1. *A total eclipse of the Sun on March 8–9* is visible as a partial eclipse from Asia, the Philippines, the north-western part of the Pacific Ocean, Alaska, north-western Canada and the Arctic Ocean. The eclipse begins on March 8 at $23^h 17^m$ and ends on March 9 at $03^h 31^m$. The track of the total phase starts on the borders of Russia, Sinkiang (China) and Mongolia, and then sweeps north-eastwards through eastern Russia, ending in the Arctic Ocean. The total phase begins at $00^h 41^m$ and ends at $02^h 06^m$: the maximum duration from any one location is $2^m 50^s$.

2. *A partial eclipse of the Moon on March 24* is visible from Africa, the western part of the Malagasy Republic, western Asia Minor and western Asia, Europe, the Atlantic Ocean, Iceland, Greenland, the Americas, the eastern Pacific Ocean and part of Antarctica. The eclipse begins at $2^h 58^m$ and ends at $6^h 21^m$. At maximum eclipse, 92% of the Moon's diameter is obscured.

3. *A partial eclipse of the Sun on September 1–2* is visible from Australasia, the South Pacific Ocean (including New Caledonia and Vanuatu) and part of Antarctica. The eclipse begins on September 1 at $21^h 44^m$ and ends on September 2 at $2^h 23^m$.

4. *A total eclipse of the Moon on September 16* is visible from the western Pacific Ocean, Australasia, Asia, the Indian Ocean, Africa, Europe, Iceland, eastern Greenland, the Atlantic Ocean, the eastern part of South America and Antarctica. The eclipse begins at $17^h 08^m$ and ends at $20^h 25^m$. Totality begins at $18^h 16^m$ and ends at $19^h 18^m$.

Occultations in 1997

In the course of its journey round the sky each month, the Moon passes in front of all the stars in its path, and the timing of these occultations is useful in fixing the position and motion of the Moon. The Moon's orbit is tilted at more than 5° to the ecliptic, but it is not fixed in space. It twists steadily westwards at a rate of about 20° a year, a complete revolution taking 18.6 years, during which time all the stars that lie within about 6½° of the ecliptic will be occulted. The occultations of any one star continue month after month until the Moon's path has twisted away from the star, but only a few of these occultations will be visible from any one place in hours of darkness.

There are five lunar occultations of bright planets in 1997, two of Mercury, one of Venus, one of Mars and one of Saturn.

Only four first-magnitude stars are near enough to the ecliptic to be occulted by the Moon: these are Regulus, Aldebaran, Spica and Antares. Only Aldebaran undergoes an occultation (thirteen times) in 1997.

Predictions of these occultations are made on a worldwide basis for all stars down to magnitude 7.5, and sometimes even fainter. The British Astronomical Association has just produced the first complete lunar occultation prediction package for microcomputer users.

Recently, occultations of stars by planets (including minor planets) and satellites have aroused considerable attention.

The exact timing of such events gives valuable information about positions, sizes, orbits, atmospheres and sometimes of the presence of satellites. The discovery of the rings of Uranus in 1977 was the unexpected result of the observations made of a predicted occultation of a faint star by Uranus. The duration of an occultation by a satellite or minor planet is quite small (usually of the order of a minute or less). If observations are made from a number of stations it is possible to deduce the size of the planet.

The observations need to be made either photoelectrically or visually. The high accuracy of the method can readily be appreciated when one realizes that even a stop-watch timing accurate to $0^s.1$ is, on average, equivalent to an accuracy of about 1 kilometre in the chord measured across the minor planet.

Comets in 1997

The appearance of a bright comet is a rare event which can never be predicted in advance, because this class of object travels round the Sun in enormous orbits with periods which may well be many thousands of years. There are therefore no records of the previous appearances of these bodies, and we are unable to follow their wanderings through space.

Comets of short period, on the other hand, return at regular intervals, and attract a good deal of attention from astronomers. Unfortunately they are all faint objects, and are recovered and followed by photographic methods using large telescopes. Most of these short-period comets travel in orbits of small inclination which reach out to the orbit of Jupiter, and it is this planet which is mainly responsible for the severe perturbations which many of these comets undergo. Unlike the planets, comets may be seen in any part of the sky, but since their distances from the Earth are similar to those of the planets their apparent movements in the sky are also somewhat similar, and some of them may be followed for long periods of time.

The following periodic comets are expected to return to perihelion in 1997, and to be brighter than magnitude +15:

Comet	Year of discovery	Period (years)	Predicted date of perihelion 1997
Wirtanen	1948	5.5	Mar. 14
Wild 2	1978	6.3	May 6
Encke	1785	3.3	May 23
Hartley 1	1985	6.0	May 28
Gehrels 2	1973	7.2	Aug. 7
Wolf–Harrington	1925	6.5	Sep. 29
Hartley 2	1986	6.4	Dec. 21

Minor Planets in 1997

Although many thousands of minor planets (asteroids) are known to exist, only a few thousand of these have well-determined orbits and are listed in the catalogues. Most of these orbits lie entirely between the orbits of Mars and Jupiter. All of these bodies are quite small, and even the largest, Ceres, is only 913 km (567 miles) in diameter. Thus, they are necessarily faint objects, and although a number of them are within the reach of a small telescope few of them ever reach any considerable brightness. The first four that were discovered are named Ceres, Pallas, Juno and Vesta. Actually the largest four minor planets are Ceres, Pallas, Vesta and Hygeia (excluding 2060 Chiron, which orbits mainly between the paths of Saturn and Uranus, and whose nature is uncertain). Vesta can occasionally be seen with the naked eye and this is most likely to occur when an opposition occurs near June, since Vesta would then be at perihelion. Ephemerides for these minor planets in 1997 are:

1 Ceres

2000.0

		Right Ascension		Declin- ation		Geo- centric distance	Helio- centric distance	Phase angle	Visual magni- tude	Elong- ation
		h	m	°	′	AU	AU	°		°
July	2	23	19.79	−17	24.0	2.395	2.980	17.9	8.6	115.7W
	12	23	21.49	−18	4.8	2.282	2.981	16.3	8.4	124.7W
	22	23	20.96	−18	58.5	2.183	2.982	14.1	8.2	134.2W
Aug.	1	23	18.14	−20	2.4	2.102	2.982	11.6	8.1	143.8W
	11	23	13.11	−21	12.1	2.042	2.982	8.8	7.9	153.3W
	21	23	6.25	−22	21.2	2.006	2.982	6.2	7.7	161.4W
	31	22	58.17	−23	22.9	1.997	2.982	5.2	7.7	164.5W
Sep.	10	22	49.69	−24	10.7	2.015	2.981	6.6	7.8	160.0E
	20	22	41.76	−24	40.1	2.060	2.980	9.3	7.9	151.4E
	30	22	35.18	−24	49.5	2.129	2.979	12.1	8.1	141.6E
Oct.	10	22	30.55	−24	39.1	2.219	2.978	14.5	8.3	131.7E
	20	22	28.22	−24	11.1	2.325	2.976	16.5	8.5	122.1E
	30	22	28.25	−23	28.2	2.445	2.974	17.9	8.6	112.8E
Nov.	9	22	30.55	−22	32.8	2.574	2.972	18.9	8.8	103.9E
	19	22	34.91	−21	27.5	2.708	2.970	19.3	8.9	95.5E

2 Pallas

2000.0

	Right Ascension		Declin- ation		Geo- centric distance	Helio- centric distance	Phase angle	Visual magni- tude	Elong- ation
	h	m	°	′	AU	AU	°		°
June 2	19	55.65	+19	49.3	2.793	3.369	15.6	9.9	116.4W
12	19	51.41	+20	35.8	2.714	3.376	14.6	9.8	123.0W
22	19	45.47	+21	1.7	2.650	3.383	13.5	9.7	129.0W
July 2	19	38.22	+21	3.2	2.603	3.389	12.5	9.6	134.0W
12	19	30.20	+20	37.9	2.576	3.395	11.7	9.6	137.4W
22	19	22.12	+19	45.8	2.571	3.400	11.4	9.6	138.5E
Aug. 1	19	14.63	+18	29.1	2.588	3.404	11.7	9.6	137.2E
11	19	8.35	+16	52.1	2.628	3.408	12.4	9.7	133.7E
21	19	3.75	+15	.9	2.689	3.411	13.4	9.8	128.4E
31	19	1.08	+13	1.8	2.769	3.414	14.5	9.9	122.1E

3 Juno

2000.0

	Right Ascension		Declin- ation		Geo- centric distance	Helio- centric distance	Phase angle	Visual magni- tude	Elong- ation
	h	m	°	′	AU	AU	°		°
Jan. 3	1	16.39	−5	39.2	1.685	1.990	29.6	9.0	92.7E
13	1	30.05	−4	.5	1.786	1.986	29.6	9.1	86.5E
23	1	45.24	−2	13.7	1.887	1.983	29.3	9.2	80.7E
Feb. 2	2	1.72	−0	22.0	1.987	1.982	28.8	9.3	75.3E
12	2	19.32	+1	31.8	2.087	1.983	27.9	9.4	70.2E
22	2	37.91	+3	25.1	2.184	1.985	26.9	9.5	65.3E
Mar. 4	2	57.35	+5	15.5	2.280	1.990	25.7	9.6	60.6E
14	3	17.54	+7	.9	2.373	1.997	24.4	9.6	56.1E
24	3	38.39	+8	39.4	2.464	2.005	23.0	9.7	51.7E
Apr. 3	3	59.79	+10	9.3	2.552	2.016	21.4	9.7	47.5E

4 Vesta

	Right Ascension h	m	Declin-ation °	′	Geo-centric distance AU	Helio-centric distance AU	Phase angle °	Visual magni-tude	Elong-ation °
							2000.0		
Aug. 21	2	10.70	+3	1.0	1.816	2.437	21.9	7.3	116.1W
31	2	12.46	+2	32.2	1.721	2.446	19.7	7.1	125.2W
Sep. 10	2	11.39	+1	50.1	1.637	2.455	16.8	6.9	135.1W
20	2	7.46	+0	57.5	1.570	2.464	13.4	6.8	145.4W
30	2	.92	−0	1.1	1.523	2.472	9.5	6.6	156.0W
Oct. 10	1	52.37	−0	59.4	1.501	2.480	5.9	6.4	165.3W
20	1	42.82	−1	50.0	1.506	2.488	4.8	6.4	167.8W
30	1	33.41	−2	26.1	1.537	2.495	7.6	6.6	160.5E
Nov. 9	1	25.26	−2	43.2	1.595	2.503	11.4	6.8	150.1E
19	1	19.23	−2	39.6	1.675	2.510	14.8	7.0	139.5E
29	1	15.76	−2	16.1	1.775	2.516	17.7	7.2	129.1E
Dec. 9	1	15.02	−1	34.9	1.890	2.523	19.9	7.4	119.3E
19	1	16.89	−0	39.0	2.015	2.529	21.4	7.6	110.1E
29	1	21.12	+0	28.5	2.148	2.534	22.4	7.7	101.5E

A vigorous campaign for observing the occultations of stars by the minor planets has produced improved values for the dimensions of some of them, as well as the suggestion that some of these planets may be accompanied by satellites. Many of these observations have been made photoelectrically. However, amateur observers have found renewed interest in the minor planets since it has been shown that their visual timings of an occultation of a star by a minor planet are accurate enough to lead to reliable determinations of diameter. As a consequence many groups of observers all over the world are now organizing themselves for expeditions should the predicted track of such an occultation cross their country.

In 1984 the British Astronomical Association formed a special Asteroid and Remote Planets Section.

Meteors in 1997

Meteors ('shooting stars') may be seen on any clear moonless night, but on certain nights of the year their number increases noticeably. This occurs when the Earth chances to intersect a concentration of meteoric dust moving in an orbit around the Sun. If the dust is well spread out in space, the resulting shower of meteors may last for several days. The word 'shower' must not be misinterpreted – only on very rare occasions have the meteors been so numerous as to resemble snowflakes falling.

If the meteor tracks are marked on a star map and traced backwards, a number of them will be found to intersect in a point (or a small area of the sky) which marks the radiant of the shower. This gives the direction from which the meteors have come.

The following table gives some of the more easily observed showers with their radiants; interference by moonlight is shown by the letter M.

Limiting dates	Shower	Maximum	Right Ascension h	Right Ascension m	Declination °	
Jan. 1–4	Quadrantids	Jan. 3	15	28	+50	
Apr. 20–22	Lyrids	Apr. 22	18	08	+32	M
May 1–8	Eta Aquarids	May 4	22	20	−01	
June 17–26	Ophiuchids	June 19	17	20	−20	M
July 15–Aug. 15	Delta Aquarids	July 29	22	36	−17	
July 15–Aug. 20	Piscis Australids	July 31	22	40	−30	
July 15–Aug. 25	Capricornids	Aug. 2	20	36	−10	
July 27–Aug. 17	Perseids	Aug. 12	3	04	+58	
Oct. 15–25	Orionids	Oct. 21	6	24	+15	M
Oct. 26–Nov. 16	Taurids	Nov. 3	3	44	+14	
Nov. 15–19	Leonids	Nov. 17	10	08	+22	M
Dec. 9–14	Geminids	Dec. 13	7	28	+32	M
Dec. 17–24	Ursids	Dec. 23	14	28	+78	

Some Events in 1998

ECLIPSES

There will be two eclipses, both of the Sun.

February 26: total eclipse of the Sun – the Americas.
August 21–22: annular eclipse of the Sun – SE Asia, Australasia.

THE PLANETS

Mercury may be seen more easily from northern latitudes in the evenings about the time of greatest eastern elongation (March 20), and in the mornings around greatest western elongation (August 31). In the Southern Hemisphere the corresponding most favourable dates are around January 6 (mornings) and November 11 (evenings).

Venus is visible in the evenings for the first ten days of January. It is visible in the mornings for the last ten days of January and until late in September. It is again visible in the evenings for the second half of December.

Mars is at conjunction on May 12.

Jupiter is at opposition on September 16.

Saturn is at opposition on October 23.

Uranus is at opposition on August 3.

Neptune is at opposition on July 23.

Pluto is at opposition on May 28.

A Robotic Telescope on the Internet

JOHN E. F. BARUCH

It is a truth universally acknowledged, that an astronomer in possession of new technologies will change the face of astronomy. With a core of new technologies, robotic telescopes are already providing innovative solutions to old problems and bringing the excitement of astronomy to many people. The Bradford Robotic Telescope is leading the way. Since December 1993, the Engineering in Astronomy Group at the University of Bradford's Department of Industrial Technology have been operating this robotic telescope on the Internet. The address or URL of the telescope base station, which is called Baldrick, is: http://www.telescope.org/rti. The robotic telescope has attracted Internet surfers from all over the world. On a typical day about 10,000 people take information from the site. At the time of writing, a total of over 16,000 people from 72 countries have registered as users and have submitted observing requests. The Bradford robotic telescope was the first robotic telescope on the World Wide Web. It has recently been joined by robot systems on the Web run by the University of Iowa and University of California at Santa Barbara.

Introduction

It was Isaac Asimov who popularized the concept of a robot. His robots were human-like figures which were able to perform many of the tasks normally undertaken by people. That was science fiction, but the word has stuck. The robotic telescope is not human, but it has its own defined 'character and autonomy' around its simple limited capabilities. It is able to record and analyse CCD images of areas of the sky to create a list of the relative brightnesses of the star-like objects within the borders of the image. In order to perform this simple task without human interference, the telescope exists within an environment which not only links it to the outside world but also continuously monitors the observing conditions in order to schedule the observing requests that it receives.

The Bradford instrument is a technology prover to demonstrate the concept of an autonomous robotic telescope. It was built for defined limited astronomical objectives, but has stumbled on a new world – perhaps the future world of astronomy.

Astronomy with a robotic telescope

The incentive to design and build a robotic telescope was an interest in eruptive variables, particularly gamma-ray bursters and cataclysmic variables. I had been working in cosmic-ray physics for many years, and it seemed to me that progress was very slow and that a new approach was needed. Gamma-ray bursters and cataclysmic variables posed considerable problems in their own right, and they appeared to be the most likely sources of the highest-energy gamma-rays, protons and electrons. Observations to monitor these objects in the visible wavebands would help to understand them and possibly provide a key to finding the source of high-energy cosmic rays. But there was a problem.

Observing time on available telescopes was subject to competitive bids from astronomers, and was awarded on the general basis of the results they were likely to achieve. Results means publications. A request for two nights' observing time with the likely publication of two or three papers would be granted. A request for six months' observing time to observe two or three objects and with the likely publication of only one paper would not fare well. Neither should it, bearing in mind that with few telescopes one project monopolizing a telescope for months at a time would exclude many others. The issue of quality is really an issue of hindsight. Committees which made judgements on likely quality would be institutionalizing mediocrity. The only feasible route to studying the objects I wanted to was to build a dedicated low-cost telescope.

The fact that it should be low-cost was possibly the most important parameter, provided that the astronomical specification was not compromised. Robotic telescopes had to be attainable not only for my particular programme, but also for others who had similar selfish programmes. But were these programmes selfish? For the past hundred years most astronomy has followed the same route. The days of the private observatory with one or two astronomers pursuing their own pet interests have long since gone. Apart from surveys by the Palomar, ESO and UK Schmidt telescopes and by satellites operating in new wavebands, astronomical research has sought the maximum number of publications from the minimum observing time. It may be that observing programmes that left this route would find many new opportunities. Perhaps even new astronomy? Can it be that our perception of the Universe has been distorted by a preoccupation with rapid results, a culture of more and more papers of decreasing substance?

Robotic telescopes must move into new areas of science, but what are the most fertile places to look?

Flare stars which produce unexplained electromagnetic storms in their coronæ, such as U Geminorum and UV Ceti, require parallel multi-waveband observing in the visible wavebands to monitor the rapid energy transport processes taking place. U Geminorum, like our Sun, generates flares. Flares from the Sun interfere with electric power grids, railway systems and long-distance communications. Flare stars are in the serious business of flares, and serious study may lead to a better flare forecasting service for outback Canada and other places whose electricity supply is vulnerable to solar storms.

Cataclysmic variables, along with flare stars, are rapidly varying objects. Observations in a single waveband provide only part of the story. Often, single-waveband observations are made with satellite observatories costing many hundreds of millions of pounds. The scientific returns are limited without the photometric visible waveband signatures that link the objects with the rest of astrophysics. An additional small expenditure on robots would provide this information. (Of all the requests for observing time on the X-ray satellite Exosat, 60 per cent involved simultaneous observations in other wavebands from the ground; in only 25 per cent of these cases were these concurrent ground-based observations achieved.) Robotic telescopes can also be used to patrol cataclysmic variables to look for objects coming out of quiescence.

Cepheid variables are one part of the ladder which we construct to establish the Universe's distance-scale, the Hubble constant and the age of the Universe. Cepheid variables have an absolute brightness which is related to the period of their variability. If you measure how bright they appear to be and you measure their period, then you can calculate how bright they really are and you can deduce their distance. From nuclear physics we are able to measure the age of the oldest stars to be around 15 billion (15 thousand million) years. Using Cepheid variables, we determine the Hubble constant from the redshifts of these galaxies. We then calculate how long the Universe can have been flying apart at this speed, and we get as a crude answer for the age of the Universe around 8 billion years. Something is wrong – the oldest stars cannot be older than the Universe.

A better understanding of Cepheid variables would give us more confidence in that rung of the distance ladder, and that understanding requires thousands of observations of Cepheid variables – a good job for robots. Many other regular and irregular variable stars would become better understood with regular and frequent monitoring on a long-term basis using robotic telescopes.

Satellite observatories, working in many new windows not available from the ground, are making enormous contributions to our understanding of the Universe, but they also generate many new questions. Ground-based follow-up observations would greatly increase the scientific returns that we get from our satellite observatories. ROSAT found many new objects in its wavebands, but ground-based observations are needed to determine what they are; similarly with the ALEXIS EUV satellite and the Compton Gamma Ray Observatory.

Supernovæ may be acceptable in the Large Magellanic Cloud, but nearer home they are tinged with danger. Young, hot, massive stars like Eta Carinæ are living in the fast lane. Some will explode as supernovæ in the next few hundred years. Only a serious study of these objects will warn us. Robotic telescopes are the best tools we have to unlock the secrets of these monster stars.

Planetary systems. Searches are currently fashionable, and one spectroscopic method is based on looking for the small movements of a star as it orbits a common centre of mass with a planet. These searches have produced three credible planetary systems, 51 Pegasi, 70 Virginis and 47 Ursæ Majoris, to supplement the incredible neutron-star systems PSR 1257+12 in Virgo and PSR B0329+54 in Camelopardalis. The only other suspected planetary system at the time of writing, Beta Pictoris, is indicating its presence by perturbations in the disk of dust surrounding the star. Robotic telescopes could add to these searches by looking for transits of

Jupiter like planets across solar type stars. (See Paul Murdin's article in this *Yearbook*.)

Gamma-ray burster source searches were a major spur to building the Bradford Robotic Telescope. The objective was to search for repeating gamma-ray burster sources with an approximate position supplied by gamma-ray detectors on board satellites. By the time work had started on a dedicated robotic telescope, the consensus view on gamma-ray bursters was that they were unlikely to repeat on a short time scale, unless they were in fact X-ray bursters with much 'softer' spectra. These did appear to repeat, but were they the same things as gamma-ray bursters? The reason for continuous monitoring was now not as powerful, but there was still much to discover with cataclysmic variables and a host of other objects. It was these requirements that generated the specification for the robotic telescope.

It is interesting that with gamma-ray bursters we have come full circle, for the Bradford Robotic Telescope is the only telescope in the world that can accept co-ordinates over the Internet and have an arc-second resolution telescope pointing at a source within 20 seconds. To find the source with 1 arc-second errors requires an intermediate camera to ride piggy-back on the telescope and match the 10° error box from the satellite with the 12 arc minute field of the telescope. The Bradford team is working very hard to find the £30,000 that such a camera will cost.

Telescope specification: a model 'T'

A model 'T' telescope
The essential requirement is a low-cost telescope which does not compromise the astronomy. In economic terms, the technology must ensure that the cost of collecting photons falls considerably, possibly by a factor ten or more. Thus for what it costs to collect 100,000 photons with a standard 1-metre telescope, robotic telescopes will collect a million or ten million photons. The gain on the Hubble Space Telescope will be even more dramatic. Of course, astronomy is more than collecting photons, and ground-based robotic telescopes will not equal the Hubble Space Telescope in resolution or UV sensitivity for many years, if ever.

The new generation of large telescopes with 8-metre-plus diameter mirrors will be used for imaging, but primarily they will be used as light buckets, collecting photons for spectroscopy. Arrays of inexpensive robotic telescopes linked by fibre optics will be able to compete effectively. These large telescopes are costing about half a million pounds per square metre of light collecting power. Arrays of robotic telescopes should be able to reduce this by a factor of three or more, but this would be a bonus. Robotic telescopes must prove themselves by opening up new areas of astronomy.

To make robotic telescopes accessible on the Internet for research astronomers, for students of all ages, for amateur astronomers and for the public who are involved with astronomy either through an astronomy club or just because they have visited a planetarium or a museum, they must be inexpensive. This requires that they are designed to a standard. The standard robotic telescope would be a model 'T' Ford of a telescope that can do serious astronomy anywhere in the world where there is a supply of electricity and a telephone line. These services could be provided with small generators, or even batteries and solar cells, and a satellite phone or Internet link.

To be assembled by two people on a mountain top
To keep the costs as low as possible, robotic telescopes should be designed around the same basic model 'T' Ford mechanical system. This does not mean that they will all end up the same, because of the great inventiveness of astronomers in putting additional instruments on telescopes or even linking them together into arrays to imitate a large aperture. This basic system should be such that it can be dispatched from the manufacturers as a kit, loaded in parts on the backs of mules if necessary, and assembled at the top of a mountain by two people without heavy lifting gear. The heaviest part of a telescope is the mirror cell. This limits the telescope to an aperture of about 1.2 metres. If a honeycomb mirror is used, the complete mirror assembly will weigh about 80 kg.

Design studies indicated a number of new approaches to telescope construction that could be exploited for robotic systems in which people would not be part of the data collection process. The main technology that supports this approach is the rapidly growing power of inexpensive computers, used individually or linked together in a network. This makes it possible not only to computerize many aspects of the telescope operation, but also to keep the software simple and modular. In this way the software can be run in different modules on different independent computers. It then becomes much more robust, reliable and maintainable. It also can be written to specified interfaces, an approach which supports co-operative working and the integration of software from different sources.

A telescope that is 80 per cent software

An evaluation of the effort required to build a working robotic telescope indicated that 80 per cent of the total cost is in the software; experience has shown that this is probably an underestimate. This completely changes the economics of telescope construction. A robotic telescope in cost terms comprises 20 per cent hardware and 80 per cent software (not including all the site costs for the erection and commissioning of the telescope). The rapid changes in computer technology and software mean that at the moment the system starts operating it will be out of date. This would not matter if the system were a stand-alone system used by astronomers who were content to learn how to use it with all its idiosyncrasies. Robotic telescopes are not like that. They will be linked to the rest of the world, and to be successful they will have to be user friendly for all comers. They will have to respond to rapid developments in computer hardware and software, as users will expect upgrades and new facilities. One effective way of dealing with such a problem is to adopt the method used with the operating system Linux, the public domain version of Unix. Linux has been developed by a user group and is being continually supported and enhanced by that group. It is the Unix of preference for many PC users of Unix systems, primarily because it has a large and enthusiastic support group.

Any telescope manufacturer that is going to respond to the software problem will have to employ software staff. Customers and users of their telescope systems will not readily share their updates if they believe that the telescope company will be selling their ideas for a profit. On the other hand, if the software is free and written to standard interfaces, not only will users share their software, but this group of software engineers will soon become much larger and more effective than the software team supporting any commercial supplier of telescopes. The only way to exploit this situation is to sell the telescope hardware and computing systems and to provide the software free to the members of the club. The software systems supporting the Bradford Robotic Telescope have been designed with communal use in mind.

Telescope hardware

The telescope hardware for a robot is also different. There is no eyepiece, although a TV camera could be made available at one focus position. There are significant advantages in using an altazimuth mounting system, and no disadvantages. The 'zenith hole' is effectively dealt with by an automatic scheduling system that does not schedule through the zenith. This is a trivial addition to the scheduler, and has no associated costs. The resolution of the field rotator required for currently available CCDs is an order of magnitude less than that required for the telescope control system, and the rotator drive instructions are easily derived from the telescope control software. The main advantage of an altazimuth mounting system is a much simpler and lighter construction. The mechanical stresses are much less complex and easier to accommodate with a simple and inexpensive mechanical design.

The telescope has a simple three-point mounting set into a thick concrete floor. The yoke rotates on a central bearing with a cable hole, and the telescope tube is mounted at the top of the yoke and counterbalanced with 84 kg.

An essential requirement for the drives of a robotic system is the elimination of backlash. This ensures that the position of the telescope is known at all times. A relatively easy method of driving the telescope without backlash is by the use of direct friction drives. Steel wheels drive steel wheels directly on the axis of the telescope. It is necessary to ensure that the axes of these drive systems are perfectly parallel so as to minimize any slippage.

The encoders should be placed directly on the telescope axes. The Bradford Robotic Telescope uses circular interference gratings on glass disks attached to the telescope axes. Since these systems were installed, inexpensive tape encoders have become available which would outperform the interference gratings to give sub-arcsecond resolution. Fiducial markers are also required to provide absolute calibrations to the incremental encoders. The whole position system can be driven by stepper motors, which naturally generate an incremental position indicator and provide a check on the encoders.

The telescope imperfections are modelled in a computer. This corrects errors in pointing and tracking due to limitations of the mechanical system, i.e. telescope axes are not perfectly perpendicular, drive axes are not perfectly centred. In this way the effects of the imperfections are removed and the telescope appears 'perfect' to the outside world to point, track and slew precisely.

The Bradford team adopted an innovative optical system which has considerable benefits for an autonomous instrument. The innovation was to use a Newtonian optical arrangement with the focus taken through the altitude axis. The flat can be rotated, and so two foci are available. It has been called a 'pseudo-Nasmyth' arrangement. A standard Nasmyth is applied to telescopes with slow focal ratios and uses two secondary mirrors to bring the image out through the altitude or declination axis at a point along the telescope tube which is relatively close to the primary mirror. The system described here is relatively fast with a focal ratio of f/4.4. The telescope tube is weighted to make the altitude axis pass through the centre of the secondary Newtonian mirror which is relatively far from the primary mirror. The benefits are that it does away with one cable wrap and it provides two instrument locations with few restrictions on size or weight or access. This is ideal and much better than a conventional Cassegrain arrangement. With this arrangement polarimetry is not possible, but there appear to be no other penalties.

The telescope initially had a single 12-position filter wheel with Johnson broad-band filters. This system is now being supplemented with a second wheel to house neutral density filters. The system is focused from a stored matrix of focal positions for each filter at a range of temperatures. The temperature is taken from a sensor on the telescope yoke.

Autonomy for the robot
The word 'robotic' as applied to the telescope is used to describe a system that is autonomous, and to differentiate it from automatic, automated and remote systems. A robotic system that is autonomous is able to assess its environmental conditions in conjunction with its current task list, and optimally match the two. It performs this optimization continuously, responding to changes in both the task list and the environmental conditions without outside intervention. It is able to schedule its tasks, process the data to include an assessment of the quality of its work, and return the results to the person who requested them.

Autonomous systems require complete sensor systems to monitor the environment and ensure that the telescope operates safely and efficiently in all conditions of weather and human presence, and all the failure modes are fail-safe modes. There are over 40 sensors supporting the operation of the telescope. At the core of the system is a fail-safe roof operation. The initial design had the roof driven through an uninterruptable power supply (UPS) module which was significantly underrated. Roof sensors monitored the position of the roof, a sensor monitored the mains and a watchdog monitored the activity of the computers. If the power failed or any of the computers crashed, the roof was closed using the UPS to provide power. All worked well until the first winter and the formation of ice on the roof wheels. At this point the initial surge of current required to move the roof overloaded the UPS, which closed down and failed to move the roof. This has now been changed for a d.c. motor driven from a battery with an electric wheelchair control system. This is much more robust, and so far has worked well under all conditions.

The weather sensors are in a hierarchy. At the top are wind and rain (precipitation). The wind must be less than 40 mph (65 kph), and there must be no precipitation for the telescope to operate safely. These sensors are supplemented by multiple humidity, temperature, dew, cloud, pressure and light sensors to provide an overall picture of the environmental conditions. There is also a complete security system to ensure the safety of people working there and the security of the systems left unattended. The telescope itself also looks for bright stars in a test mode to provide a supplementary check on observing conditions.

The communications from the telescope to the outside world are of great importance. Normal telephone connections cannot be relied upon without checking their suitability. When the Bradford Robotic Telescope was designed, it was envisaged that images would be taken, but few would be sent to the observers. They would be analysed on site, the key parameters being extracted to provide enough information to give the observer confidence in the quality of the system. The data file for each observation would be less than 5 kb. It soon became clear that everyone wanted images, and each observation exploded into 250 kb. A robotic telescope could make 3000 observations in one night – that is 750 Mb to send down a telephone line without any communication overheads. Old telephone lines were happy working at 2400 baud; a poor line might have difficulty working at 300 baud. A 20 kbaud line would take over 10 hours to send 750 Mb. Realistically, at 14.4 kbaud, which only a good line could reach, 3000 images would take two days to download.

This is not a trivial problem. Observatories are often far from a

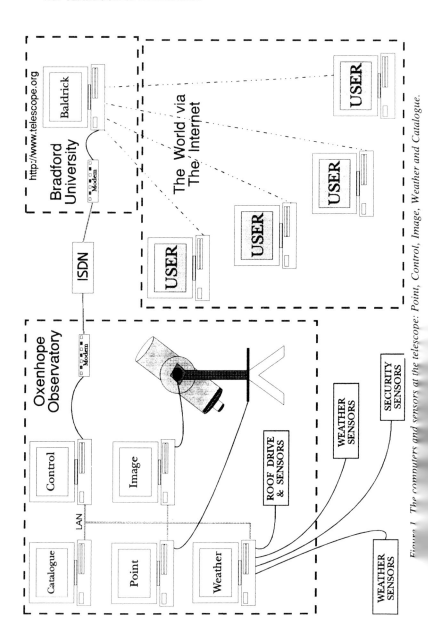

Figure 1. The computers and sensors at the telescope: Point, Control, Image, Weather and Catalogue.

telephone exchange. The telephone lines to the observatory could have been added years after the original lines were laid. The technology of the new lines, the size and material of the wires, may be completely different to the systems it is being linked to. All these factors affect transfer speed. People can understand one another's speech over appalling telephone lines. Computer modems either collapse, or the more sophisticated ones will lower their communication speed until data is being transferred. If a cut-out speed is not inserted, this transfer rate could be as low as 75 baud. Eventually an ISDN digital phone line was installed. This has a guaranteed transmission speed of 64 kbaud. BT installed a microwave link to achieve this level of service.

The Bradford Robotic Telescope lives in an environment of five computers networked together and linked to Baldrick, the base station Unix computer, via an ISDN line as shown in Figure 1. The five computers are designated Control (with the link), Weather, Point, Image and Catalogue. Weather provides a complete environmental monitoring system for the telescope (Figure 2) and provides an 'OK_for_observing' signal to the system.

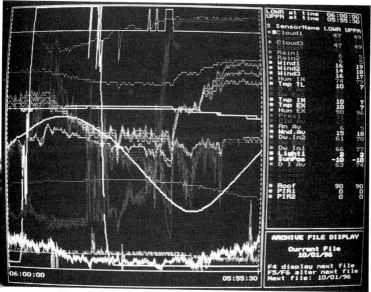

Figure 2. The weather screen, showing sensor information.

A telescope for photometry

The initial objective of the telescope was to provide comparative or relative photometry of stars in the same CCD image. It was envisaged that the telescope could monitor variable objects with comparison stars in the same field. The monitoring could be on time scales from minutes to years. Since the commissioning of the telescope the team has demonstrated drift-scan observing, in which the shutter is opened on the target field and the CCD is clocked vertically and read out continuously. Very rapid variability can be monitored in this way.

The automatic calculation of exposure times for stars is relatively easy, but for diffuse objects with only a known integrated magnitude it is not simple: for them it is necessary to know the surface brightness. Efforts are being made to include surface brightness in the catalogues and so automatically calculate exposures. The Moon and planets provide other problems of magnification. The Moon is too large to fit onto a single CCD image, and so demagnification is required. With a plate scale of 100 arc seconds per millimetre, and 24 μm pixels, Jupiter is only 12 pixels in diameter. Image magnification is also required.

Comparative photometry requires there to be at least two stars in the field. The stellar number density indicates that for stars fainter than 12th magnitude there is a high probability of there being two stars in an image covering about 200 square arc minutes. It was for stars fainter than 12th magnitude that the telescope was designed. For deep images there will be many faint stars. At magnitude 18 there will be upwards of 30 stars in 200 square arc minutes in directions away from the galactic centre. It is important that there should be no confusion, and that the telescope can point with sufficient precision (about 5 arc seconds) to ensure that pattern recognition programs will work in crowded fields.

A large proportion of the cost of most telescopes is due to the requirement that they are able to support every type of instrument. Robotics is a relatively new science. There are relatively few robots in operation and very few autonomous robots. There are none that operate in the open air on the tops of mountains with complex systems like a telescope. A great deal of science is possible with a robotic telescope that only provides for its users comparative photometry of stars on the same CCD image and straight images. An effective robot will initially only be able to utilize one instrument. In this case it is a CCD camera operated as a photometer.

Robotic telescopes have the problems of normal telescopes, plus their own. The severe problems of autonomous robots include spiders making homes on LEDs to benefit from the warmth, spinning webs in filter apertures, birds roosting on heated rain sensors and fouling them, mice nibbling cables, and condensation in electronic systems. Improved design and sensor integration will eventually eliminate these problems, but at present there are no books on good practice, and the lessons are being learned.

The Bradford Robotic Telescope has been built as a technology prover to investigate the design of robotic telescopes, demonstrate that autonomous robotic telescopes are possible and indicate the major difficulties that have to be overcome. The telescope was constructed at the University Experimental Station on the Moors near Haworth at an altitude of 440 metres. It is a 46 cm Newtonian with a pseudo-Nasmyth optical arrangement (Figure 3). It has a CCD camera with 585 × 385 pixels and is able to point and track with arc second precision. First light was in September 1993, and the telescope system was linked to the Internet in November 1993.

A telescope on the Internet
The telescope is available to all on the Internet. The address http://www.telescope.org/rti should be easy to remember. The interface is

Figure 3. The Bradford Robotic Telescope.

designed to be helpful and supportive, with comments and default values always available. Objects are available on browsable lists and can be selected as Messier, IC, SAO or NGC objects, or with an RA and dec. Observations are returned to the requester in gif and FITS format with a complete header and partial data reduction. A FITS viewer is also available from the site.

The base page provides access to:

- the telescope;
- a list of other interactive hardware that is available on the Web;
- the Nuffield project, which is a series of school projects and a vast amount of astronomical information, games and worksheets;
- stars and galaxies (taken from a commercial multimedia CD-ROM produced by Bradford Technology Ltd and Armagh Observatory); contains many images of astronomical objects and is a learning resource in its own right, with moving images, audio and hypertext;
- the home pages of the Engineering in Astronomy team who have made it all possible;
- the University of Bradford's information system.

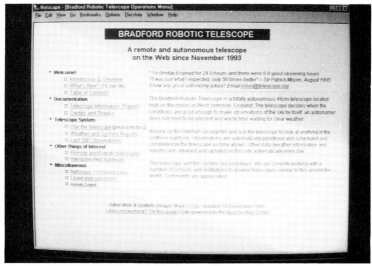

Figure 4. The Internet home page.

The whole system is cross-linked with hypertext, so the parts of the Nuffield project that require the telescope have the links available.

The telescope page brings you into the system page, which tells you that the telescope has been on the Web since November 1993. It gives the observing time over the previous 24 hours and any weather that limited observing. The links on the system page are divided into *Welcome!*, *Documentation*, *Telescope System*, *Other things of interest* and *Miscellaneous*, as shown in Figure 4. The *Welcome* gives access to the *Introduction Page* (Figure 5) which shows the location of the telescope on a map. It contains a picture of the telescope and the sort of background information given in this article. *What's New?* provides news of telescope and system development, and a *Table of Contents* is a comprehensive list of the available sets of documents. *Use the telescope*, under *Telescope System*, gives information about using the system over the Internet, and the option to register if you are a new user or to log in if not. If you have forgotten your password, this is where you can change it automatically. The registration procedure provides the information necessary to e-mail you with results, to enable you to have your own observing space and to provide some administration information to assist us in developing the service.

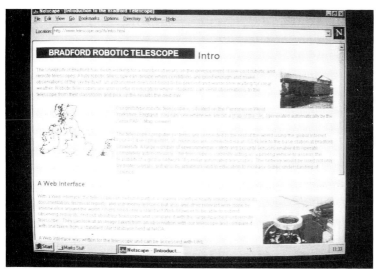

Figure 5. The Introduction page.

When you have registered you are sent the user name that the system will use. This is required to log on in future. When you log on you get into the *User Menu*, which welcomes you and indicates your level of authority and the type of user that you have been classified as. There are ten levels. Users are divided into professionals, guests, students and admin. Initial log-on will get you into level 10. If you are collaborating with us in a general way, you will be put into level 9.

Service observing

The User Menu includes the submission of observing requests. These can be done by browsing a list of Solar System objects, a list of objects selected from the Messier Catalogue and a list of star names, described on the page illustrated in Figure 6. Alternatively you can submit an observing request by providing the NGC, IC or SAO number of the object. The requested observations are placed in a pool scheduler. A macro schedule is produced every afternoon for the following evening. The scheduler places the top levels first and then fits in the lower levels to produce a schedule to fill 150 per cent of the available time. This provides a small pool for the micro scheduler at the telescope to select the most appropriate objects to

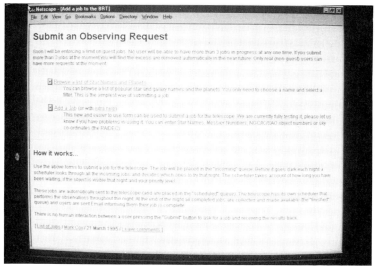

Figure 6. The observing request submission page.

observe whenever the conditions are suitable. This schedule is loaded up to the telescope every evening and the telescope waits for the 'OK_for_observing' signal from the Weather computer. The Control computer then generates a micro schedule fitting the highest-priority objects, even if they are not at their best observing position. These are followed by the lower-priority objects. This is an easy task performed within seconds, and the system is ready to observe.

Apart from the few objects that have a high enough priority to be observed if possible, all the other objects are observed on the southern meridian. The telescope works very fast, moving up and down the meridian to obtain images. An analysis of the telescope operation indicates that most of the time is spent reading out the CCD (about 10 seconds per image). In an average observing session the telescope makes more than 200 observations per hour.

Other techniques have been developed for the telescope in addition to the standard service observing described above. These modes include eavesdropping, prompt observing and engineering mode. In the engineering mode the telescope can be driven remotely, but this is hardly ever used; when it is used, it is usually for TV demonstrations.

Prompt observing

Prompt observing has been developed to search for gamma-ray bursters in outburst. Co-ordinates of the outburst error box are calculated at the Compton Gamma Ray Observatory base station in the USA and distributed over the Internet within six seconds of the onset of the burst as detected by the satellite. The information is sent in coded form to the base station computer Baldrick, which processes the information and calculates if the error box is above the horizon and if it is dark at the observatory. If the answer to these questions is 'yes', Baldrick opens the link and within 10 seconds of receiving the information it is transferred to the Control computer at the telescope. If the telescope is observing, the program is interrupted and the telescope is slewed to the new co-ordinates while the CCD is reset. The process requires an intermediate CCD camera because the co-ordinates as supplied at present have an uncertainty of 10 degrees and the current CCD is only 20×12 arc seconds. An intermediate camera would have a field of $10°$ square. It would be mounted piggy-back on the telescope and provide a much smaller error box with which to guide the main telescope.

Calculations indicate that this whole process, to the opening of the shutter of the main CCD camera on the telescope, can be accomplished within 60 seconds. At 60 seconds, 30 per cent of gamma-ray burster sources are still in outburst.

Eavesdropping
Eavesdropping is operational, but not available on the Internet because the observing conditions at the Bradford site are so unpredictable that it would not be of any use. The development team have access to the base station from home and can operate the eavesdropping mode to check how the telescope is working. They are also able to operate the engineering control mode to institute observations. Eavesdropping gives access to the computer screens in a read-only mode.

The future
The most amazing part of the whole Bradford Robotic Telescope development has been the ever-growing public interest. When the information requests received over the Internet reached 1000 a few weeks after starting, we were surprised. At the time of writing we often have weeks with 120,000 information requests for the telescope alone. Most of the 16,000 registered users are in the USA; the UK is second with over 1600, followed by Canada, Sweden, Australia, Germany, the Netherlands and Italy, each with over 250. At the other end of the scale there are ten countries each with one registered observer, including Fiji, Lithuania and Kuwait.

Most of the observing requests are for the Moon, Jupiter, Venus, Mars, Saturn and the Andromeda Galaxy. There is a continual stream of e-mail messages, typically 30 over a weekend, which is about 0.1 per cent of the people who have accessed the system. The e-mail exposes to us the vast interest there is in astronomy from people of all ages and interests, the only common factor being that they have access to the Internet.

We get many helpful suggestions and comments, as well as questions like 'Why will the telescope not accept my request for. . . ?' for a range of objects that never rise at a latitude of 53°N, and 'Why do you not have a list of black holes for us to select from?' We certainly appreciate the limitations of our system, and the immense advantages there would be in having a telescope anywhere in the world, operating from a good site and accessible over the Internet. The weather on the moors above Haworth is atrocious, both in its lack of clear skies and the extreme conditions in which our systems have to survive and operate.

Astronomy for school students

The scale of interest in the system has led us to develop astronomy projects for school students using the telescope. One set of projects funded by the Nuffield Foundation is associated with hundreds of pages of information about astronomy, linked to projects, information, games, worksheets and puzzles, supplemented by observations provided by the telescope. There is also a series of research projects funded by the Particle Physics and Astronomy Research Council (PPARC) that are still under development. These research projects are real scientific projects, involving professional astronomers, which school students can undertake using the telescope. For the projects to be effective, the students have to let us know what they would like to do so that they can have an appropriate level of priority for telescope use. The projects include the follow-up observations required by astronomers observing with satellites or other telescopes outside the optical wavebands, the search for rapid transient events on low-energy X-ray stars, the monitoring of light pollution, and the search for transits of Jupiter-like planets orbiting solar-type stars.

Daytime observational astronomy

A telescope at a good site on the other side of the Earth, e.g. in Hawaii or Australia, would enable school students in the UK to see the dark sky from their classrooms. A telescope in Australia would show them a sky they have never seen from home. The teaching of science would greatly benefit from eavesdropping observations using robotic telescopes on good sites linked to clear supporting material placed on the Internet. The supporting material could be investigated at any time, but the eavesdropping observations could be programmed (e.g. the study of the velocity of light by the occulting of Jupiter's moons by the planet itself).

Requests and comments from school students convince me that a robotic telescope should have a constellation camera with a 10° or 20° field of view which can ride piggy-back on the main telescope and provide images of the constellations as they really are, and also through filters.

The provision of background material means that students can develop their interest at a speed and a depth that suits them. This provision will also support the thousands of amateurs who regularly inspect our site, and the many parents who are interesting their children in astronomy. Robotic telescopes on the Internet will completely change the teaching of science and astronomy.

New challenges at the leading edge of research
Eavesdropping also opens up a new avenue to enthuse the public with astronomy. Professional astronomers using the largest telescopes in the world could open their observing to eavesdropping on the Internet. Astronomers could be required to produce Internet public explanatory pages of their work. These could be presented to the committee awarding the observing time, and could form part of the assessment of applications. Successful applicants would use their Internet pages to take the public through the logic of their request for observing time, and indicate what results they expected and what the implications of the different possible results would be. The public could have access to the excitement, thrill and tedium of research. Astronomers could thus become media stars, and their work would be enhanced and protected. Access to computer screens does not give the details of the data necessary for publication or access to the calibration data necessary to confirm the quality of the data.

Robotic telescopes are about to revolutionize astronomy. They can increase the observing time available for the long-term programmes for investigating many of the cornerstones of astronomy. These could include a serious search for planetary systems. Robotic telescopes would rescue much science currently lost from satellite observatories through the difficulty of making follow-up or concurrent observations. They would open observational astronomy to school students, who would be able to work from their classroom to pursue their own research programme or merely observe the sky on the dark side of the planet. For millions of people access to research as it takes place through eavesdropping on the astronomer observing at the telescope is an exciting prospect. Robotic telescopes are about to bring millions more people into an intimate relationship with astronomy. Let us hope that it is a fruitful marriage.

James Nasmyth: Astronomer of Fire

ALLAN CHAPMAN

For most of the 19th century, fundamental astronomical research in Britain was dominated by Grand Amateurs: men of ample fortunes who had the resources to innovate in the field of instrument design, and devise equipment that was tailored to the demands of original lines of investigation. Professional astronomy, by contrast, was much more restricted in its scope: the Astronomer Royal at Greenwich, for instance, was kept to the strict routine of positional astronomy required by the Admiralty. Similarly, the university observatories were tightly controlled, under-funded, understaffed, and expected to keep to the straight and narrow of positional work.[1]

If you wanted to become involved in *real* research, therefore – to study planetary and lunar surfaces, search for asteroids or satellites, examine sunspots and flares, or attempt to resolve nebulæ – you had to pay for it yourself. Not only that, but you would probably have had to devise a specialist technology with which to do it, for suitable instruments were not available through commercial channels. Such research needed ingenious and inventive individuals, and James Nasmyth (1808–1890) became one of the most distinguished of the type, for his contributions to astronomy were the direct products of his success as an engineer and as a businessman.

Nasmyth was fortunate to be born into an environment that aroused and regularly stimulated his talents throughout his early years. His happy and encouraging childhood, spent at 47 York Place, Edinburgh, no doubt contributed greatly to that confidence and resourcefulness that were such conspicuous features of his adult life. His father was Alexander Nasmyth, the leading Scottish artist of the day, and generally considered the founder of Scottish land-scape painting, while his mother Barbara came from the well-connected Foulis family. Alexander, who was 50 years old when James was born, had known Robert Burns (whose portrait he painted), and moved on equal terms among the scientists, doctors, statesmen and philosophers of the 'Scottish Enlightenment'.[2] When

Figure 1. James Nasmyth, as pictured in the frontispiece to the Autobiography. *Some artistic licence was exercised by the engraver in softening the lines of the subject's face in this portrait. The original photograph on which it is based shows a less avuncular, much harder countenance. Perhaps it was this innate toughness, and possible abrasiveness of manner, which lay at the heart of Nasmyth's often ambivalent relations with the genteel world of London science.*

James Nasmyth supplied an account of his life to his autobiographical editor, Samuel Smiles, he claimed that he first became fascinated by astronomy as a boy when his father showed him the Moon's craters through his Dollond refractor.[3] Moreover, with scientists like Sir David Brewster among his father's friends, James would not have lacked informed guidance on technical matters. Alexander gave his son the sound artistic training that he was to find invaluable in his later careers as engineer and astronomer, as well as providing an environment of remarkable tolerance. When the young James first acquired his life-long passion for metal-casting and turning, he was allowed to build a smelting furnace into his bedroom fireplace, though his father kept a long cane with which to tap on the drawing-room ceiling below the bedroom if operations went on too long past midnight.

The young Nasmyth attended Edinburgh High School, the School of Arts and some of the science lectures at Edinburgh University, though it was soon clear that his passion was for engineering and applied science. After receiving some engineering training in Edinburgh, he went to London in 1829 to become the pupil and personal assistant of Henry Maudslay, whose machine-tool factory was then the most advanced in the world. Nasmyth worked as Maudslay's 'Gentleman' Assistant for three years on the nominal salary of 10 shillings (50p) per week; while his father was well off, he decided as a point of honour that at the age of twenty-two it was about time that he lived off his own earnings. He always took pride in the thrift and discipline which enabled him to live well off this small salary, so Smiles reported, though we must never forget that incomes are always relative to expectations. There were, after all, thousands of labourers in England in 1830 who kept whole families on less than 10 shillings per week.

We know that, during his time with Maudslay, astronomy and telescopes figured prominently in Nasmyth's life. By 1827 he was already a skilled caster of speculum mirrors, and had produced a fine 6-inch 'metal' while living in Edinburgh. Nasmyth soon developed his 'chill' method of casting telescope mirrors, whereby the molten metal was poured from its crucible on to a flat iron plate within an iron mould-ring. To ensure an even flow and cooling of the metal, the molten speculum mix entered the mould-ring via a spout-hole, losing its heat at a uniform rate. In this way he was able to produce a mirror blank of remarkable metallurgical homogeneity, so that when it had cooled, and the mould-ring and plate were knocked away with a hammer, a beautiful speculum was ready for figuring. This basic technique was to be used by Nasmyth for all his subsequent mirrors. He was also assisting Maudslay with the design for an observatory for his retirement home outside London, when his master died suddenly in 1831. At this juncture in his life, the enterprising Nasmyth seized upon an offer recently made to him by the Dale brothers of Manchester. The previous September, when he had travelled up to Lancashire to attend the opening of the Manchester to Liverpool railway (the first public steam railway in the world) and meet George and Robert Stephenson, the mercantile Dale brothers had offered to lend him £500 so that he might establish an engineering factory in their city. This led to the founding of the famous Bridgewater Foundry at Patricroft, near Manchester, which happened to lie alongside the newly opened railway. Over the next quarter of a century this factory became world-famous for the manufacture of large precision steam-engines. Its ideal location beside the railway lines made it possible to import raw materials and deliver finished products anywhere in Britain – or, via Liverpool, the world – by 1845.

The Bridgewater Foundry made a large fortune for Nasmyth by 1856 (indeed, a multi-million fortune in modern money[4]), but what won him his first real fame was the invention of the steam hammer in 1839. Using the power of a large piston and steam cylinder in a vertical frame to deliver precision hammer-blows, Nasmyth invented the machine which made heavy iron forging possible. When it was in operation, the giant steam hammer-blows could be heard a quarter of a mile away, and shook the earth as they forged the paddle-shafts of ships. Yet so precise were the adjustments that, when Nasmyth was showing visitors around his factory, he demonstrated that the hammer could also be used to crack an egg without even damaging the wineglass in which it was set.

If the invention and use of the steam hammer brought Nasmyth his first fame, it was astronomy that brought his second. As soon as his foundry was running successfully, and he had built his house nearby (appropriately called 'Fireside'), he set up his own observatory in the grounds. With the vast resources of the Bridgewater Foundry at his command, it is hardly surprising that he built remarkable telescopes. His factory, after all, was world-famous for the fact that it could machine ten-ton blocks of iron to one-thousandth of an inch, and construct railway locomotives that were as exact as clocks; so one should not be surprised that Nasmyth set about constructing big telescopes that could be accurately controlled with hand-operated gears.

His first attentions were paid to optics, and by the early 1840s he was able to figure and polish virtually identical specula 10 inches in diameter. Since boyhood he had been a skilled mirror-grinder, and when he started to experiment with large blanks at Bridgewater he turned his thoughts to machine figuring. But it was a problem that was far from easy to solve, for it was first necessary for him to analyse carefully, in geometrical terms, the subtle convolutions of hand that were necessary to give a perfect finish to a speculum, and then invent machinery with which to replicate and scale up the process.

The machine figuring of large mirrors became of special concern to Nasmyth after he formed what was to become a life-long friendship with the Liverpool brewer and astronomer, William Lassell, in 1840. In 1844, Lassell was designing a 24-inch equatorially mounted reflecting telescope (to become the largest equatorial telescope of the day), and realized that only a precision machine could impart the exact curves that were necessary for such a large piece of metal. Lassell was already impressed by Nasmyth's hand-polished 10-inch mirrors – claiming that their perfection 'made my mouth water'[5] – and proposed a design for a large figuring machine. Nasmyth built this machine for his friend (no doubt, as a professional engineer, adding some improvements); when a small steam-engine was connected to it, beautiful 24-inch specula could be produced with relative ease.[6]

Nasmyth's brilliant and beautifully figured mirrors impressed everyone who saw them, and were further responsible for sparking the initial interests of a man who would in turn become one of the Grand Amateur astronomers of the third quarter of the nineteenth century. In 1842, Nasmyth entertained a business client who was commissioning new machinery for an industrial process, and who happened to see a freshly figured 13-inch speculum. From this chance encounter at the Bridgewater Foundry, Warren De La Rue ordered a reflecting telescope for himself, and began a career that was to secure his reputation as a pioneer of solar astronomy, and of the newly invented art of astronomical photography.[7]

Since he was a professional engineer, it goes without saying that one of Nasmyth's obvious astronomical interests was telescope design. He developed a speculum alloy consisting of 15 parts tin, 32 parts copper and 1 part arsenic, and found that it gave an excellent blank capable of taking a fine white polish. In addition to the optics, Nasmyth devoted a great deal of attention to the design of mounts that were both stable and easy to use.

It may seem strange to a modern observer that early-19th-century astronomers who were willing to invest such time and energy into their specula often mounted them in large wooden structures where limited altazimuth motions, jamming pulleys and slippery ladders made them awkward and dangerous to use. Sir William and Sir John Herschel, John Ramage, and Lord Rosse all built such telescopes. Indeed, one of the main reasons why reflecting telescopes were so often considered to be idiosyncratic amateur instruments, unsuitable for professional observatories, was that they were invariably custom-built to an individual's special needs, and required a lot of maintenance, and 'knack' in their usage. A battleship-rigged structure of wood and cordage had to be nudged, tweaked and coaxed by its loving owner to make it perform to optimum advantage, and no professional observatory could afford the time this took – only a rich amateur could. Like racehorses and Stradivarius violins, 'Herschel-mounted' reflectors were one-man telescopes: perfect symbols of the individualism of early-19th-century British astronomy.

Nasmyth's reflectors, and those of his friend Lassell, were in this one-man-telescope tradition, though their designs were transitional between the Herschel-type telescopes and the professional observatory reflectors of Melbourne and Mount Wilson. And this link was made by the use of precision-engineered iron and gunmetal mounts in place of wood, stone and rope. The heavy engineering technology that was necessary to mount a large mirror on a geared metal mount would not have been possible until the Industrial Revolution was well advanced, and it should not be forgotten that, of the two men who pioneered it, one built railway locomotives and marine engines for a living, and the other was his close friend.

Although Lassell came to pioneer the large iron equatorially mounted reflector, Nasmyth stayed with altazimuth mounts for all his large instruments. But they were altazimuth mounts of extremely original design and facility of usage. In many ways, Nasmyth's big reflectors were the ancestors of modern computer-controlled altazimuth telescopes, where two simple mechanical motions, in azimuth and altazimuth, in conjunction with the correct 'program', can track in right ascension and declination. The 'program', one might say, was inside Nasmyth's head, and it was turned into an easy tracking motion by two simple endless screws that could

*Figure 2. What Nasmyth called his 'comfortable' telescope of 1848. This used the triple-mirror Nasmyth focus, the eyepiece being located on the altitude axis through the support trunnion. All parts of the sky could be reached without the observer having to leave his seat. (*Autobiography, *p. 338.)*

be operated by each of the observer's hands when his eye was at the eyepiece. This was the essence of Nasmyth's 'comfortable telescope' of 1848, which embodied an optical system whereby the image was formed at an eyepiece inserted into the hollow trunnion that supported the tube, so that the entire sky could be reached and tracked without the observer needing to change position. It goes without saying, however, that such an instrument required the very highest standards of balance and engineering if it was going to work at all. And it worked superbly, as Nasmyth proudly informed his Sheffield scientist friend Clifton Sorby in 1848, when inviting him over to Manchester to enjoy a 'scamper over the sky' at the finished instrument.[8] This remarkable telescope is still preserved in the store of the Science Museum, London.[9]

Nasmyth's 'comfortable telescope', originally of 10 inches aperture, contained a 20-inch-diameter primary speculum by 1850, though it lost some 62 per cent of its incident light by having to have two secondary mirrors in order to form an image inside the tube trunnion. But the amount of light that an astronomer wants is entirely relative to the things that he wishes to study, and because Nasmyth's chosen objects of research were the Sun and the Moon, he no doubt felt that he could waste light in the interests of ease of operation. Even after squandering light by reflecting it off three metal surfaces, there was still enough left to give him prodigious magnifications, especially when looking at the solar surface.

It is interesting how differently his friend Lassell approached light-economy in the design of his big reflectors. Wishing to observe the giant planets and their satellites, Lassell needed every available photon, and used equatorial mounts because they enabled him to maintain long periods of unbroken concentration at the Newtonian focus of his 24- and 48-inch mirrors as he awaited brief snatches of perfect visibility. Good friends and skilful mirror-casters and clever mount-devisers Nasmyth and Lassell may have been, yet their astronomical interests stood at opposite ends of the light-demand scale!

In 1852, the British astronomical community was seriously considering the possibility of setting up a large reflecting telescope in a 'prime sky' location in the Southern Hemisphere, in Australia or South Africa, for deep-space work. The moving spirit behind the project was Lord Rosse, who was currently President of the Royal Society; as one might expect, he invited his fellow Grand Amateurs, Nasmyth and Lassell, who were also big-reflector users, to join the

Figure 3. Nasmyth's comfortable telescope, situated in the grounds of his house, 'Fireside', in Manchester, in about 1850. (Autobiography, p. 315.)

'Southern Telescope' committee. At first, on December 15, 1852, Nasmyth begged leave of absence, because of 'the pressure of Commerical Engagements' in Manchester, but relented even while writing his letter of apology, and soon threw all of his energies into the scheme.[10]

By December 30, he was into the project hammer and tongs, and had already dispatched preliminary sketches for a giant equatorial to Lassell (who was by then observing in Malta) along with a letter to Lord Rosse proposing an 81-point mirror-support system, a hinge arrangement for removing the 48-inch mirror for repolishing and a specially sprung railway vehicle to convey it to the workshop. Nasmyth made no attempt to land the order for the 'Equitorial' telescope (his spelling was often unusual) for his own firm, but recommended Maudslay's for the heavy parts, while estimating that £3000 would not be enough to build such an instrument.[11]

By July 1853, Nasmyth had submitted two beautifully coloured sets of engineering drawings (the products, no doubt, of the Bridgewater Foundry Drawing Office) for a 48-inch-aperture, equatorially mounted Newtonian reflector in iron.[12] Its conical polar axis and roller-bearing tube mounts he fully acknowledged to have been inspired by his friend Lassell's 24-inch reflector. Although it did not use his 'Nasmyth' focus, he clearly aspired to make it a 'comfortable' telescope by seating the observer in an enclosed 'snug box' which swivelled about the eyepiece, to protect him from the inconvenience of standing in the open for hours at a stretch. He was of the opinion that a comfortable observer observed the best, though when Lassell saw the sketches that had been sent out to him in Malta he declared the swivelling 'snug box' to be unworkable. Yet the 'Southern Equitorial' came to nothing in 1852–3, and it was to be more than a decade before a large southern reflector became a reality, in Melbourne, though this 48-inch-aperture Cassegrain reflector, by Grubb of Dublin, was never a success.

The concept of a large-aperture comfortable telescope was later to capture the imagination of another ironmaster amateur astronomer. Henry Bessemer, the pioneer of steel manufacture, built an enormous 48-inch-aperture 'Nasmyth' focus reflector for his private observatory at Denmark Hill, London, in the 1890s, though there is no evidence that this massive suburban observatory ever did any useful work.[13]

Nasmyth's first astronomical interest was the Moon. Indeed, his willingness to rise in the middle of the night to make use of clear skies soon gave rise to the belief that the grounds of his house, 'Fireside', were haunted by a ghost seen wandering in the moonlight carrying its own coffin. This tale must have started quite early in Nasmyth's astronomical career, before the completion of his permanent large telescope, when the nightshirt-clad 'ghost' still carried a portable instrument around the gardens of 'Fireside', inadvertently frightening the barge-men on the nearby Bridgewater Canal, who would carry accounts of the apparition as far south as Wolverhampton. By 1842, however, when his first large mirrors were coming into use, Nasmyth was examining the lunar surface with very high magnifications. To record features with the greatest accuracy, he made drawings at the eyepiece with white chalk on grey paper. In June 1844, Nasmyth sent his first letter to the RAS, which accompanied lunar drawings made in black and white chalk, '*from Nature*, i.e. the actual Moon', along with a model of part of the lunar surface. The drawings and model were made 'with my home made Newtonians of 8¾ and 12 inches aperture, powers 240 and 360 . . .'[14]

Over the years, he had drawn the lunar surface with great detail and made micrometer measurements of the features, and what especially came to interest him was the geological history of our satellite. We must remember that by the 1840s terrestrial geology itself was advancing rapidly, and it was only natural that Nasmyth (who also happened to be a skilled amateur geologist, especially of Scotland) should come to look at the Moon in developmental terms. While he considered the Moon to have become a dead world by the present day, he tried to find explanations for those topographical features that are unique to the lunar surface.

Like the Highlands of Scotland, the Moon's surface seemed to Nasmyth to be the product of volcanic activity and internal heat. Indeed, his was very much an ironmaster's concept of lunar geology, as he saw parallels between the behaviour of molten iron and its solidifying dross in the foundry crucible, and that of terrestrial and lunar features. He was impressed by the way in which cooling metals can suddenly expand and form cracks in solidifying crusts, to produce miniature 'lunar' surfaces. What was more, when examining the recently erupted Vesuvius crater in 1865 he observed the way in which the diminishing power of the eruption had created a small central peak in the crater. Could not the walls and central peaks of lunar craters have been formed by similar processes?[15] But where the Moon differed most radically from the Earth was in its lack of an atmosphere, causing it quickly to lose its heat early in its geological history. The Earth's heat loss, by contrast, had been slowed by its thick atmospheric blanketing, producing a gradual shrinking of the crust around the terrestrial core that resembled the wrinkled skin of a desiccated apple.

But lunar geological features showed all the signs of activity produced by internal heat, with cracks, rays, craters and intruded mountain formations, such as Pico, which appeared to have penetrated the crust from below. The lunar crust, because it was effectively *in vacuo*, must have hardened quickly, for the smaller mass of the Moon would have been unable to retain its internal heat for as long as the water and gas-blanketed Earth. As the internal heat and pressure subsided, it was likely to collapse, buckle and split, to form the jagged and un-eroded features that are so characteristic of the lunar landscape. The remaining outbursts of internal pressure would produce the volcanic craters. Though Nasmyth did not deny that meteoritic bodies had hit the Moon, he argued that the central mountains and walls of many craters clearly indicated a volcanic origin.[16]

Nasmyth's deeply practical turn of mind naturally made him seek the best available techniques by which to communicate his lunar studies to the learned world. His black-and-white relief drawings were fine, but since at least 1844 he had been experimenting with exquisitely detailed three-dimensional plaster models of the lunar surface, which could be photographed against a low light for engraving and publication. These models were used to illustrate his *magnum opus*, *The Moon* (1874), as well as being used by Robert Ball in *The Splendour of the Heavens* (1892) and other works. Several of the original models, on boards just under a foot square, are still preserved in the Science Museum store.

In 1850, Nasmyth presented his initial findings on lunar topography and geology to the Edinburgh meeting of the British Association for the Advancement of Science, where he displayed his lunar drawings, along with a lunar map six feet in diameter.[17] Nasmyth's address to the Association caused something of a stir, for no one else in Britain (and relatively few elsewhere) was devoting such detailed attention to the Moon as an object with a geological and a topographical history. It was really this meeting that caused the public to look at Nasmyth in a different light: not just as a famous inventor and manufacturer, but also as a scientist. In 1850 Nasmyth was forty-two years old, in excellent health and vigour, happily

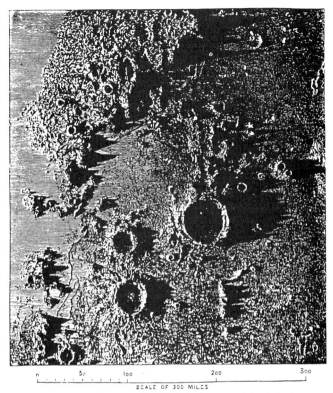

SCALE OF 300 MILES

Figure 4. One of Nasmyth's superbly detailed plaster models of the lunar surface. (Autobiography, *p. 322.*)

married and rich beyond all of his imaginable needs. The prospect of simply making yet more money rather bored him, and being a man in whom a roving intellect and an inventive genius were the primary mainsprings of life, he planned a very early and active retirement.[18]

Astronomy, by this stage in his life, had long ceased to be a hobby and was now his 'chief daily occupation', though cultivated alongside his interests in geology, archaeology and ancient history. In 1849 he had complied with a request from the Royal Institution of London to supply a teaching model of his 20-inch 'comfortable telescope',[19] and in the wake of the Edinburgh meeting of 1850 he was entertained by the Duke of Argyll, an active amateur geologist.

At the Great Exhibition of Art, Science and Technology held in the Crystal Palace, London, in the summer of 1851, he received a medal not only for his steam hammer, but also for his lunar maps. These maps had clearly aroused considerable interest, for when Queen Victoria and Prince Albert were staying with the Earl of Ellesmere near Manchester in October 1851, Her Majesty specifically requested to be introduced to Nasmyth, and to see the now famous lunar drawings, which Nasmyth brought to Worsley Hall in his carriage. Queen Victoria recorded in her diary how much she had been impressed by Nasmyth and by 'the charm of his manner, in which the simplicity, modesty, and enthusiasm of genius all strikingly combined are warmly dwelt upon'.[20] Before travelling to Manchester, the Queen had been in Liverpool, where she had specifically requested that Liverpool's most eminent scientist, William Lassell, be presented to her.[21]

Nasmyth was now quite a celebrity, and when he was finally able to disentangle himself from the engineering business in 1856 at the age of forty-eight, he resolved to use his 'active leisure' to pursue useful scientific and technical projects as a private individual. And the most consuming of these projects was to be astronomy. At this juncture in his life he decided to move to Kent, primarily to escape the polluted skies of industrial Manchester, purchasing a mansion at Penshurst. 'Hammerfield', as Nasmyth called it, was to be his home and scientific base for the rest of his long life. It was here that he completed the extensive course of observations and beautifully sculpted illustrative topographical models for his book *The Moon* (1874). It was also at 'Hammerfield' that he developed a friendship with his illustrious fellow Kent resident, Sir John Herschel, who was impressed with Nasmyth's ingenuity, and strongly encouraged him to write *The Moon*.[22] It was also in Kent that he came to use his 20-inch telescope to examine the Sun.

During the 1840s, astronomers across Europe had become fascinated by the 'pink flames' that had been observed during totality at the solar eclipse seen in northern Italy in 1842. Although glimpsed at previous eclipses, the decisive identification of the solar prominences that year set a whole new agenda for solar studies and astrophysics. Astronomers wanted to know the relationship between the 'pink flames', sunspots and faculæ, not to mention their combined relationship to the solar atmosphere and the prodigious heat-mechanism of the Sun. And, as everyone agreed, if these questions were going to be answered it would be necessary to devise an 'artificial eclipse' instrument that would make the flames available on demand.

In the wake of the total eclipse of 1851 observed by William Lassell and others in southern Sweden, when the 'pink flames' were seen again, the need to devise an instrument whereby the prominences could be observed at any time grew in importance.[23] Piazzi Smyth in Edinburgh thought that he was able to see them in September 1851, and Mrs Richarda Airy, the wife of the Astronomer Royal, who was staying with the Smyths in Edinburgh, described Piazzi's instrument on September 3, 1851. Piazzi was trying out a device using obscuring disks to blot out the brightness of the Sun's face, and while Mrs Airy thought she saw prominences 'in size, proportion and character just like those, which I saw in 1842', they were later traced to optical aberrations.[24]

The pressure to devise a prominence-observing instrument was clearly on by early September 1851, for while Mrs Airy (who appears to have had a sound understanding of astronomy and knew many of the leading scientists of Europe) was in Edinburgh, James Nasmyth in Manchester was corresponding with her husband, the Astronomer Royal, in Greenwich, about an instrument of his own devising. Nasmyth's prominence-observing apparatus consisted of a black-lined projection box with baffles set over the eyepiece of a refracting telescope, similar to the arrangement generally used to observe sunspots. But there was a circular diaphragm through which the solar image was to pass, and as the diaphragm could be adjusted so as to bring it into precise correspondence with the solar limb, it could 'catch' the prominence while the full force of the solar image was deadened by the black baffles in the middle of the field.[25] Airy and Nasmyth corresponded in some detail about the prominences, and especially about the validity of Piazzi Smyth's results. At first, Airy had been inclined to accept Piazzi's Edinburgh prominences, especially as he trusted Richarda's judgement; she, after all, seems to have been the only person present in Edinburgh in 1851 to have seen the 'pink flames' both during the 1842 eclipse, from Turin, and through a projection apparatus. By September 12, 1851, however, Airy was expressing his doubts about seeing prominences artificially, for the key optical feature of a total eclipse was that the 'pink flames' are seen 'through dark air', and he was coming to think that what Piazzi and Richarda had seen were secondary reflections.[26]

Even so, Airy was glad to have Nasmyth's projection apparatus sent to Greenwich for official testing, though Nasmyth apologized for the delay in finishing it, as his factory was closed for 'our village holiday week and I have let all our Foremen and the greater part of the workmen get to London to see the Great X [Exhibition] which has caused us to put out our Fires and down our Boilers . . .'.[27] Nasmyth must have been quite an enlightened employer if he was willing to pack off his workforce to London to visit the Great Exhibition. One wonders whether Nasmyth or the men themselves paid for the trip.

Nasmyth's device was far more than a simple projection box, however, and consisted of an entire apparatus with finely machined parts that could also track the Sun in right ascension. He realized that his apparatus, the success of which hinged upon maintaining the diaphragm's critical alignment with the entire solar limb, would work only if exact tracking were achieved, and that was an engineering job. But it is interesting to see that Piazzi Smyth and James Nasmyth approached the problem of getting rid of the bright solar image from different directions: Smyth by using obscuring disks that would enable the solar atmosphere beyond the limb to shine out on its own, and Nasmyth by first catching the limb's image on his diaphragm, and then 'losing' the full disk in his baffle-chamber. But it is clear that Nasmyth had the greatest regard for Professor Piazzi Smyth, and when Smyth announced his plans for making astronomical observations from the top of the high peak of Teneriffe in 1856 (to become thereby the first mountain-top astonomer), Nasmyth loaned him a precision heliometer.[28]

In January 1853, Airy wrote to Nasmyth saying that all the detailed trials through which the solar projection apparatus had been put at Greenwich in 1852 had failed to produce the desired prominences. Nasmyth never recorded being able to make the apparatus work either, and seems to have abandoned his experiments by 1853, though Piazzi Smyth gave it a high-altitude trial at Teneriffe in 1856.[29] It was not until 1868 that Janssen and Lockyer succeeded in seeing the solar prominences 'artificially' through the slit of a spectroscope applied tangentially to the solar limb.

But what is significant is the line of endeavour that was pursued once the solar prominences were decisively identified at the eclipse of 1842. It was not a university professional who first set about seeing them artificially (for Piazzi Smyth was inspired by Nasmyth), but a Manchester ironmaster and Grand Amateur astronomer; in 1851, such men were the ones most likely to possess the time, observing experience and manufacturing capacity to take the matter in hand. Nasmyth's correspondence with Airy, and the Royal Observatory's willingness to test his apparatus independently, indicates the seriousness with which he and his fellow Grand Amateurs were taken in high scientific circles. The 'Steam Hammer', as Nasmyth was popularly known, was making the transition in the public eye to what Cardinal Manning would soon call 'the Man in the Moon'.[30]

During the 1850s, Nasmyth came to pay increasing attention to the Sun in the wake of his interest in the prominences. Like many astronomers, he was puzzled by the source of the Sun's prodigious energy output, though he argued that this energy was probably not constant through time. Nasmyth pointed out that one could find evidence for fluctuations in the solar energy output in terrestrial history, such as the Ice Ages, which in the 1840s geologists were learning to identify from rock strata. The Earth had clearly been cooler during the Ice Ages, argued Nasmyth, probably because of a drop in solar output. He also suggested that there was a form of energy, or matter, spread throughout space which caused the Sun, or stars, to burn. In some respects this was similar to the ideas of John Herschel, who suggested that the zodiacal light, comet tails and nebulæ were all fuelled by a fine cosmic matter that suffused space.[31]

The Sun seems to have occupied much of Nasmyth's attention when he retired to Kent in 1856, and, as with his interests in lunar geology, one sees that love of fiery phenomena that was never far from the ironmaster's mind. He was still occupied with the problems of relating the 'pink flames' to other solar phenomena, in spite of his failure to produce them artificially, and in 1861 Nasmyth suggested to his friend Mr Grove that the flames be viewed in polarized light to see if they showed different characteristics from the rest of the solar atmosphere.[32]

When looking at sunspots at very high magnifications, Nasmyth was able to see deep into their interiors, which seemed to be layered. And then he observed that they were sometimes crossed by filaments or 'bridges', as an individual spot developed or broke up. In 1861 Sir John Herschel confirmed the existence of these bridges. Then, in June 1860, when observing the high Sun under conditions of great atmospheric clarity, Nasmyth noticed a granular appearance on the solar surface, which appeared to be composed of innumerable lenticular or 'willow-leaf' shapes (now known as the solar granulation).

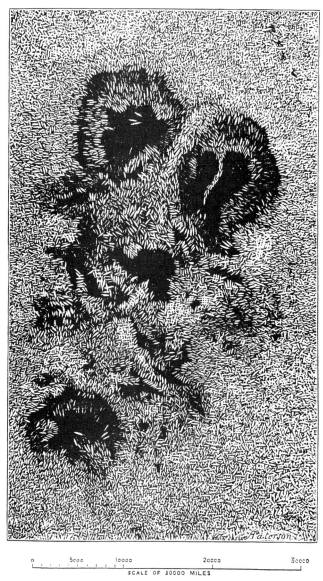

*Figure 5. The 'willow leaves', or granulation, of the Sun's surface, and the interior structure of sunspots. (*Autobiography, *p. 370.)*

These 'willow leaves' were very hard for other observers to confirm, for they were visible only at very high magnifications when the air was exceptionally steady and clear in high summer. Though no longer resident in Manchester, Nasmyth still maintained close contacts with the city, and he wrote a paper on them for the Manchester Literary and Philosophical Society.[33] The existence of the 'willow leaves' was officially confirmed, however, by E. J. Stone at the Royal Observatory on June 5, 1864, and the Astronomer Royal commissioned a special reflecting eyepiece to study them. Yet other astronomers had reported glimpses of the 'willow leaves' prior to the Greenwich confirmation, and Nasymyth's old astronomical protégé, Warren De La Rue, claimed to have seen them in March 1864. The 'willow-leaf' (sometimes called 'rice-grain') structure of the solar surface was perhaps Nasmyth's greatest astronomical discovery.[34]

There is no evidence to suggest that Nasmyth was ever personally active in deep-space astronomy; however, in a paper which he presented to the Royal Astronomical Society in 1855 he argued that the spiral shapes of the nebulæ such as the 'Whirlpool' seen through Lord Rosse's 72-inch telescope indicated that they were *rotating*, and that the laws of universal gravitation no doubt operated in the depths of stellar space. Nor was he especially a planetary astronomer, though at the Mars opposition in the autumn of 1862 he made detailed drawings from Penshurst. He identified green and sandy-coloured regions on the planet, an 'island', and a 'cliff' formation around the south polar cap. Nasmyth suspected that the Martian polar caps were eccentric to the axis of the planet, and compared the superior colour-resolution of his 20-inch reflector against that of his 8-inch Cooke refractor.[35] On September 26 and 27, 1878, he used his large reflecting telescope to compare the luminosities of Venus and Mercury when they were so close together as to be visible simultaneously in the instrument's field. In spite of Mercury's greater proximity to the Sun, he found it to be the colour of zinc or lead, whereas Venus shone like silver.[36]

Even when one makes allowance for the overtly heroizing tone of Samuel Smiles's biography of James Nasmyth, it is hard to avoid the conclusion that Nasmyth lived his long life with zest, profit and great enjoyment. Possessing as he did an immense capacity for creative work, combined with a powerful ruthless streak, Nasmyth was never happier than when devising and inquiring. His first passion, for industrial invention, made him rich and famous by the age of forty, and after that it was to scientific research that his energies moved. Whether he was corresponding with Clifton Sorby or Michael Faraday about making artificial diamonds in his blast-furnace, the Astronomer Royal about the solar prominences, Lord Rosse about the Southern Telescope, or 'my Excellent friend' Lassell about specula and lunar vulcanism, the boyish enthusiasm never left him.[37] The capacity for playfulness also came out in the inky-blob stylcd 'James Nasmyth, hys mark' which he sometimes added beneath his signature on letters to friends. Indeed, the enthusiasm for communicating science and invention, so evident at the Edinburgh meeting in 1850, and in the construction of subsequent plaster models of the lunar surface, further enchanted the Manchester author, Mrs Elizabeth Gaskell, in 1856. She, and a group of her friends, were treated to a 'lesson in geology' at Nasmyth's Patricroft Works, 'illustrated with impromptu diagrams drawn on the wall alternately with a piece of white chalk and a sooty fore-finger'.[38] Mrs Gaskell also used Nasmyth as the inspiration for her Mr Manning, the charismatic railway surveyor, in her novel *Cousin Phillis* (1864). As Nasmyth had a Manchester business partner named Gaskell, it is possible that the author could have known the engineer-astronomer through various social channels over many years.

In spite of this homespun enthusiasm, one suspects that there was something about Nasmyth that antagonized certain types of people: perhaps a forthright bluntness which could also go along with the charm, and a sense of the value of money which could have offended some gentlemen. It is hard, otherwise, to understand the undisguisedly 'catty' remark made by the Anglo-Irish clergyman-scientist, Thomas Romney Robinson, who was Director of the Armagh Observatory. Writing to Lord Rosse in 1845, he castigated Nasmyth as 'a man who works for profit', rather than for 'love', in spite of Nasmyth's entirely amateur status as an astronomer, which contrasted with Robinson's academic salary and ecclesiastical benefice.[39] Perhaps Robinson was a straightforward snob, while Nasmyth in turn mellowed between his Steam Hammer and his Kent days!

One suspects that mellowing had indeed taken place, for when Sir John Herschel and his daughter Bella were guests of the Nasmyths at Penshurst in May 1864, Sir John recorded being introduced to the High Sheriff of Kent at Nasmyth's dining table. The Nasmyths, moreover, were clearly received in the houses of the leading Kentish gentry, for on the same 1864 visit, Mrs Nasmyth took Miss

Bella Herschel to call on Lady de Lisle, who lived nearby.[40]

Indeed, what makes Nasmyth so interesting to the historian are the contrasting sides of his nature: the inventor, the powerful man of business, the apparently generous employer, the passionate scientist. For a man who could take an invitation to attend upon Queen Victoria in his stride, he never failed to be strangely flattered when distinguished scientists acknowledged him as an equal. When visiting Rome in 1865, for instance, he clearly felt delighted when the eminent Jesuit astronomer Angelo Secchi praised his discovery of the 'willow leaves'. Nasmyth continued his astronomical observations and correspondence with the leading scientists of the day virtually up to the end of his life. He was still making regular observations of the solar surface at the age of seventy-four, reporting to Norman Lockyer that 'I was fortunate yesterday during *islands* of tranquility of the atmosphere to catch glimpses of my old acquaintances the willow leaves scattered over the penumbral surface.'[41]

I suspect that, in spite of his many years spent in astronomy, James Nasmyth always thought of it as his 'second career'; and, 'Grand' and distinguished as he undoubtedly was, he never failed to think of himself as first and foremost a *lover* of the science, and in the noblest and Latinate traditions of the word, an *amateur*.[42]

Acknowledgements

I wish to express my thanks to the Archivists and Librarians of the following collections for their assistance and for access to primary sources: The University Museum, Oxford; Exeter University; Salford City Libraries; and Sheffield Literary and Philosophical Society. Special thanks are owing to the staff of the Royal Society Library; to the Earl and Countess of Rosse; to Adam Perkins of the RGO Library, Cambridge University; to Peter Hingley and Mary Chibnall of the RAS Library; to Kevin Johnson of the Science Museum, London; to St Andrews University; to the National Library of Scotland; and to Tony Simcock, Museum of the History of Science, Oxford. My particular thanks, however, are due to Dr David Gavine of Edinburgh, for supplying me with Nasmyth material in Edinburgh and St Andrews.

Notes

1. A. Chapman, 'The Victorian Amateur Astronomer', *Yearbook of Astronomy 1994*, ed. Patrick Moore (Sidgwick & Jackson, London, 1993), pp. 159–77.

2. Martin Kemp, 'Alexander Nasmyth, and the Style of Graphic Eloquence', *The Connoisseur*, Feb. 1970, pp. 93–9.

3. The most complete life is still *James Nasmyth Engineer, An Autobiography*, ed. Samuel Smiles (John Murray, London, 1889). The early life story comes down through this book, no doubt as Nasmyth outlined it to Smiles. Smiles reworked Nasmyth's autobiographical account in his own inimitable way to produce an overtly reverential text intended to form edifying as well as factually informative reading. Yet Smiles left one wondering how such a rôle model of virtuous self-help made such a fortune so quickly. Smiles' account, sadly, passes over the driving energy and ruthlessness that were also fundamental parts of Nasmyth's character. See also Dr David Gavine, 'James Nasmyth', Lorimer Lecture 1996; *Astronomical Society of Edinburgh Journal* 35 (July 1996) 4–10. This article contains a pedigree for the Nasmyth family.

4. Various figures have been given for Nasmyth's fortune: John Cantrell, in *James Nasmyth and the Bridgewater Foundry* (Chethams Society, Manchester University Press, 1985), gives it as £400,000, though at his death he left only £244,000. Upon retirement, he still retained a £110,000 share in the Foundry. John Cantrell's handlists to Nasmyth's papers, dealing largely with commercial documents, are preserved in Salford City Library, Local Studies Section, Greater Manchester. If one applies the '50 times factor' to 1850 and 1990, one sees that £100,000 then would be roughly equal to £5 million today.

5. Nasmyth, *Autobiography* (n. 3), p. 313.

6. William Lassell, 'Description of a Machine for Polishing Specula, &c. . . .', *Memoirs RAS*, XVIII (1849), 1–20. Gerard Gilligan, *William Lassell* (North-West Astronomers series, Liverpool Astronomical Society, 1994). A. Chapman, 'William Lassell (1799–1880): Practitioner, Patron, and "Grand Amateur" of Victorian Astronomy', *Vistas in Astronomy*, 32 (1988), 341–70.

7. Nasmyth, *Autobiography* (n. 3), p. 314.

8. Nasmyth to Clifton Sorby, October 13, 1848: Sheffield Literary and Philosophical Society Manuscript. Nasmyth sent a detailed sketch of 'My comfortable telescope', showing the Bridgewater Canal at the bottom of his 'Fireside' garden, to John Phillips in Oxford: University Museum, Oxford, Phillips Papers 1851–3. This earlier version of the 'comfortable telescope' contained only a 10-inch mirror. The 20-inch was not finished until 1849–50, though even then Nasmyth was imagining its scaling-up to 60 inches or more: Nasmyth to J. D. Forbes, May 14, 1849. St Andrews University Library, Forbes Letter Book, 1849/25. (I thank Dr Gavine for this reference.)

9. In 1994, when a grant from the Royal Insurance Company made it possible to build a full-size, fully working replica of Lassell's 1845 reflector of 24 inches aperture, Nasmyth's 20-inch 'comfortable telescope', preserved in the store of the Science Museum, London, was

used as a guide in the reconstruction. It is, after all, a slightly younger contemporary of Lassell's instrument, and one presumes that the iron tube, gearing, mirror-mount and other features of the two instruments would have been similar with regard to the craft skills needed to construct them.

10. Much of this correspondence is preserved in the Royal Society archives. Nasmyth to Rosse, December 15, 1852, R. Soc. Misc. Ms. 12:66. Some of the letters were also published in *Correspondence Concerning the Great Melbourne Telescope, in Three Parts, 1852–1870* (Royal Society, London, 1871).

11. The letter of December 15, 1852 (n. 10) contained a preliminary sketch for the 48-inch 'Equitorial', indicating that during the course of writing this letter Nasmyth had switched from absenting himself to submitting a rough drawing. See also Nasmyth to Rosse, December 30, 1852, R. Soc. Misc. Ms. 12:74. There is an additional copy of this letter in the Rosse Archives, Birr Castle: Ms. K. 17:20, reproduced in *Correspondence Concerning . . .* (n. 10, p. 15. See also Lassell (Valetta, Malta) to Thomas Bell, December 30, 1852, R. Soc. Misc. Ms., reproduced in *Correspondence Concerning . . .*, pp. 15–18.

12. Nasmyth to Thomas Bell, July 2, 1853. Between December 28, 1852 and July 2, 1853, Nasmyth prepared two large-scale sets of drawings for his proposed southern 'Equitorial': R. Soc. Misc. Ms. 12:84, Misc. Ms. 19:117. These beautiful 38×35-inch coloured drawings are now *very* fragile, but a reduced-size engraving was published in *Correspondence Concerning . . .* (n. 10), p. 38.

13. Henry Bessemer, *An Autobiography* (*Engineering Journal*, London, 1905), pp. 348–54. Nasmyth and Bessemer, ironmaster astronomers as they were, had corresponded in the 1880s.

14. Nasmyth to Richard Norris, Secretary, RAS, June 11, 1844 (RAS Letters, 1844). Nasmyth, not yet an FRAS himself, said that 'my Excellent friend Mr. Lassell' and the Reverend Dawes had recommended him to send the lunar model and drawings to the Society.

15. James Nasmyth and James Carpenter, *The Moon, considered as a Planet, A World, and a Satellite* (John Murray, London, 1874). This book gives an elegant and amply illustrated exposition of the internal heat theory. For the Vesuvius eruption, see pp. 102–3.

16. Nasmyth, *The Moon* (n. 15). But Nasmyth was already discussing a well-developed theory for volcanic lunar crater formation in his letter to Clifton Sorby in Shcffield by July 9, 1850 (Sheffield Literary and Philosophical Society Manuscript). He told Clifton Sorby (July 9, 1850) that he intended 'to hold forth a bit' on Earth and lunar geology at the following British Association meeting in Edinburgh (Sheffield Lit. and Phil. Soc. Ms.).

17. This map probably ended up at the Radcliffe Observatory, Oxford, where they hung it on the wall in the late 19th century. Nasmyth was a

correspondent of Professor John Phillips of Oxford, and in the 1850s sent him sketches of sunspots made at high magnification, and a drawing of the 20-inch 'comfortable telescope' (Nasmyth to John Phillips, September 6, 1859, John Phillips Papers, University Museum, Oxford).

18. As early as 1848, when he was only forty, Nasmyth was planning to 'take down my sign board' and retire (Nasmyth to Clifton Sorby, October 4, 1848, Sheffield Lit. and Phil. Soc. Ms.).

19. Nasmyth did not seem happy with the treatment this model received, however, and by February 22 (? month not certain on letter) 1852 was complaining to John Williams, Assistant Secretary of the RAS, about his lack of acknowledgement, and demanding it back (RAS Letters, 1852).

20. Nasmyth, *Autobiography* (n. 3), p. 333. Smiles quotes from Queen Victoria's unpublished Diary; cited by Sir Theodore Martin, *The Life of the Prince Consort* (Smith, Elder & Co, London, 1876), II, p. 398, for an account of the very favourable impression that Nasmyth made on Her Majesty.

21. Lassell's 'Obituary', *The Daily Post*, October 9, 1880, contains an account of Lassell and the Queen (cited also in A. Chapman, 'William Lassell' (n. 6), pp. 347–8).

22. Nasmyth, *Autobiography* (n. 3), pp. 379–80.

23. William Lassell, 'Observations of the Total Eclipse of July 28, 1851', *Memoirs RAS*, XXI, 1 (1852), 42–50.

24. Richarda Airy to George Biddell Airy, Edinburgh, September 3, 1851 (Royal Greenwich Observatory Manuscript, Cambridge University Library Ms. RGO 6 113/131).

25. Nasmyth to G. B. Airy, August 18, 1851 (Cambridge University Library Ms. RGO 6 113/123–4).

26. G. B. Airy to Nasmyth, Greenwich, September 12, 1851 (Cambridge University Library Ms. RGO 6 113/163).

27. Nasmyth to G. B. Airy, September 5, 1851 (Cambridge University Library Ms. RGO 6 113/146–7).

28. H. A. and M. T. Brück, *The Peripatetic Astronomer: The Life of Charles Piazzi Smyth* (Adam Hilger, Bristol, 1988), p. 51.

29. Airy to Nasmyth, Greenwich, January 25, 1853 (Cambridge University Library Ms. RGO 6 113/163). See also Brück and Brück, *Peripatetic Astronomer* (n. 28), p. 59.

30. Nasmyth, *Autobiography* (n. 3), p. 381. Following this meeting Nasmyth sent Cardinal Manning a complimentary copy of *The Moon*, the reply to which was published in the *Autobiography*.

31. John Herschel, *Treatise on Astronomy* (Longman, Rees, Orme, London, 1833), pp. 406–7; *Outlines of Astronomy* (Longman, Brown, Green, London, 1847), Art. 897. A. Chapman, 'An Occupation for an Independent Gentleman: Astronomy in the Life of John Herschel', *Vistas in Astronomy*, 36 (1993), 92–4. [Because of typographical

errors, this article was reprinted by *Vistas* as a corrected Supplement (1994): pp. 11–12.]

32. Nasmyth to Grove, June 4, 1861 (Royal Institution Library, London).

33. *Memoirs of the Literary and Philosophical Society of Manchester*, 3rd series, Vol. I, p. 407. See also Nasmyth, *Autobiography* (n. 3), p. 370.

34. On January 9, 1864, Nasmyth mentions having dispatched to the RAS a case of 'my drawings in relation to my discovery of the Willow Leaf shaped objects which I find to form the Luminous Envelope of the Sun . . .' (RAS Letters, 1864).

35. Nasmyth to John Phillips, (?) January 20, 1863 (R. Soc. Ms. A.P. 45:10).

36. Nasmyth, *Nature*, XIX (1878–79), pp. 22–3. Agnes M. Clerke, 'A Popular History of Astronomy During the Nineteenth Century, (Adam and Charles Black, London, 1893).

37. In the 1840s, Nasmyth undertook experiments attempting to make artificial diamonds: Nasmyth to Clifton Sorby, October 4, 1848 (Sheffield Lit. and Phil. Soc. Ms.).

38. Catherine Winkworth to Emily Shaen, March 18, 1856, published in Jenny Uglow, *Elizabeth Gaskell, A Habit of Stories* (Faber & Faber, London, 1993), p. 544.

39. Robinson to Rosse, November 19, 1845 (Rosse Archives, Birr Castle, K 5:6).

40. The 'Diary' of Sir John Herschel (Royal Society Manuscript, 585).

41. Nasmyth to J. N. Lockyer, April 17, 1882 (Exeter University, Joseph Norman Lockyer Archive).

42. Nasmyth became an FRAS on June 8, 1849, and paid his £4 4s 0d (£4.20) subscription by a postal order dated June 26, 1849 (RAS Letters, 1849). He resigned from the Fellowship in a letter to the Secretary dated October 25, 1858, and his departure was noted without comment at the meeting of November 12, 1858 (RAS Letters, 1849, 1858). Whatever the cause of his resignation, he still corresponded with the Society, and on December 29, 1888, at the age of eighty, he dispatched a collection of photographs of his 'willow leaves' to the Secretary (RAS Letters, 1888). In spite of his apparent sociability, Nasmyth never became a member of the RAS Club, and only dined as a Visitor on one occasion, March 12, 1858, when he was seated between the Rev. Professor Baden Powell (the astronomer father of the First Scout) and Admiral Smyth. He must have been the guest of one or other of these gentlemen (*Records of the RAS Club, 1820–1910*, ed. H. H. Turner (Oxford, for private circulation, undated), p. 70).

One Half of Astronomy: Supernova Remnants

CHRIS KITCHIN

It has been said that astronomy divides into the astronomy of the Crab Nebula and the astronomy of everything else, and that, of the two, the former is the more important! While this is clearly something of an exaggeration, it does serve to highlight just how fascinating the Crab Nebula and other remnants of supernova explosions can be. Supernova remnants (SNRs) are the rapidly expanding clouds of hot gaseous debris flung out during supernova explosions. Supernovæ themselves are just as fascinating as their remnants, but there is not space here to cover them as well, except where the details of the supernova explosion affect what we see of the SNR.

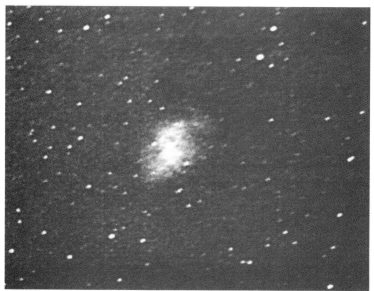

Figure 1. The Crab Nebula (M1, NGC 1952) (University of Hertfordshire image).

Neutron stars, pulsars and possibly black holes are also remnants of supernovæ, but again lack of space prohibits any discussion of them.

The Crab Nebula (Figure 1), the first object in Messier's list, is visible as a faint amorphous glow a degree or so north-west of the star Zeta Tauri. It can be seen in quite small telescopes and even in binoculars, but the filamentary structure which led to its name is very difficult to detect by eye. A typical visual appearance is shown in Figure 2. On images taken some years apart, it can be seen to be expanding. The outer edges of the nebula move outwards by a second of arc every seven or eight years. At its distance of about 6500 light-years, this corresponds to a linear expansion velocity of 1200 km/s. It is roughly 4.2 arc minutes along its long axis, and so at its observed rate of expansion it must have originated some 900 to 1000 years ago. This gives us the clue to its origin, for in AD 1054 a bright new star was observed for a few weeks by Chinese and other astronomers in the area of sky which we now call Taurus. That new star was a supernova exploding, and the bulk of the star's material was flung out into space to form the nebula. Near the centre of the

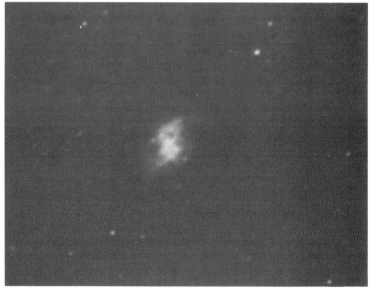

Figure 2. The Crab Nebula as you may expect to see it in a small telescope (University of Hertfordshire image).

nebula is a 16th-magnitude star. That star can be observed to be flashing on and off 33 times a second. It is the other remnant of the original star: its collapsed core, now forming one of the few pulsars that can also be seen in the visible part of the spectrum.

The Crab Nebula is probably the best known SNR, but it is not typical. Most SNRs are shells and so are seen as rings, rather than having the filled-in appearance of the Crab. Moreover, relatively few are detectable in the optical part of the spectrum: most are found only from their radio emissions. The difference between the Crab and other SNRs probably arises from the pulsar continuing to supply energy to the material in the nebula to keep it glowing throughout its whole volume. The Crab and other 'filled' SNRs are known as plerions. The nebula IC 433 (Figure 3) shows the more typical appearance of an SNR.

When a supernova explodes, a vast amount of energy is released: up to 10^{46} J over a year or two, most of it in the form of neutrinos in

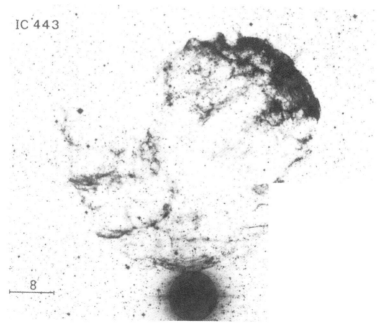

Figure 3. The nebula IC 433 – a typical SNR (reproduced courtesy of the European Southern Observatory).

the first few seconds of the explosion. This is a hundred times the amount of energy that our own Sun will radiate over its entire lifetime. Even though only 1 per cent or so of the total energy is in the form of light, a Type I supernova at its peak brightness may reach an absolute magnitude of -19, which equals the brightness of a moderate-sized galaxy such as the Large Magellanic Cloud. With such energies and brightnesses, it is tempting to think of a supernova as an enormously amplified version of an explosion on the Earth, but this would be quite misleading. The increase in brightness, though large, occurs quite slowly. The rate of increase is typically between a quarter and half a magnitude per day, compared with five magnitudes or so per day for an 'ordinary' nova. The increase occurs because the outer layers of the star have been flung outwards at velocities of up to 20,000 km/s. The outer surface of the star is therefore expanding, and so more and more energy is radiated as it becomes larger. However, the energy of the supernova radiated as electromagnetic radiation (as opposed to the neutrino burst) does not come directly from the explosion. It is in fact radiated by the expanding outer layers, and so is coming from the SNR in its earliest stages.

The first clue to the energy source for these early stages of the SNR comes from the light curves of supernovæ (Figure 4). These show a decrease in intensity with a 'half-life' of about six or seven days initially, lengthening after a few weeks to about 70 or 80 days. Now, an exponential decay of this sort immediately suggests radioactivity as a likely energy source, and that idea fits in well with the

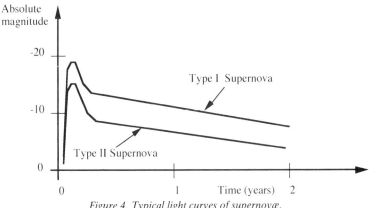

Figure 4. Typical light curves of supernovæ.

theories of supernovæ. The theories suggest that a supernova should produce a large amount (a solar mass or more) of the radio-active isotope nickel-56.[1] This decays with a half-life of 6.1 days, and produces cobalt-56. However, cobalt-56 is also radioactive, and decays with a half-life of 77 days to the (stable) isotope iron-56. Confirmation of this as the energy source for the early stages of the developing SNR finally came with spectroscopic observations of the 1987 supernova in the Large Magellanic Cloud (of which more later). These observations detected both gamma-ray and infrared emission from cobalt which decreased in line with the 77-day half-life of the cobalt-56 isotope.

The short half-life of nickel-56 means that its energy is deposited into the expanding gas very quickly, forming a small hot bubble at the centre. The pressure from this hot gas is much higher than can be contained by the surrounding material. The SNR is now highly unstable, and long protuberances of the hot, nickel-rich material are forced out into the surrounding gases. These 'nickel bullets', as they have been called, cause the SNR to become very hetero-geneous, and mix the products of nucleosynthesis originating from near the centre of the star throughout the whole nebula.

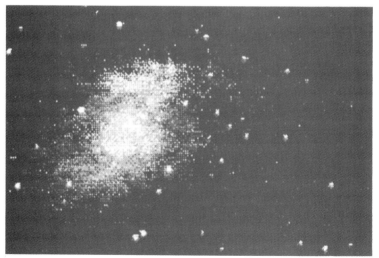

Figure 5. A false-colour image of the Crab Nebula, showing light polarized vertically as green, and horizontally as red (reproduced courtesy of Mr S. Ford, University of Hertfordshire Observatory).

Now, with its half-life of two and a half months the cobalt-56 will soon decay away to almost nothing. Yet we can observe SNRs for tens of thousands of years after the supernova explosion, so where does the continuing energy supply come from? The clue to the answer lies in the polarization[2] of the radiation from SNRs. The emitted radiation is highly linearly polarized, in both the optical (Figure 5) and radio regions. Now, such polarization is characteristic of synchrotron radiation,[3] produced when rapidly moving charged particles, such as electrons, spiral around magnetic fields (Figure 6). Most of the energy from SNRs thus originates from electrons moving close to the speed of light and following tortuous paths among the tangled web of magnetic fields left after the explosion. To begin with, the electrons' velocity arises from the explosion. Later, the electrons may be accelerated to velocities high enough for the radiation to occur, as the material passes through the turbulence and interacting magnetic fields within the supersonic shock front where the expanding SNR meets the interstellar medium. The Crab Nebula and other plerions, however, emit radiation throughout their whole volume, rather than from the interaction zone with the interstellar medium. This is probably

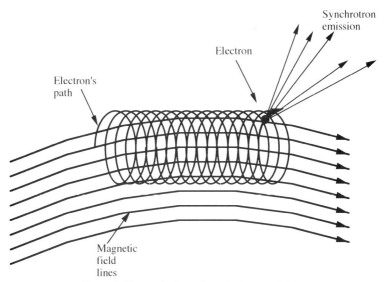

Figure 6. The production of synchrotron radiation.

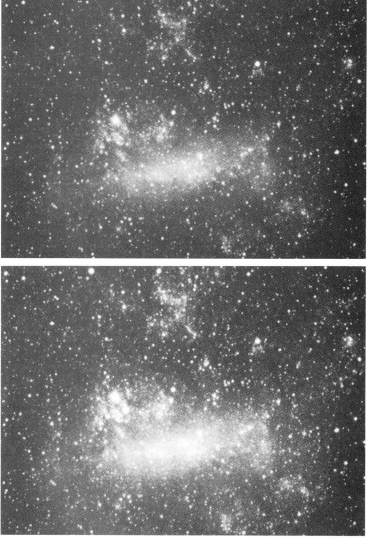

Figure 7. Before and after pictures of Supernova 1987A in the Large Magellanic Cloud, visible in the lower image below and to the right of the Tarantula (30 Doradûs) Nebula, which is itself to the left of centre (reproduced courtesy of the European Southern Observatory).

because the central pulsar is still emitting copious quantities of high-energy electrons, and these supply sufficient energy to power the central parts of the nebula.

The study of supernovæ and SNRs is dominated by two objects: the Crab Nebula, and the 1987 supernova (SN 1987A, Figure 7) in the Large Magellanic Cloud. Much has already been said about the Crab, but what is the significance of SN 1987A? Simply that, at 170,000 light-years from us, it is the nearest supernova to have been observed since the invention of the telescope. Supernovæ of all types occur at a rate of perhaps five to ten per century in a large spiral galaxy such as the Milky Way. But in the visible, we are restricted by absorption in interstellar dust clouds to observing only about 10 per cent of all the stars in the Galaxy. Thus we might have expected to see two or three supernovæ in the last few centuries, and have been unlucky that none have occurred since Kepler observed the last nearby supernova in 1604 (we have also been lucky – a really close supernova would probably wipe out most life from the land surfaces of the Earth!). SN 1987A has not had much time to form its SNR. Most observations so far thus relate to the supernova itself. None the less, the SNR has been detectable from radio observations since 1990. These show a roughly spherical but rather irregular shell of gas expanding outwards at some 30,000 km/s. By the end of this century those expanding gases should start to collide with slower material ejected from the star prior to its explosion, and the radio emissions should then become very much stronger.

Although not strictly a part of the SNR, a number of intriguing observations of light echoes have been made, revealing much about the environment into which the SN 1987A SNR will expand. Light echoes occur when the pulse of light from the explosion is scattered towards us by gas and dust clouds to one side of the line of sight (Figure 8). The light echoes have revealed a ring of material one-third of a light-year from the star – the ring centred on the supernova in Figure 9. This is probably produced by material flung off the star before it exploded. The other two rings in Figure 9 may not be from the supernova precursor, but from another nearby star losing mass in the form of jets and spinning to create the rings. Further out, other light echoes (Figure 10) reveal two sheets of gas and dust some 400 and 1050 light-years closer to us than the supernova. Clearly there are a lot of complex gas and dust clouds near SN 1987A, but this should not surprise us, because it is on the

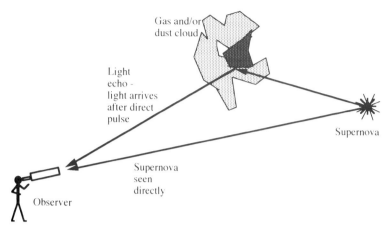

Figure 8. The production of light echoes.

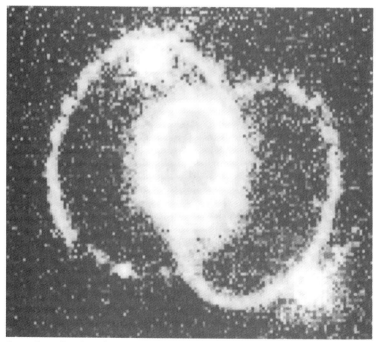

Figure 9. Light echoes from close to supernova 1987A (reproduced courtesy of NASA/ Space Telescope Science Institute).

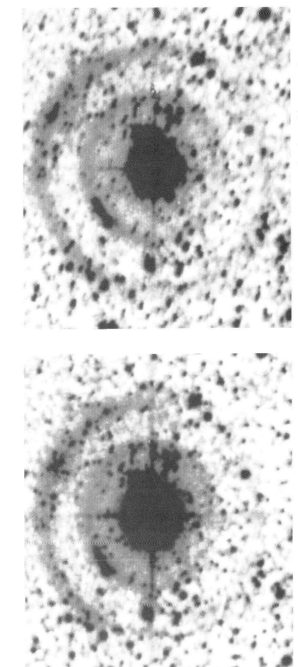

Figure 10. More distant light echoes from Supernova 1987A (reproduced courtesy of the European Southern Observatory).

Figure 11. The Tarantula Nebula in the Large Magellanic Cloud – also known as the 30 Doradûs complex (reproduced courtesy of the European Southern Observatory).

outskirts of the Tarantula (30 Doradûs) Nebula (Figure 11), the largest and most tangled star-forming region currently known.

Apart from their intrinsic interest, do supernova remnants have any wider significance? The answer is an emphatic 'Yes!', and some considerable personal significance to every one of us, for without SNRs occurring some 4.5 to 5 billion years ago, the Solar System might never have been formed, and even if it had there might well have been insufficient of the heavier elements to form the Earth, and ultimately ourselves.

The expanding SNRs blow huge bubbles of very hot rarefied gas into the normal interstellar medium or into the denser clouds within which their precursor stars have formed. Since there are many such bubbles (they can also be produced around very hot stars), sometimes overlapping or touching each other, the interstellar medium is compressed and swept into the spaces left between the bubbles. The interstellar medium thus resembles the soap film in a bowl of soapsuds, rather than the evenly distributed, low-density gas hitherto expected by most astronomers (Figure 12). The Sun, for example, is close to the centre of a bubble which is about 200 light-years across. Frequently, however, a supernova will occur while it is still embedded in the dense gas of a star-forming region (Figure 11). Then the ram pressure of the expanding SNR will compress the gas of the surrounding nebula and perhaps precipitate a phase of rapid star formation. There is evidence (from isotope ratios) that just such a process triggered the formation of the Solar System.

Then there are cosmic rays. These are subatomic particles, mostly protons, electrons and atomic nuclei, travelling very close to the speed of light, permeating the whole of the Galaxy and possibly also the space beyond. Impacts of high-energy cosmic ray particles with the Earth's upper atmosphere produce much of the back-

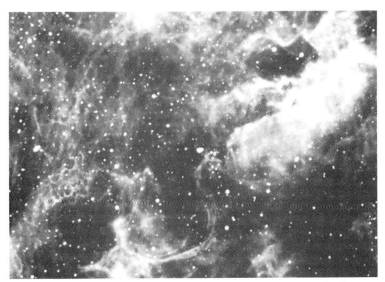

Figure 12. Bubbles in the interstellar medium in the Large Magellanic Cloud (reproduced courtesy of the European Southern Observatory).

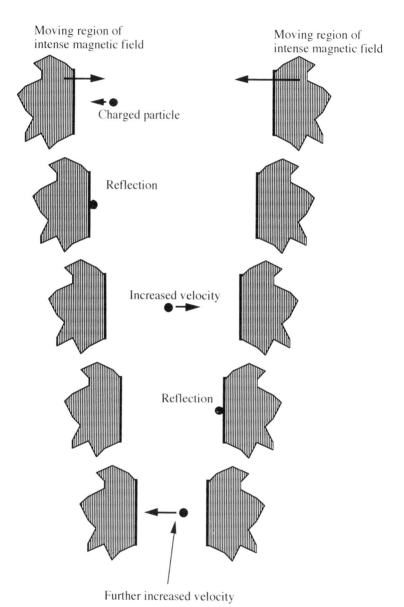

Figure 13. The Fermi mechanism for accelerating cosmic ray particles.

ground radiation which stimulates evolution via the effects of mutations. The cosmic rays also produce the radioactive isotope carbon-14 from atmospheric nitrogen which is used by archaeologists to date their finds. The cosmic ray particles are thought to be accelerated by supernovæ, and also later within SNRs. The acceleration is thought to be via the Fermi process (Figure 13), where charged particles are reflected many times between moving magnetic fields. When the magnetic fields are moving together, the particles gain energy, but they lose it when the fields move apart. However, more energy is gained than lost on average, so in the roiling turmoil of an SNR as it interacts with the surrounding material, particles can be accelerated to very close to the speed of light indeed (a speed of $0.999\,999\,999\,999\,c$ has been observed).

The Universe shortly after the Big Bang contained matter almost only in the form of hydrogen and helium. The heavier elements were gradually made from these first two by the nucleosynthesis reactions which power the stars. By the time the Solar System was forming 5 billion years ago, about 2 per cent of the material was then in the form of elements heavier than hydrogen and helium. Nowadays, these heavier elements account for perhaps 4 per cent. The Earth, and ourselves of course, contain only tiny amounts of hydrogen and helium, so without the production of the heavier elements the Earth could never have been formed. Now, though heavy elements are created inside stars (the Sun, for example, currently converts hydrogen to helium, and will probably go on to produce carbon, oxygen and possibly neon), for most stars those elements will remain locked inside them, unavailable for the formation of planets. The supernova precursor, however, produces elements up to iron, and then produces the elements heavier than iron during the supernova explosion itself. Those heavy elements are then flung out into the SNR and mixed into it by the turbulence produced by the nickel bullets. Thus it is only in SNRs that we find all the elements up to and beyond uranium that are needed to form the Earth and ourselves. Without an SNR estimated to have occurred about 200 million years before the formation of the Solar System, which provided the heavier elements in the Solar System, we would not be here thinking about it!

Notes

1. The nuclei of atoms contain protons and neutrons. The number of protons determines the chemical element, for example 28 for nickel, 27 for cobalt and 26 for iron. The number of neutrons in a nucleus, however, can vary without changing the chemical nature of the element. The nucleus of nickel, for example, can contain from 28 to 39 neutrons, giving the isotopes nickel-56, nickel-57, etc., where the number indicates the total number of protons and neutrons in the nucleus.
2. Electromagnetic radiation, including light, behaves some of the time as though it is a wave with an electric field oscillating back and forth at the frequency of the radiation. Radiation from most sources (such as an electric light bulb) has the direction of oscillation of the electric fields randomized. In linearly polarized radiation, however, the direction of oscillation is the same for all the waves. In circularly and elliptically polarized radiation the instantaneous direction is common to all waves, but that direction changes (rotating through 360°) with the frequency of the radiation.
3. Synchrotron radiation is named after the type of particle accelerator used by atomic physicists from which it was first detected.

Fifty Years, and Still the Eighth Wonder of the World: The Palomar 200-inch Reflector

RON MADDISON

Introduction

Just four days before Christmas 1947, a select group of astronomers and engineers gathered under the great telescope as the last bolts were tightened. These were the fixings holding the huge mirror cell in its place at the lower end of the enormous steel frame of the 200-inch (5.08-m) reflector on Palomar Mountain. This was the moment the telescope offically came to life – a simple event that has become known as 'first light'.

Known universally as the Hale 200-inch, the Palomar Mountain Telescope was the realization of a dream of George Ellery Hale, who had died almost a decade earlier in 1938. If birth certificates were provided for such feats of construction, then December 21, 1947 would have been the date written for the completion of this gigantic engineering project, first envisaged in an article that Hale wrote for *Harper's* Magazine in 1928 – almost 20 years before first light.

No one pretends that a few of the construction team and an optician or two had not already experienced the thrill of 'first sight' as they looked into the mirrors while making the final coarse adjustments. But when John Anderson, who had headed the project throughout the greater part of the design work, was elevated in a chair-lift nearly five metres above the observatory floor, and used a hand-held magnifying lens as eyepiece for this first view, there must have been a very pregnant silence as all those present waited for his reaction. Then somebody asked, 'What did you see?' and he replied, after a thoughtful pause and in a very far-away fashion, 'Oh, some stars.'

We now know that he was most likely very disappointed with what he saw. The image was much worse than he had expected, and the anticlimax of such a sight must have sapped his enthusiasm after such a long wait. On the other hand, no one would seriously have expected the thing to behave perfectly first time, because many fine adjustments are necessary after assembling such a delicate piece of optical equipment. It was soon realized that the enormous mono-lithic mirror was flexing under its own weight, and that the specially designed supporting mechanisms were not working as planned.

Early in the design phase, it had been anticipated that such a large single mirror would probably exceed the maximum possible size for the maintenance of a rigid parabolic surface. As the telescope turns, there are apparent variations in the direction of the force of gravity that distort the glass by several wavelengths of light and play havoc with the image quality. Great care had been taken in developing a system of balance-weighted levers and supports within the mirror cell that should have counteracted these varying stresses and strains, but first light had indicated that something was seriously wrong. As it turned out, the mirror support pivots and bearings were sticking, and not moving smoothly as they were supposed to. The forces involved were so great that the soft lubricant was being squeezed out of the bearings at times when the telescope was not in use. Minor redesigning of the bearings and a different lubricant completely solved the problem (Figure 1).

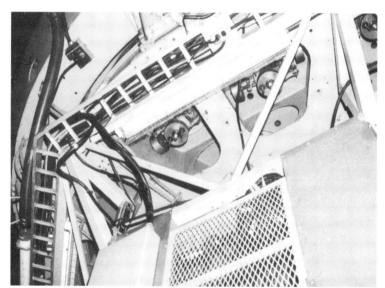

Figure 1. The underside of the 200-inch primary cell. Three of the balance-weighted mirror support mechanisms are visible between the struts supporting the Cassegrain cage.

This sort of thing is a common fault with many of the older single-mirror telescopes. It is normal to have to 'wake them up' when they seem to be asleep at the beginning of a run, usually by swinging the telescope through a full range of positions to loosen the balance-weight bearings. (Large telescope mounts are now made with a new generation of anti-friction materials and improved lubricants, so that this sort of treatment is seldom necessary.) As soon as the back and side supports of the prime mirror come to life, the quality of the images immediately improves.

In addition to the effects of mechanical distortion, there are those due to heat changes. Variations in temperature can affect the shape of the mirror, so to lessen the effect the 200-inch's observatory building is air-conditioned in order to keep the inside temperature as close to the anticipated outside night temperature as possible.

The telescope's prime mirror was made from a specially developed low-expansion Pyrex glass. It was made as thin as possible by means of a hollow honeycomb structure at its back so that maximum mechanical rigidity could be obtained from the smallest possible volume of glass. To keep the temperature steady, air is circulated around the mirror by means of a dozen small fans set into the back of the cell. In recent times optical materials have undergone a fundamental revolution, and zero thermal expansion coefficients are now commonplace. The hours of waiting while mirrors cool and finally settle to their proper shapes have now been entirely eliminated.

The 200-inch is neither the largest nor the last monolithic mirror to be made: there is, of course, the 6-metre (236-inch) Russian giant at Zelenchukskaya in the Causasus Mountains that was completed in the mid-1970s. But a good case can be made for regarding it as one of the first of the new generation of 'active' telescopes in which the design takes full account of the fact that the prime mirror actually flexes during operation. The support mechanisms compensate for flexure by automatically adjusting the thrusts that they deliver as the attitude of the telescope changes. The significant difference between the 200-inch and, for example, a fully 'active' instrument like the New Technology Telescope at La Silla in the Chilean Andes, is that the latter has a mirror that is deliberately designed to flex and a support mechanism that is instantaneously controlled by the actual quality of the image. In such an 'active' device, the shape of the image wavefront is constantly monitored and effectively checked for focus over the entire field. If part of the image drifts from sharp focus then the actuators and thrusters that control the matching part of the primary mirror are brought into action and the correct surface shape is quickly restored. Modern wavefront monitors operate so quickly that it seems as if they are able to correct minute deviations almost before they occur! On the other hand, the 200-inch support system was designed by first anticipating what corrections would be necessary and then arranging for their application as they happened. This is a much slower process. The distortions are not detected and measured – they are predicted and allowed for in advance when they are expected to occur.

The polar axis
These problems of maintaining the shapes of the optical surfaces were not the only ones that were encountered in building the 200-inch. Perhaps the most important was the problem of mounting and moving 500 tonnes of telescope smoothly and without vibration to point it in any direction in the sky. Conventional ball or roller bearings could certainly not operate smoothly enough because of the huge pressures that would have been exerted at the points of contact between the metal surfaces. The residual friction would have been much too great to handle, and movement would have inevitably been a series of short jerks rather than a smooth glide.

The elegant solution was simply to float the telescope on oil. A total of seven thin films of oil in specially designed pad systems were used so that the whole moving structure had no direct point of contact with any part of the supporting mounting. This notion of floating a telescope was by no means original, but the method involved was a breakthrough in heavy engineering.

A. A. Common had experimented in England with both mercury (1879) and water (1891) flotation, and the 100-inch Hooker Telescope on Mount Wilson, completed in 1917, still uses steel tanks containing mercury in which the ends of the polar axis float as a means of relieving most of the weight on both the North and South bearings. However, this arrangement is strictly intended as a weight-sharing mechanism. Conventional bearings are still required to confine the shaft accurately to the polar direction.

The oil-pad pressure bearings on the 200-inch work like inverted hovercraft, so that the telescope is actually elevated into position on a film of oil that is about 0.075 mm thick. The surfaces of the bearing pads are machined with great precision so that they match one another over as large an area as possible. Oil is forced into the space between the surfaces under a pressure of about 3.5 MPa (500 lbs per square inch) and slowly flows out at the pad edges. Enough hydraulic force is exerted to elevate the floating component and to maintain a slow continuous flow of oil, so that the two surfaces are kept separated by an extremely low friction fluid.

The arrangement is as follows. The open lattice tube of the telescope is supported between the arms of a giant fork system made from two 3.2-m diameter cylindrical girders some 15 m in length, which are joined together by a cross-beam at the southern end. The South polar bearing is a 14-tonne, 2-m diameter polished steel hemisphere which is held by three matching pressurized oil-pads (Figure 2). These pads are positioned so that they share both the vertical component of the weight of the whole instrument and also the thrust component along the polar axis caused by the steep angle of tilt of that axis. This polar angle is, of course, the inclination due to the latitude of Palomar Mountain, which is about 33°N.

The North end of the fork is made into a yoke by fixing the girders to the opposite ends of an enormous horseshoe-shaped support, some 14 m in diameter, which has a polished cylindrical bearing surface on its outer edge. The opening in the centre of the horseshoe is big enough to allow the telescope to swing between the yoke tubes so that it can see the entire northern sky, including the area around the pole. The edge bearing surface rests in two pairs of balanced oil-pads that share the weight of the whole top end of the instrument (Figure 3).

When this revolutionary oil-pad system was first tried, the result was outstanding. When properly balanced the whole of the moving structure, weighing as much as 530 tonnes, could be turned by hand, and it was claimed that the weight of a milk bottle on one of the ends of the horseshoe was sufficient to move the instrument – though that may be just a bit of the mythology that has developed over the years! In truth, the motor that is normally used in star tracking is rated at just 60 watts (one-twelfth of a horsepower)!

Problems with the drive

One consequence of having bearings of such low friction was totally unanticipated. As the telescope is driven, the entire torque is transmitted from the drive wheel, which is about 4.3 m in diameter, to the yoke by means of a steel torque tube some 4 m long and 1 m in diameter (Figure 2). Partly because of the inertia of 500 tonnes of

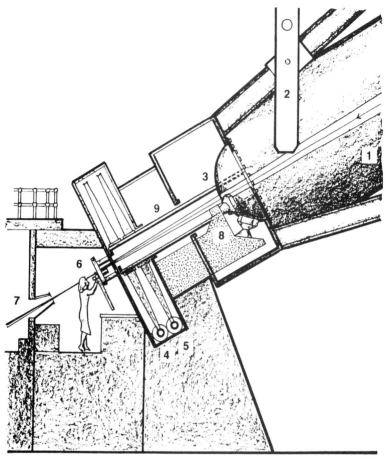

Figure 2. Cross-sectional schematic diagram of the South polar bearing and the coudé focus station: 1 yoke tube; 2 arch support for fourth mirror, used when observing close to the North celestial pole; 3 hemispherical oil-pad bearing fixed to the telescope; 4 slewing gear; 5 tracking gear; 6 coudé eyepiece frame; 7 coudé spectrograph room; 8 base support for three oil-pad bearings (mating with 3); 9 torque tube for transmitting drive power from gears to telescope.

telescope, and also the virtual absence of any damping friction, a gust of wind or a small movement of the observer in the prime focus cage would set up a twisting oscillation in the torque tube that would build up to a visible amplitude of about half a millimetre and a

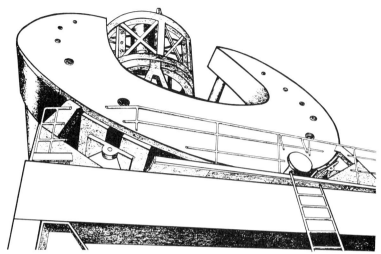

Figure 3. Schematic cutaway of North polar axis horseshoe bearings, showing the two pairs of oil pads on the machined outer edge of the horseshoe. Also visible, at the top of the ladder, is the anti-vibration friction unit (the thin disk-shaped object) that bears on the outer rim of the horseshoe.

period of about 1.4 seconds. At a focal length of 16.75 metres, this is equivalent to a swing of about 6 arc seconds – enough to ruin any high-resolution observations and make effective guiding imposs-ible. The reason for the oscillation was the unexpectedly low bearing friction, which was not large enough to dissipate the excess energy and dampen the vibration.

The cure was simple. A set of metal disks immersed in oil was coupled by means of a 38-mm diameter rubber-covered roller to the outside edge of the horseshoe bearing (Figure 3). This device adds resistance to the system. It can be automatically uncoupled when the telescope is being slewed, but is kept engaged at all other times. It is also valuable in accident prevention! Such a perfectly balanced system of such enormous weight with so little frictional drag could very easily be unbalanced by carelessly leaving a piece of equip-ment, or even a bag of books, in the wrong place. The whole thing could be set in motion and could easily collide with someone, causing dire consequences. Some sort of automatic brake is essen-tial under these circumstances. This small unit provides enough extra damping during an observing run to stop the resonance and completely eliminate all the irritating oscillations.

The declination axis
One other problem that was solved with great ingenuity was the design of the declination bearings. For normal applications in which ball or roller bearings are used for heavy loads, those loads are nearly always applied in steady and fixed directions. However, for a large telescope the declination axis swings from East to West in the course of a night's observing, so that the full weight of the telescope first acts downwards through the East bearing, and then progressively changes until, after passing through the zenith, it begins to act downwards through the West bearing. This change in direction generates considerable distortion of the shape of the telescope tube, together with the entire yoke structure, and this in turn affects the declination bearings.

It must be remembered that in the 200-inch the declination axis is not just a single shaft. It is made from two short shafts which, inevitably, are almost impossible to maintain in perfect alignment. Each short shaft is held rigidly in one of the two cyclindrical yoke pieces by a separated pair of ball races. The mutual alignment of the two shafts is impossible to adjust, but allowance is made by means of flexible couplings at each side of the telescope tube which take the form of sets of spokes like those that locate the hub of a bicycle wheel (Figure 4). If the two short shafts were held rigidly, as if they were a single shaft, then the bearings would be placed under extremely high loads if their alignment was forced to vary due to changes in shape of the telescope tube. This would greatly increase the friction and lead to eventual binding which, in turn, would make tracking and guiding in declination virtually impossible. With spoked couplings the axis centres are fixed radially at the telescope, but there remains a small amount of angular flexibility that can accommodate slight misalignment of the two declination half-shafts.

The tube
Unwanted optical misalignments caused by flexure of the telescope tube were anticipated and dealt with by Marc Serrurier early in the design stage, when he introduced the system that now bears his name. The 'Serrurier truss' system compensates for any sagging at the top end, which carries the secondary mirrors and the prime focus cage, by arranging for equal sagging at the bottom end, which carries the primary mirror in its cell. This is done by carefully calculating the required strut lengths so that the optical surfaces

Figure 4. The lower end of the telescope tube. One of the spoked declination-bearing flexible couplings is visible between the top of the cell and one of the Serrurier truss components.

each move by the same amount as any sagging takes place. These lengths depend on the relative weights of the two ends. The strutting has to be arranged so that the telescope tube has a square section, and the struts on opposite sides of the square form a parallelogram in which any movement would still maintain the same mirror plane. Since the two pairs of sides are free to move only at right angles to one another, great rigidity is generated and only a small amount of sagging occurs. When sagging does occur the primary and secondary mirror surfaces still stay parallel to each other, and the optics remain accurately collimated.

Over the years, this design has proved so successful that it is now used for most telescopes, from the cheapest portable amateur instruments through to the largest professional observatory telescopes.

Using the telescope

So much for the design of this magnificent telescope. For me, there is another reason for remembering the early days of the 200-inch reflector. The monster Pyrex glass disk came out of the annealing oven in early 1935. That was the culmination of years of hard work solving the problems of making, casting and cooling such a large mass of low expansion glass.

I too came out of the annealing oven in early 1935, and grew through childhood to maturity following the ground-breaking work that the telescope was doing. I was a keen young astronomer in 1947, almost thirteen years old, when the 200-inch saw first light, and it was partly the promise of what it would achieve, and the gradual realization of that promise, that influenced me to become a professional. Palomar Mountain became for me a Mecca that I had to visit. I had to see for myself what had become the eighth Wonder of the World and had provided so many fundamentally important observations and measurements.

It is only in recent years that 'active' and 'adaptive' optical systems have become commonplace; that 8-m diameter flexible mirrors and multi-mirror systems have become operational; that we have CCDs and photon-counting detectors that have converted amateur size telescopes into serious research tools. Obviously, the 200-inch has kept up with all these developments, but it is still difficult to believe that since late in 1989 photography has only rarely been used to record images. Observers now seldom sit in the prime focus cage, or hand guide with button paddles. Today's observer monitors activity from an isolated and comfortable side-room, within sight of the vast telescope and connected to it by cables.

If there is an eyepiece at all, then it is found at the coudé focus (Figures 2 and 5), where an observer can scan the very small field of view and accurately fix on a particular target before the image is allowed through to the coudé spectrographs in the dust-free room behind the South polar bearing. The main drive motors and gears can be seen behind the desk unit below the coudé focusing frame, and under a desk (Figures 2 and 6) is the original 'phantom' telescope that mechanically converted the attitude of the 200-inch into signals that controlled the dome drive motors. In this way the dome opening was magically kept in line with the main telescope axis. Today this simple mechanical computer has been replaced by electronics.

Inside the dome

The 200-inch remains one of the most sophisticated light collectors in the world, and it works better and more efficiently today than

Figure 5. The eyepiece frame at the coudé focus station. The light enters the coudé spectrograph room to the left of the picture. Note the hand-paddle, used for fine setting.

Figure 6. The original 'phantom telescope' in the desk under the coudé eyepiece frame that was used to synchronize the dome with the telescope.

George Ellery Hale could ever have dreamt possible. My own dream came true in 1994, when Jean Mueller, Night Assistant at Palomar, guided me through the intricacies of this beautiful structure. She joked that an unwritten part of her job description is that she should 'protect the telescope from the astronomers' – and, knowing many astronomers as I do, I knew exactly what she meant!

From the entrance to the building at ground-level, most of the space seems to be taken up with the base section of the three-storey-high massive steel framework on which the telescope stands. A short elevator ride brings you to the main observing level, and as one walks out on to the spotlessly clean and highly polished floor one is taken aback by the immensity of the enormous mounting as it looms above and disappears from sight high in the top of the dome (Figure 7).

The huge dome is rather poorly lit, and the view from inside the glass-enclosed public gallery is very dim and a little disappointing. Photography from there is impossible, because of all the reflections from the surrounding glass. However, on the main observing floor all is very quiet, and the lack of any obvious activity reminds one of

Figure 7. The great telescope looms above and disappears from sight high in the top of the dome.

the nave of a large cathedral. Conversation is soon moderated to a respectful level partly because of the way that sound reverberates and echoes around the walls and dome as in some huge whispering gallery. Above the centre of the floor, the Cassegrain observing cage, fixed to the back of the mirror cell, hangs down from the darkness above and the great mirror cell itself seems eerily suspended some 5 m in the air. Closer inspection reveals the red cooling fans and the many delicate mirror support mechanisms that can be clearly seen around the outer edge of the cell.

Inside the Cassegrain cage, reached by means of a tall ladder on a mobile platform, the detectors at the focus are being readied and adjusted for the coming night's work. The 'cage' fixed under the 'cell' certainly gives the impression that it was designed to confine the 'wild astronomer' of the night – a notion that might not be too far from the truth! But it is very unlikely that anyone will actually be in the cage while measurements are being made. A human body gives off about 150 watts of heat energy, and is best kept separated from the cold precision of the very sensitive optics.

Off the observing floor, the elevator takes one to the base of the dome from where there is a magnificent overall view of the mounting and telescope, which seems to fill the entire 39-m diameter arena. The outer part of the floor at this level is fixed to the dome, and as the 1000-tonne structure turns smoothly and silently, one gets the distinct impression that it is the telescope on its own floor section that is really turning. There is no perceptible vibration or sense of movement because the rollers and rails under the dome's edge are precision-ground, and the drive is applied through two pairs of rubber-covered wheels pressed onto the lower dome foundation ring – and they operate in utter silence!

At this level there is access to the outside balcony. There is a sort of airlock as one passes through the 1.2-m thick air-conditioning layer between the inner and outer dome walls, but the view outside over the San Bernardino Mountains is stunning. Jean tells of those times at the end of a night's observing when she has gone aloft to check the telescope before closing the dome, and the sky begins to lighten in the East. The view of the sky from Palomar Mountain is truly out of this world, and the presence of the giant telescope seems to add to the feeling of the overwhelming vastness of the Universe that it scans.

Postscript

One envies the small group of astronomers in the early days of the 200-inch who were able to look over the edge of the tube at the end of a night's run and see a sea of stars made by the 'Great Reflector' and seeming to float in the mouth of the tube before their eyes. This was how William Herschel used to use his own much smaller telescope when he began to make detailed charts of the Milky Way for the very first time. Nowadays there are many interlock devices that are designed to protect the mirror from all possible hazards, and access to the top end of the tube is not possible while the mirror is uncovered. After the first 50 years it would be particularly sad if any small accident should damage this priceless eye.

The 200-inch occupies a special place in the history of astronomy, and if it is looked after as well in the future as it is today then we can look forward to celebrating its centenary in 2047.

Comet Hyakutake: The 'Great Comet' of 1996

JOHN MASON

Really brilliant comets seem to have been rare during the present century, certainly in comparison with the 19th century when there were about a dozen remarkable comets, some of which were reportedly visible in daylight. Of course, there have been quite a number of prominent naked-eye comets during the past 40 years, such as Arend–Roland in 1957, the sungrazer Ikeya–Seki in 1965, Bennett in 1970 and West in 1976, but these were in no way comparable with the great comets of the last century. With the exception of the Great Daylight Comet of January 1910, there has been nothing in our own century to rival the great comets of 1807, 1811, 1819, 1823, 1835 (Halley's Comet), 1843, 1845, 1858, 1861, 1865, 1881 and 1882. The Great Comet of March 1843, for example, was so brilliant that it apparently cast shadows.

With the exception of Halley's Comet – which was not bright last time around in 1985/86 – and perhaps Comets Swift–Tuttle and De Vico, which last returned in 1992 and 1995 respectively, none of the so-called 'short-period' comets, with periods of less than 200 years, can be brilliant. The most spectacular comets, those of 'long period', take so long to go round the Sun – many thousands of years or much longer – that we have no past records of them on which to base predictions for their reappearance, and so they turn up quite unexpectedly.

Frequently, new comets are discovered by enthusiastic and committed amateur astronomers who spend long hours sweeping the night sky in the hope of making just such a discovery. Some amateurs have been remarkably successful in these endeavours. The Australian amateur Bill Bradfield has found no fewer than 17 new comets, and even in the UK, retired Peterborough schoolmaster George Alcock has seven new comets to his credit. The Japanese also have teams of dedicated amateurs who devote a considerable amount of time to searching for new comets.

It was one of these Japanese comet hunters who, early in 1996,

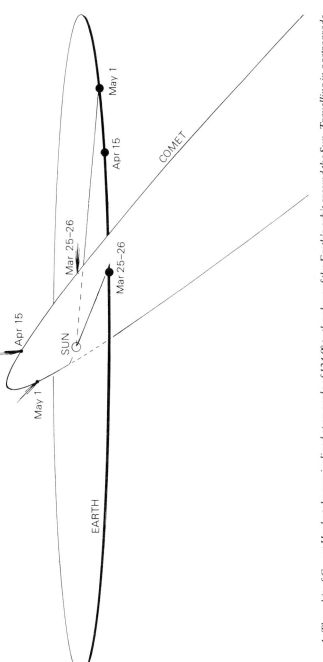

Figure 1. The orbit of Comet Hyakutake was inclined at an angle of 124.9° to the plane of the Earth's orbit around the Sun. Travelling in a retrograde, or 'wrong-way' direction, the comet swept just 15 million km above the Earth on March 25, 1996 on its way in towards the Sun. The comet passed within 35 million km of the Sun, at closest, on May 1, 1996, and at this time it was closer to the Sun than the planet Mercury.

made the first visual observation of the previously unknown comet that is the subject of this article. It was first observed by Yuji Hyakutake from Hayato-machi in Kagoshima-ken, using a pair of giant 25 × 150 binoculars, on January 30, 1996. At that time the comet was more than 300 million km from the Sun, in the constellation of Libra, and appeared as an 11th-magnitude object, with a head, or coma, about 2.5 arc minutes in diameter.

Coincidentally, just over a month earlier, on Christmas Day 1995, Hyakutake had found another new comet in a position less than 4° (eight Moon diameters) from that of his later discovery. However, though a modest binocular object at best in February 1996, this comet was nowhere near as exciting as his subsequent discovery.

In accordance with accepted practice, the second comet was also named Hyakutake after its discoverer, but it received the new designation C/1996 B2, indicating that it was the second comet to be discovered in the second half-month of January (the letter B plus number 2) in the year 1996. In accordance with the new system brought into use for designating comets on January 1, 1995, the 24 half-months of the year are indicated by letters of the alphabet: A indicates January 1–15; B, January 16–31; C, February 1–15, and so on; I is omitted, and Z is not needed. The prefix 'C/' indicates that this is a long-period comet, with a period of more than 200 years.

As precise positional observations of the new comet were received from observers around the world by the Central Bureau for Astronomical Telegrams in Cambridge, Massachusetts, it became possible to compute the comet's orbit around the Sun. In fact, the comet had been photographed by another Japanese amateur as early as January 1, 1996, and these pre-discovery observations permitted the comet's orbit to be determined more accurately. As soon as an initial orbit for the comet was worked out, it became clear that the comet would pass within 35 million km of the Sun at perihelion passage on May 1, 1996 – much closer than the planet Mercury. Moreover, it proved to be heading almost directly towards the Earth, and was to make a close approach to the Earth in late March, with the potential to become the brightest comet for several decades.

Calculations showed that, at its closest on March 25, 1996, Comet Hyakutake would pass just 15 million km above the Earth. This sounds a long way, but it is quite a 'near miss' on the cosmic scale – though there was never the remotest chance of a collision! Indeed, there have been other, much closer cometary encounters. In April AD 837, Halley's Comet passed within 5 million km of the Earth, and this was its most spectacular return in recorded history. The maximum magnitude of the comet's head has been calculated as -3.5, almost as brilliant as the planet Venus, while the tail extended over an angular distance of more than 90°. The closest cometary approach on record occurred in July 1770, when Lexell's Comet came within just 2.2 million km of the Earth, and was visible with the naked eye. More recently, in May 1983, Comet IRAS–Araki–Alcock passed only 4.6 million km from the Earth. That too was a naked-eye object, but rather large and diffuse.

Although other comets have made closer approaches to the Earth, what made Hyakutake so special was that no comet on record had ever passed close to the Earth and then gone on to make such a close approach to the Sun. It was also intrinsically the brightest comet to pass so close to the Earth since the year 1556. Another point of interest is that Hyakutake has an elliptical orbit, although the eccentricity is only just less than 1, so its return period must be very long – about 14,000 years, after passing through the inner Solar System. When Comet Hyakutake is at its furthest from the Sun, it is a hundred times more remote than Halley's Comet at its most distant. Its elliptical orbit meant that Comet Hyakutake was not a 'new' comet approaching the Sun for the first time, but had most probably already made several returns to the inner Solar System from the distant Oort Cloud of comets.

Comets have a reputation for being notoriously unreliable, and so there was great interest in the predictions of how bright Hyakutake was likely to become. The brightness of any comet depends upon a number of factors: its absolute magnitude (a measure of its intrinsic brightness), and its distance from both the Sun and the Earth. As a comet nears the Sun, jet activity on the surface of the dirty-iceball nucleus causes it to lose gas and dust into the coma at an increased rate. The rate at which material is lost varies from one comet to another, so predicting the brightness of any particular comet, especially one that has never been observed before, can be a difficult matter.

The activity of a comet also depends on whether it is a first-time visitor or not. Because Comet Hyakutake had already been around the Sun several times before, there was every reason to believe that its behaviour – in particular its brightness – might be more predictable. Experience has shown that comets coming in to the inner Solar

System from the Oort Cloud for the first time frequently perform disappointingly in that they brighten less rapidly than expected due to the presence of different chemical materials on the surface of such comets' dirty-iceball nuclei. The best-known example of this was Comet C/1973 E1 Kohoutek, and another was C/1989 X1 Austin. These comets increased rapidly in brightness at first, but their brightness then levelled off so that they ended up several magnitudes fainter than predicted.

During February and early March, as it appeared to move very slowly among the stars of Libra, Comet Hyakutake brightened steadily and 'normally' for a comet that has made previous returns to the inner Solar System, becoming a naked-eye object by the end of February. Based on its performance up to this time, various predictions were made for its expected brightness during March and April. Calculations showed that the brightness curve of the comet would display a double peak: the first as the comet approached and then receded from the Earth in late March/early April, and the second as it passed closest to the Sun on May 1.

Even 'pessimistic' predictions at this time indicated that the comet might reach a total magnitude of $+0.5$ when closest to the Earth on March 25, and magnitude -1 at perihelion, though it would then be within just $10°$ of the Sun. The more optimistic forecasts had the comet reaching magnitude -1 when passing closest to the Earth, and a brilliant -4 at perihelion. The magnitudes predicted by such forecasts refer, of course, to the total brightness of the comet's head. When closest to the Earth, the comet's coma would appear large and diffuse. A diffuse comet of 1st magnitude will appear much fainter than a 1st-magnitude star because its light will be spread out over an area of several square degrees. Consequently, it will never be as prominent as a star or planet of the same magnitude, because these objects have all of their light concentrated essentially at a point, or into an area of very small angular diameter.

By early March, Comet Hyakutake was a 5th-magnitude object with a coma about 15 arc minutes in diameter and a narrow gas (or ion) tail $1°$ long, visible in binoculars. During mid-March the comet moved northwards, its apparent motion against the background stars becoming increasingly rapid as its distance from the Earth decreased. By the time it crossed the celestial equator in eastern Virgo on March 20, the comet had brightened to 2nd magnitude and the gas tail exceeded $15°$ in length. From this time, right through until the end of April, the comet was destined to be an easy naked-eye object for observers in the northern hemisphere, being particularly well placed in late March and early April for observers in northern temperate latitudes. It was also very fortunate that the Moon was New on March 19. Consequently, moonlight did not become a problem for comet observers until the last three or four days of March, with the comet being visible in a dark sky in the early morning hours until then.

Between March 20 and 25, the comet moved northwards through the eastern part of Virgo, and across Boötes, passing near the brilliant Arcturus early on March 23, then on into Ursa Major, past Alkaid (the star marking the end of the Great Bear's tail) early on March 25. In this period it brightened from 2nd magnitude to a peak total magnitude of -0.5 when closest to the Earth on March 25. Most of this brightening was due simply to the decreasing distance between the comet and the Earth. The apparent northward motion of the comet against the background stars near the time of closest approach was quite obvious in binoculars over a period of just ten minutes or so. The comet's apparent motion then amounted to just under 50 arc minutes (nearly two Moon diameters) every hour! The night after closest approach, early on March 26, the comet lay midway between the end of the Great Bear's tail and the Pole Star, not far from Kocab, one of the 'Guardians of the Pole'. The following night, in the early morning of March 27, it passed within just 4° of the North celestial pole, and many observers successfully took unguided photographs of the comet at this time.

For a couple of nights either side of closest approach, the comet was a wonderful sight if you were fortunate enough to have a clear, dark sky. By sheer bad luck, the weather in the UK was very poor at the time, and observers were seriously hampered by long periods of unbroken cloud. Another problem was the ever-present light pollution; many observers found that their view of the comet was spoiled by even small amounts of haze, or skyglow from artificial night-time lighting.

At its best, under dark, cloud-free, unpolluted skies, and once one's eyes had become accustomed to the dark, Comet Hyakutake was an impressive object. Its head was about 2° across, and an extremely long and highly structured gas tail could be traced across the sky for up to 70° from the comet's head! The gas tail was initially narrow near the comet's head with several discrete filaments visible, and it was generally quite straight, gradually broadening along its

Figure 2. Comet Hyakutake photographed by Nick James, Glyn Marsh and Martin Mobberley from Punta Hidalgo, Tenerife on March 23, 1996. This 8-minute exposure, commencing at 0258 UT, shows sharp rays and considerable structure in the comet's gas tail. The bright star in the tail is Arcturus, in Boötes, the fourth brightest star in the sky.

length. Many observers likened the shape of the brightest part of the comet's head, as viewed in binoculars or a low-power telescope, to a spring onion, and many remarked on the pronounced hue of the comet – a striking turquoise or blue-green colour.

The outer envelope of the coma was more or less parabolic in form. Telescopic observers reported considerable jet activity within the inner coma: one tailward jet was particularly obvious at times, but the greatest jet activity was observed on the sunward side of the nucleus and gave rise to a fountain-like feature on the sunward side of the inner coma. Although the comet's head was large, it was not as diffuse as many had expected; there was always a degree of condensation to the coma, with binoculars revealing a bright star-like point at its heart. The total magnitude of the coma at brightest was recorded as being comparable to, or even brighter than, the star Arcturus (put out of focus to resemble the comet's head).

Comets generally display two types of tail – gas tails and dust tails. Gas tails tend to be the more common of the two, but to the naked eye they usually appear fainter than dust tails. This is because the

Figure 3. A disconnection event in the gas tail of Comet Hyakutake is discernible in this photograph by Nick James, Glyn Marsh and Martin Mobberley, taken from Mount Teide on Tenerife early on March 25, 1996. This 4-minute exposure, commencing at 0019 UT, shows a 'knot' marking the point of disconnection in the 'old' tail moving away from the head of the comet, while a new tail 'grows' behind it. The bright star above and to the right of centre is Alkaid, the end star in the Great Bear's tail.

light from gas tails comes from gas atoms which are 'excited' to fluoresce under the action of solar ultraviolet radiation. The fluorescent light in comets' gas tails is very blue, which is difficult for the human eye to perceive. The dust tail, which consists of extremely small dust particles emitted from the nucleus and blown away from it by solar radiation pressure, is often curved and is usually much brighter than the gas tail since it shines by reflected sunlight. There was little dust activity evident in Comet Hyakutake when it was at its closest, but this was no great surprise. Dust tails tend to become prominent in comets when (or if) they approach the Sun closer than the Earth's orbit, where the warming solar radiation incident upon the ices in the comet's nucleus causes much greater jet activity, leading in turn to much greater coma and tail activity. Most of the really 'bright' comets, such as Comet C/1975 V1 West, displayed prominent naked-eye dust tails.

By the end of March, the comet had faded slightly and was passing the familiar 'W' of stars that make up Cassiopeia. The Moon became an increasing problem at the end of March and in early April, the moonlight making it impossible to view the comet in a dark sky. However, a convenient total eclipse of the Moon on the night of April 3/4 provided a further opportunity for comet observers. For the 1^h 27^m that the Moon was totally eclipsed, it was possible to view the comet in a fairly dark sky, although it was somewhat inconveniently placed rather low in the north-western sky in the constellation of Perseus. At this time, the head of the comet appeared noticeably smaller than before – less than a degree across – on account of its greater distance from Earth. However, the tail was still quite obvious, although considerably shorter than when at its best only 10 days previously.

By the end of the first week of April, the comet was an evening object. With the Moon being past Full, there were three weeks of relatively moonlight-free skies in which to observe the comet as it sank lower into the north-western sky on its way in towards perihelion on May 1. Hyakutake was not expected to show a noticeable dust tail until mid-April at the earliest, as it drew rapidly nearer to the Sun. As has already been explained, a prominent dust tail is a necessary requirement if a comet is to become a bright naked-eye object as it nears the Sun. Unfortunately, by mid-April Comet Hyakutake was still showing little sign of increased dust activity. Consequently, though it remained a fairly obvious naked-eye object, visible in the north-west in the evening twilight sky an hour or two after sunset in mid-April, it was no brighter than 2nd magnitude and the apparent length of the gas tail was still further reduced on account of the comet's increased distance from Earth. On the evening of April 17, the comet made an interesting grouping with Mercury and Venus in the late evening twilight. By April 21 the comet lay near the border between Perseus and Aries, only 10° above the horizon in Britain, due north-west about an hour after sunset. It was becoming ever more difficult to see in the bright twilight sky, and the comet's brightness did not increase as expected as it approached the Sun. It remained between 2nd and 3rd magnitude towards the end of April, though it was difficult to estimate its brightness against the light sky.

Comet Hyakutake passed perihelion on May 1, but at this time its elongation from the Sun was only 7.5°. On re-emerging from perihelion and solar conjunction, the comet headed southward, passing rapidly from Aries into Cetus, and on through Eridanus and Fornax. Ten days after perihelion it became visible to Southern Hemisphere observers as a morning object in the eastern sky as twilight began. During late May and early June, comet watchers were able to observe the comet rapidly fading in the pre-dawn sky as it traversed the far-southern constellations, entering Dorado in late June.

We have had some cometary disappointments in the past, but at last we have witnessed a comet which has lived up to expectations, and provided us with a really first-class show. There seems little doubt that, in the future, Comet Hyakutake C/1996 B2 will be known as the 'Great Comet' of 1996.

On March 24 and 25, Dr Steven Ostro and his team from NASA's Jet Propulsion Laboratory successfully bounced radio waves off the nucleus of Comet Hyakutake. Using the 70-metre X-Band dish at Goldstone in California, several dozen 480-kilowatt radar pulses were directed towards the comet, which was then just over 16 million km distant. Echoes were received 107 seconds later, the first definite radar contact with a comet since the detection of Comet Halley by the Arecibo dish in 1985. The radar results indicated that the nucleus of Comet Hyakutake was very small – only 1–3 km in diameter. For comparison, the peanut-shaped nucleus of Comet Halley measures 15 km by 8 km. The very small size of Comet Hyakutake's nucleus would explain why the Hubble Space Telescope was unable to view it, despite having the ability to record details as small as 7.5 km across within the comet's coma. However, the Hubble's images showed highly energetic jets of gas and dust streaming from the nucleus, and also revealed three small fragments that had apparently broken off the comet, each forming its own tail. It tracked these small fragments as they moved away from the nucleus at around 11.5 km per second.

The Impact of Comet Shoemaker–Levy 9 on Jupiter and on the World of Astronomy

STEVEN MILLER

Introduction

The dust has settled; the new belt around the giant planet has now faded. But if the effects on Jupiter of the impact of Shoemaker–Levy 9 (SL9) have proved to be relatively short-lived, the comet's impact on the world's Solar System astronomers will last for as long as we remain interested in our particular corner of the Universe. For what happened during the week of July 16–22, 1994 was a once-in-a-lifetime event. And it has provided astronomers with so much information that it will take years to sift through it all.

SL9 was first discovered on March 23, 1993, by Carolyn Shoemaker, working her way through the few photographic plates that she, husband Gene and colleague David Levy had taken on the Mount Palomar telescope that night. Carolyn described her discovery as a 'comet that someone had stood on and squashed'. Such an unusual discovery set pulses racing through the dedicated community of comet watchers. Jim Scotti, working on the Spacewatch Telescope in Arizona and contacted by Carolyn to confirm her detection, managed to make out not just one cometary nucleus, but a whole row of them, lined up in the sky like pearls on a string.

As the measurements of this fascinating object came in, Harvard professor Brian Marsden worked out why it was that SL9 looked as it did. Some time previously, SL9 had been deflected on its way in towards the Sun and was caught up in Jupiter's enormous gravitational field. In July 1992 the comet had approached too closely to the giant planet's surface – within 30,000 km – and had literally been ripped apart. The twenty-plus fragments produced by this violent encounter then set off on what was to be their final orbit. For the calculations showed that in July 1994 SL9 would slam into Jupiter in a series of massive explosions. With 15 months' advance warning,

Circular No. 5725

Central Bureau for Astronomical Telegrams
INTERNATIONAL ASTRONOMICAL UNION
Postal Address: Central Bureau for Astronomical Telegrams
Smithsonian Astrophysical Observatory, Cambridge, MA 02138 U.S.A.
Telephone 617-495-7244/7440/7444 (for emergency use only)
TWX 710-320-6842 ASTROGRAM CAM   EASYLINK 62794505
MARSDEN@CFA or GREEN@CFA SPAN: BITNET or HARVARD.EDU)

COMET SHOEMAKER-LEVY (1993e)

Cometary images have been discovered by C. S. Shoemaker, E. M.
Shoemaker and D. H. Levy on films obtained with the 0.46-m Schmidt
telescope at Palomar. The appearance was most unusual in that the comet
appeared as a dense, linear bar ~ 1' long and oriented roughly east-west;
no central condensation was observable, but a fainter, wispy "tail" extended
north of the bar and to the west. The object was confirmed two nights later
in Spacewatch CCD scans by J. V. Scotti, who described the nuclear region
as a long, narrow train ~ 47'' in length and ~ 11'' in width, aligned along
p.a. 80°-260°. At least five discernible condensations were visible within
the train, the brightest being ~ 14'' from the southwestern end. Dust
trails extended 4'20 in p.a. 74° and 6'89 in p.a. 260°, roughly aligned with
the ends of the train and measured from the midpoint of the train. Tails
extended > 1' from the nuclear train, the brightest component extending
from the brightest condensation to 1'34 in p.a. 286°. The measurements
below refer to the midpoint of the bar or train.

1993	UT	α2000	δ2000	m₁	Observer
Mar.	24.35503	12ʰ26ᵐ39ˢ27	-4°03′32″9	14	Shoemaker
	24.43072	12 26 37.21	-4 03 23.0		
	26.29531	12 25 42.24	-3 57 55.7	13.9	Scotti
	26.30479	12 25 42.09	-3 57 53.7	16.7	"
	26.31448	12 25 41.63	-3 57 53.7		"
	26.41291	12 25 38.70	-3 57 34.8		

C. S. Shoemaker, E. M. Shoemaker, D. H. Levy and P. Bendjoya (Palomar).
Measures D. H. Levy, J. Mueller, P. Bendjoya and E. M. Shoemaker.
J. V. Scotti (Kitt Peak). Last observation made through cirrus.

The comet is located ~ 4° from Jupiter, and the motion suggests that
it may be near Jupiter's distance.

SUPERNOVA 1993E IN KUG 0940+495

D. D. Balam and G. C. L. Aikman report a measurement of V =
20.3 ± 0.1 and B − V = +0.51 on Feb. 26.28 UT, using the 1.85-m reflector
(+ CCD) at the Dominion Astrophysical Observatory.

1993 March 26

Brian G. Marsden

Figure 1. Left: the International Astronomical Union announces the discovery of Comet Shoemaker–Levy 9. Right: Jim Scotti's image of SL9 shows not only the bright central region of the fragment nuclei, but also dust wings extending far out into space on either side. (Brian Marsden, IAU; Jim Scotti, Spacewatch Telescope, University of Arizona.)

theoreticians and observers alike had plenty of time to make their preparations; observatories around the world were alerted.

Predicting exactly what would happen was not going to be straightforward. Jupiter is not a planet like the Earth, and we have relatively little knowledge of the conditions which prevail there. With a diameter of over 140,000 km, it is 1300 times larger than our own planet. Composed of the same mixture out of which the early Solar System was formed some 4600 million years ago, Jupiter is a swirling ball of mixed gases. An astronaut entering Jupiter's atmosphere would encounter first atomic hydrogen, followed by molecular hydrogen and helium. In this uppermost region, the ionosphere, much of the gas would be electrically charged and the pressure would be less than one-millionth of the air pressure we experience at sea level.

After a descent of some 1500 km through the ionosphere, a point called the homopause is reached, below which gases heavier than hydrogen and helium may also be found. Going beneath this into the Jovian stratosphere, the mixture would have added to it small amounts of methane and other hydrocarbon gases such as ethane and acetylene. Eventually, after another 300 km, the pressure would reach 60 per cent of the Earth's atmospheric pressure, and a layer of clouds would be reached. But these clouds would be made of ammonia ice, not water ice as here. And these clouds really mark the end of any certainty in our knowledge of Jupiter.

Below them, our best models predict that there is first a layer of clouds formed from ammonia hydrogen sulphide. And, in a region where the pressure is about five Earth atmospheres, water ice clouds are formed. After that the pressure and temperature increase rapidly. As the gas becomes more and more dense and at a depth of some 50,000 km, the hydrogen becomes metallic. At the very centre of Jupiter there may even be a rocky core, similar to our own Earth. With so much uncertainty, however, predicting and interpreting the results of the SL9 impact was to be quite a challenge.

The comet, too, had its secrets. The reason why SL9 was detected by Carolyn Shoemaker when it was some 750 million km from the Earth was that its violent disruption by Jupiter released huge clouds of dust which surrounded each of the fragments. That dust, in turn, reflected sunlight back to watching astronomers. But while the dust proved essential in making SL9 initially visible, it hid from view the fragment nuclei, making it impossible to work out just how large –

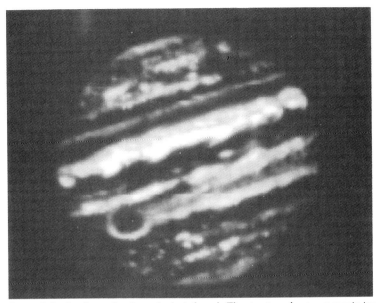

Figure 2. Jupiter imaged at 5 μm in the infrared. The structure due to ammonia ice clouds shows up clearly; the Great Red Spot is a dark circle. (Richard Baron, NASA Infrared Telescope Facility.)

and how solid – they really were. Even the best images obtainable by the orbiting Hubble Space Telescope, its vision repaired thanks to a Shuttle mission in December 1993, could only resolve objects larger than a few hundred kilometres across at the comet's distance. That was many times larger than anyone thought the SL9 nucleus could have been even before the July 1992 break-up.

Estimates of what would happen were based on assuming that an average fragment nucleus was about 1 km across, and had a density similar to that of solid ice. Hitting Jupiter at 60 km/s, such a fragment would cause an explosion equivalent to some 250,000 megatons of TNT. How large an explosion would be caused and how deep the fragment would penetrate into Jupiter's atmosphere would depend on the size and density of the nucleus. The larger the fragment, the larger the explosion; the denser the nucleus, the deeper it would get.

Since no telescope could resolve the fragments, the most reliable estimates of the sizes and densities came from calculating what

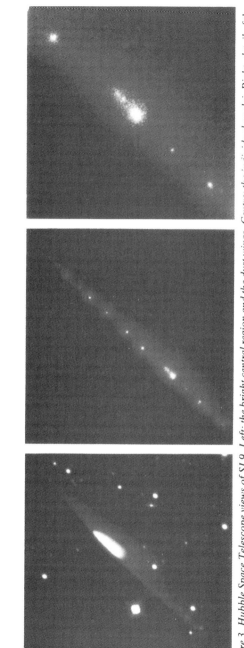

Figure 3. Hubble Space Telescope views of SL9. Left: the bright central region and the dust wings. Centre: the individual nuclei. Right: detail of the Fragment P and Q nuclei. (Hal Weaver, Space Telescope Science Institute/NASA.)

happened at break-up. These, too, were problematic. In the end, the best estimates of fragment sizes ranged from a few hundred metres to around 4 km across, and of densities from between 30 and 100 per cent of that of solid ice. But there were others who thought that none of the fragments consisted of anything but dust, and that astronomers would see nothing. 'The big fizzle is coming,' predicted the science journal *Nature* on Thursday July 14, 1994 – just two days before the first fragment was due to hit. Those of us who had made considerable efforts to record what we felt would be the astronomical spectacle of the century could only watch and wait.

To get the most information possible from the SL9 collision, observatories around the world had planned programmes to make use of various wavelength regions; as well as imaging the event, spectroscopy was also to play an important part in the campaign. Who would do what on which telescope had been decided by teams of proposers making their case to the various committees that allocate telescope time. But plans were co-ordinated to an unprecedented extent, and the University of Maryland set up an electronic bulletin board to relay e-mail information around the world to anyone who subscribed to it. During impact week itself, messages sent to the board, relating the immediate results, were to be 'exploded' to the thousands of subscribers. The Jet Propulsion Laboratory in Pasadena set up a World Wide Web SL9 home page. NASA, for the USA, and the Particle Physics and Astronomy Research Council and Royal Astronomical Society for Britain, made arrangements to keep the various media supplied with information and the latest pictures.

The news everyone had been hoping for finally came through on the e-mail exploder in Britain at around 10.30 p.m. on July 16. The team at the Calar Alto Observatory in southern Spain reported: 'Impact A was observed with the 3.5-metre telescope at Calar Alto using the MAGIC camera. The plume appeared at about nominal position over the limb (the edge of the planet) at around 20:18 UT. It was observed in the 2.3 μm methane filter brighter than Io.' 'Brighter than Io' – not a fizzle, not a whimper, but a real bang. And bang was to follow bang, later fragments often crashing into Jupiter close to where earlier impacts had left the planet darkly scarred.

In describing now what happened to typical fragments of SL9, it may be easier to depart from an earthbound astronomer's standpoint. Instead, we will follow the path of the comet itself, explaining the effects it caused and what happened to it on its suicide mission into the atmosphere of Jupiter. The results presented here were obtained by hundreds of astronomers around the world working for months on end to analyse the data they collected, and whose efforts have contributed to building up an overall picture of the last moments of the comet.

On the way in

The space of the Solar System is dominated by the solar wind, a stream of electrically charged particles sprayed out from the Sun like water from a spinning garden sprinkler. Along with its charge, the solar wind also carries the imprint of the magnetic field around the Sun, forming an interplanetary magnetic field. But around any planet which has its own magnetic field is a region known as the magnetosphere, bounded in the direction of the Sun by a shock wave where the influence of the solar wind is matched by that of the planetary field.

Our magnetopause – as this boundary is called – is about 60,000 km from the Earth. Like the Earth, Jupiter has its own internally generated magnetic field. But, as with everything Jovian, it is much more powerful than its terrestrial counterpart. Jupiter's magnetic field dominates space out to 7 million km from the planet. And in the direction away from the Sun, where the planet's field is streamed out by the passing solar wind, the Jovian magnetosphere stretches some 750 million km – all the way to the orbit of Saturn. Apart from the solar wind (and the accompanying interplanetary field) itself, the magnetosphere of Jupiter is the largest structure in the Solar System. As a result, for several weeks before impact, SL9 would be inside this giant field.

One of the key indicators of what is happening inside the magnetosphere of Jupiter is the behaviour of its aurorae, the bright lights around the northern and southern poles which are the counterparts of our own northern and southern lights. Aurorae are produced by electrically charged particles which are accelerated to great speeds, spiralling around the planet's magnetic field lines. Where these lines dip steeply into the atmosphere, near the poles, these particles smash into the atoms and molecules of the ionosphere causing them to glow. On the Earth, the greens of the aurorae are produced by excited oxygen, and the pinks by nitrogen.

Jupiter's aurorae show up best in wavelengths outside of the visible wavelengths, and are observable only by using special detectors. At short wavelengths, in the ultraviolet, the Hubble Space

Telescope has recently been able to map the auroral rings in detail on the planet's surface. The emission is due to both atomic and molecular hydrogen. In the infrared, a reactive molecular ion known as H_3^+, formed by the break-up of molecular hydrogen and subsequent reactions, is a key indicator of auroral activity.

The charged particles that are responsible for lighting up the Jovian sky come from two sources. As on the Earth, the magnetosphere of Jupiter traps particles from the solar wind. But Jupiter has an additional input. The closest of the large Galilean moons, Io, is incredibly volcanic, spewing 10 tonnes of sulphurous dust into the inner Jovian system every second. The signature of both solar wind particles and dust arising from Io can be seen in detailed images of the aurorae.

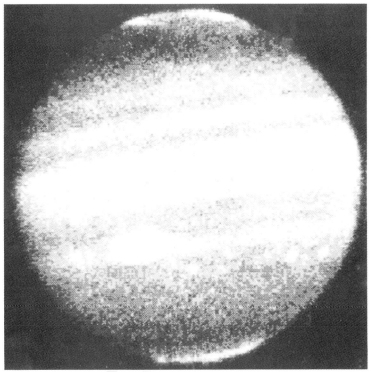

Figure 4. Infrared image of Jupiter taken at 3.8 μm showing the auroral emission in an oval around the poles. (NASA Infrared Telescope Facility.)

SL9 was bringing large quantities of dust with it, too. If the parent comet, prior to break-up, had been just 2 km across (the smallest estimate), and just 1 per cent of it was converted to dust which reached the Jovian magnetosphere, then there would be 300 million tonnes of dust dumped as SL9 arrived. Spread throughout the period for which the comet was inside the magnetosphere, this meant that SL9 would be adding material to the Jovian system at least ten times as fast as Io. And images of the comet indicated that, even as it approached Jupiter for the final time, it was continuing to break up, producing still more dust.

However, it was difficult to be sure what effect this would have. One calculation indicated that, since most of the dust would be electrically neutral rather than charged, it would have the effect of quenching Jupiter's aurorae, which are normally several thousand times as bright as anything we see here. In the end, it appeared that the Jovian aurorae, ultraviolet and infrared, were about half as bright as they had been a year earlier. To what extent this was the influence of the comet and to what extent other factors were in play is still being considered.

Io has another electrical effect on Jupiter. Orbiting just 350,000 km from the surface of the planet, Io is affected by very strong magnetic field lines. In fact, the Jovian magnetic field rotates with Jupiter once every 9^h 55^m, sweeping past the volcanic moon as it does so. Io itself conducts electricity and, according to the dynamo effect, a conductor moving in a magnetic field produces an electric current. Where the magnetic field lines which pass through Io re-enter Jupiter's atmosphere, this effect produces a current of a million amps concentrated into a bright spot.

The fragments of SL9 would also act as conductors. As some of them came in towards the planet, the Hubble Space Telescope was monitoring the aurorae, looking for the effects of the additional dust. The auroral rings were clearly visible, but the astronomers using the telescope noted another, very unusual effect. For as the fragments crossed Jupiter's magnetic field lines they generated what became known as 'blinking aurorae', bright spots of ultraviolet light which switched on and off over a period of a few minutes. Calculations of the power produced in these spots showed they were being generated by a current of between 10 and 100 million amps. The comet was giving notice of its arrival in a big way!

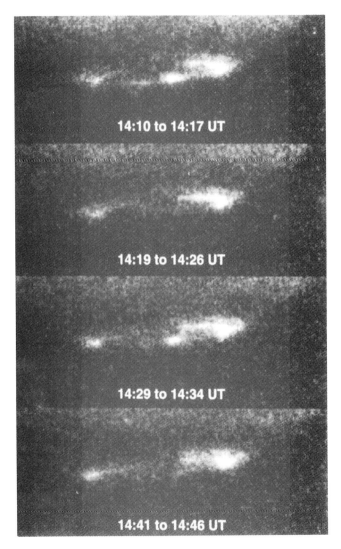

14:10 to 14:17 UT

14:19 to 14:26 UT

14:29 to 14:34 UT

14:41 to 14:46 UT

Figure 5. Hubble Space Telescope images taken during the approach of Fragment P, showing the 'blinking aurorae'. In the top image a bright spot is seen within the main auroral oval; in the next image the spot has switched off. The process is repeated in the next two images. (Renee Prange, IAS, and the Space Telescope Science Institute/ NASA.)

Analysis of the impacts

Calculations showed that the individual fragments of SL9 would strike Jupiter at a latitude of 44°S, and about 10° behind the edge or limb of the planet as seen from the Earth. The fragments would not go straight in; rather they would enter the atmosphere at an angle of around 45°. Fortunately, SL9 would hit on the dawn side of Jupiter, so that the impact sites would rotate into view within 15 to 20 minutes of the individual collisions. In the event, astronomers did not even have to wait that long. Effects were visible clearly from the first moment the comet entered the Jovian atmosphere. Many observatories took series of images or spectra which could then be analysed to bring out the detail of SL9's encounter with Jupiter. The results from several of these can be put together to build up a picture of a typical impact.

On July 18, one of the largest of the fragments, Fragment G, struck the planet. The Hubble Space Telescope took a series of images in filters that ranged from the infrared (methane band) to the violet. At the moment of impact, though it occurred behind the planet as viewed from the Earth, a bright flash was seen. A few minutes later a plume of hot gas was seen rising above the still in-visible impact site. This plume was what gave the brightest images; so intense was the radiation that, until the watching astronomers got to know what to expect, telescope detectors were regularly satu-rated. Over the next 15 minutes the plume rose to a height of some 3000 km above the cloud deck before 'pancaking' back down onto Jupiter's atmosphere.

The following day, Fragment K arrived. This was another large fragment, and was closely observed by the 10-m Keck Telescope on top of the extinct volcano Mauna Kea in Hawaii. The images of the impact Keck obtained show even more detail. For as well as a bright plume, *two* precursor flashes were seen. This was typical of other impacts, and showed up most clearly at infrared wavelengths. From the total intensity accompanying the impacts, a light curve could be constructed showing how much radiation was given off at each moment of the event. The light curve showed a 'flash' (a), 'bang' (b), 'wallop' (c) structure; (c) was called the 'main event', with often a shoulder (d) on it; (a) and (b) were called the first and second precursors to the main event.

As well as a huge plume, Fragment G produced a large, highly structured impact site. Hubble saw this clearly about 100 minutes after impact, G hitting close to where the smaller Fragment D had

Figure 6. Hubble Space Telescope image sequence of the impact of Fragment G. In the top image, a flash is seen above the dark eastern limb of Jupiter. In the rest of the sequence the plume is seen rising above the limb before collapsing back onto the upper atmosphere. (Heidi Hammel, MIT, and the Space Telescope Science Institute/ NASA.)

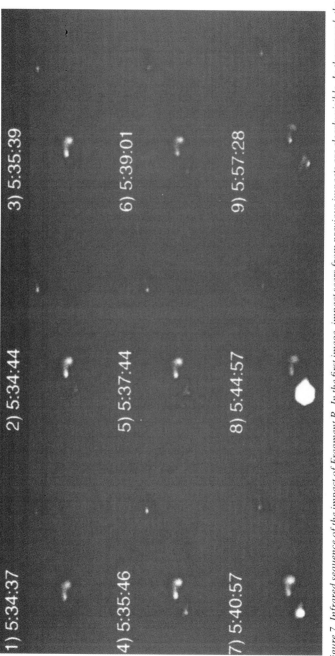

Figure 7. Infrared sequence of the impact of Fragment R. In the first image, impact scars from previous impacts are clearly visible. In the second, the first precursor can be seen in the south-east. The second precursor is visible in images 4 to 6, dying away before the 'main event' starts in image 7. (Imke de Pater, Keck Observatory, Hawaii.)

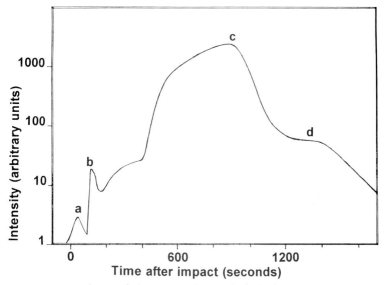

Figure 8. A typical impact light curve. Peak (a) is the flash of the meteor causing the first precursor; (b) is the explosion itself, the second precursor. The 'main event' (c) is at least a hundred times brighter than either precursor. (d) is probably caused by the impact plume 'bouncing' on Jupiter's atmosphere.

already left its mark. At the centre of the G impact site was a dark spot marking the point of entry. Surrounding it was a ring of dark material, 5000 km across, possibly due to a tarry organic chemical mix, as the 'ripple' from Fragment G's splashdown raced across the surface of the planet. And, stretching some 10,000 km from the centre, there was a dark, semicircular apron.

When the medium-sized Fragment C struck on July 17, two telescopes on Mauna Kea were carrying out complementary infrared observations. NASA's Infrared Telescope Facility (IRTF) was taking images at a wavelength sensitive to stratospheric methane, 2.4 μm. A hundred metres away, the United Kingdom Infrared Telescope (UKIRT) was taking spectra at a slightly longer wavelength, 3.5 μm, chosen to pick up four key lines of H_3^+ in the Jovian ionosphere, and follow changes in temperature. The comparison is revealing because, while IRTF could image the whole planet at one wavelength only, UKIRT could monitor a range of wavelengths, but only along the 44°S line of latitude. Thus IRTF had all the

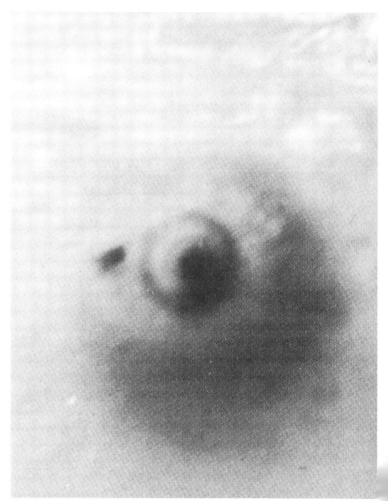

Figure 9. The impact site of Fragment G an hour after impact, showing the central impact site, the expanding ring and the crescent apron. The impact site of Fragment D is on the left. (Heidi Hammel, MIT, and the Space Telescope Science Institute/NASA.)

spatial information about the impact, but UKIRT could complement this by using spectroscopy to follow the temperature of various points on the key impact latitude.

The IRTF images produced a light curve similar to the one shown

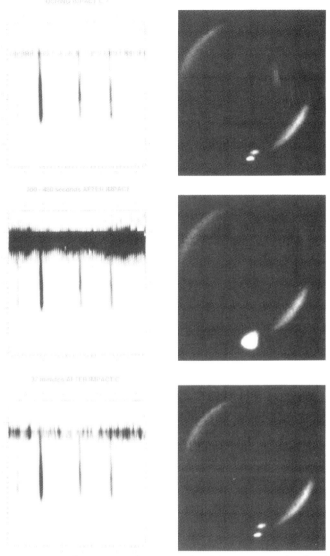

Figure 10. Spectra of the impact of Fragment C at 3.5 μm compared with infrared images. The spectra are taken with the slit aligned along the 44°S line of latitude with east at the top. As the fragment hits (top spectrum and image), the spectra at the eastern limb show a rising background as well as four distinct lines of the H_3^+ molecule undisturbed on the body of the planet. In the middle sequence, while the image shows the 'main event' occurring, a forest of hot methane lines swamp the spectrometer detectors across some 20,000 km of the planet. The impact plume and spectra die away in the final sequence. (United Kingdom Infrared Telescope and NASA Infrared Telescope Facility.)

in Figure 8, as the plume of hot gas rose to some 2800 km before falling back onto the atmosphere. The spectra from UKIRT show two key features. First, just prior to impact, the lines of H_3^+ brightened by about 70 per cent. Second, after impact the spectrum was completely swamped by lines of hot methane, which gave a temperature of nearly 1500 K a few minutes after impact. The greater sensitivity of spectroscopy over imaging meant that effects of hot methane could be seen at least 20,000 km from the central impact site. Other spectroscopic measurements showed that the explosions caused by the impacts produced cyanide, and that the plumes contained lines of hot metals such as sodium, magnesium, iron and calcium.

Nor were the effects confined to the 44°S region. About three-quarters of an hour after the arrival of Fragment K, the Hubble Space Telescope detected bright auroral spots in the *northern* hemisphere, at a location connected to the impact site by the lines of Jupiter's magnetic field. Similar events were detected by the Australian National University Telescope for many of the other

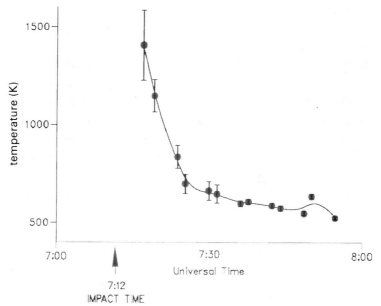

Figure 11. Temperature curve obtained from UKIRT spectra of Fragment C impact. (United Kingdom Infrared Telescope.)

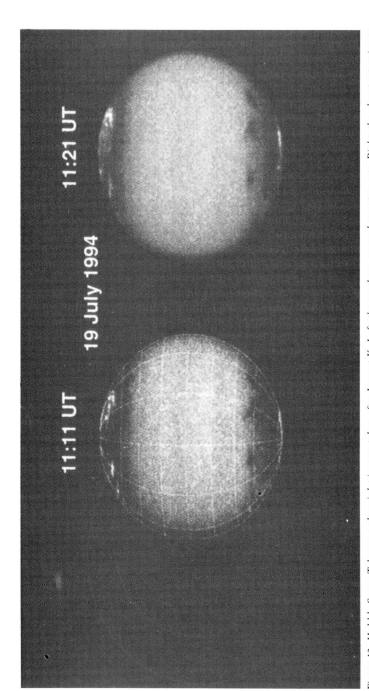

Figure 12. Hubble Space Telescope ultraviolet images taken after Impact K. Left: the northern auroral counterparts. Right: the planet returning to normal. (John Clarke, University of Michigan and Hubble Space Telescope Imaging Team.)

impacts. SL9 was clearly making its presence felt in a number of ways which could be combined to give an overall picture of the event. This is what we now think happened in a typical impact.

As the SL9 fragment hurtled in towards Jupiter at 60 km/s, it first heated the outer layer of the Jovian atmosphere, causing the lines of H_3^+ to brighten. At the same time, the fragment itself became heated by the encounter, becoming a brightly glowing meteor such as we are used to here on the Earth. This probably produced the 'flash', the first precursor seen by the Keck Telescope and shown as (a) in the typical light curve. As it plunged deeper, at an angle of 45°, the fragment punched a hole in the atmosphere, leaving a visible scar in the form of the central impact spot. Throughout the final descent, the fragment was getting hotter and hotter as a result of the friction caused by hitting atmospheric molecules, and it commenced to break apart rapidly. Finally, somewhere around the level of the cloud decks, this process of frictional heating and breaking became too much; the fragment exploded in a fireball which sent temperatures soaring to tens of thousands of degrees K, breaking apart atmospheric molecules such as methane and ammonia. The flash from this explosion, reflected from dust left high in Jupiter's atmosphere as the comet came in, is probably what caused the 'bang', light curve peak (b) corresponding to the second Keck precursor, and the first flash seen by Hubble for Impact G.

The terminal explosion sent shock waves through the atmosphere, causing a ring of chemically active, heated gas to ripple out across the surface of the planet at about 0.5 km/s, causing the ring seen in the Hubble images. (There were also predictions that some of the energy of the explosion might be fired towards the centre of the planet, where it would 'ring' Jupiter's metallic core before being reflected back to the surface. But no sign of such a seismic event has shown up so far in the data analysis.) The explosion also fired a huge plume of hot gas – like the mushroom cloud from a nuclear explosion – at 17 km/s back out along the entry hole punched by the incoming fragment. This gas swept up with it vast quantities of methane and other gases from the stratosphere. Ahead of it, it pushed electrically charged particles in the ionosphere high into the magnetic field. Once there, they sped along the field lines into the opposite hemisphere where they eventually caused the northern auroral spots, or 'counterparts', some 45 minutes later.

The plume rose clearly above the limb of Jupiter within 5 minutes, reaching to a height of 2500–3300 km above the cloud decks after 5–8 minutes, way above what is normally considered as the 'top' of Jupiter's atmosphere. As the plume rose and expanded, it cooled rapidly from ~1500 K about 5 minutes after impact, to just 600 K a few minutes later. Fragments of atmospheric molecules, broken apart by the intense, pyrochemical heat, began to recombine, probably forming the cyanide that was detected, and maybe the material of the tarry ring. Dust grains – their production monitored by the detailed behaviour of the metal spectra – also began to condense out of the hot gases.

This rising plume began to fall back again, up to 10,000 km from the impact site, after about 15 minutes. The direction of fragment entry and plume exit showed up clearly in the crescent-shaped pancake, formed as the plume material – hot dust and gas – crashed back down on the top of Jupiter's atmosphere. The collapsing plume itself heated further Jupiter's upper atmosphere, causing it to glow brightly in the infrared images and spectra. Taken together with the rising plume becoming visible, this phase gave rise to the light curve 'wallop', the main event (c). Finally, the collapsing plume 'bounced' along the top of Jupiter's atmosphere giving shoulders like (d).

After the ball was over
The dust and other chemicals produced by the explosive impacts of SL9 were to stay high in Jupiter's atmosphere for many weeks to come. Measurements made during impact week itself showed clearly defined structures, which remained hotter than the normal atmosphere by about 100 K for at least a Jovian day (9^h 55^m). Even where later impacts had occurred close to earlier ones, well-defined scars were produced. But after a few days, the structure began to break up as the strong east–west winds which blow through the Jovian stratosphere at this latitude picked up the dust and other impact material and carried it around the planet. By early August 1994, a nearly continuous belt had formed. Detailed imaging of individual sites showed that they were being drawn into the smaller storm systems which rage all over Jupiter's surface.

That Jupiter has strong zonal winds of many hundreds of metres per second has been known for some time. SL9 provided information about the meridional winds that flow north–south across the planet as well. In the first instance, detailed analysis of the Hubble images of the impact sites suggested that impact debris was drifting north–south at a rate of 30–50 m/s. This result was to be confirmed in a rather unexpected fashion, however.

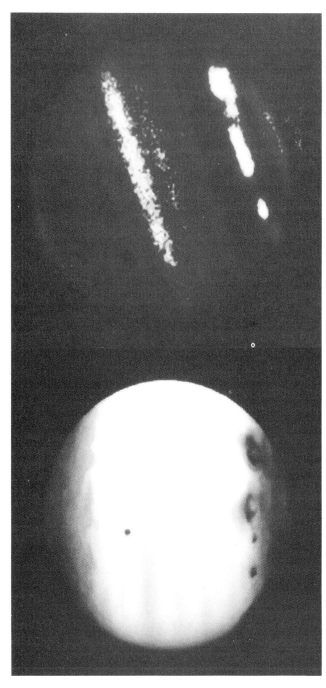

Figure 13. Left: Hubble Space Telescope ultraviolet image showing the evolution of the impact scars. Right: infrared image of Jupiter showing the belt forming. (John Clarke, University of Michigan and Hubble Space Telescope Imaging Team/NASA Infrared Telescope Facility.)

Throughout the impact period, the Jovian aurorae were being monitored to see what effects the comet might produce on them. In the week leading up to and during impact week itself, they appeared to be behaving more or less as normal, even if they were about half as bright as in the previous year. The northern and southern aurorae were of fairly similar brightness. But a few days after the impacts had finished, the northern aurora brightened slightly compared with impact week, and the southern auroral intensity dropped to just one-fifth of its previous value.

The most likely explanation for that is that as the debris from the impact drifted southwards from 44°S to the auroral zone, around 65°S, it interfered with the ion chemistry responsible for producing the bright infrared emission. The time taken to get there (the effect was first noticed in the UKIRT spectra taken on July 25) confirmed the Hubble estimate that the north–south winds were a few tens of metres per second. The suppression of the southern aurora also indicated that a fair proportion of the impact debris at that stage must have been in the form of individual molecules.

As the weeks wore on, the belt of impact sites began to fade. Three factors were at work. In the first instance, as explained above, material was drifting throughout the entire planet's atmosphere, so that the belt effect was gradually diluted. Second, heavy particles such as dust naturally tended to settle downwards under the force of gravity, gradually getting to a level where any effect they might have in producing a dark structure was masked by the cloud decks above. And third, to speed up this process, smaller grains aggregated into larger ones which settled even more quickly. By the spring of 1995, very few observers were reporting detections of the belt. By summer, none were.

The SL9 effect

The collision of Comet Shoemaker–Levy 9 with Jupiter may not have produced any long-lasting effects on the planet itself, but it has certainly provided large amounts of information that are enhancing our understanding. Models of the stratosphere and ionospheric behaviour have had many of their unknowns removed, and are constrained much more tightly. That said, SL9 has still left a number of key questions about Jupiter, as well as itself, un-answered.

For a start, it had been hoped that the impacts would dredge up material from below the ammonia cloud decks towards the surface,

July 12   July 17

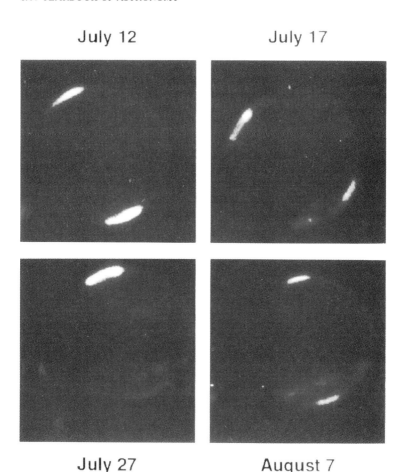

July 27   August 7

Figure 14. Infrared images showing the behaviour of Jupiter's H_3^+ aurorae. On July 12 and 17, the north and south aurorae are both clearly seen, but on July 27 the southern aurora is almost completely absent. Later, on August 7, the southern aurora returns. (NASA Infrared Telescope Facility.)

giving a first real look at the lower atmosphere. Were there really large quantities of water ice to be found just 100 km down? The water spectrum was detected by a number of observers, but it was not sufficiently intense to rule out the possibility – indeed the probability – that the material seen was brought in by the comet itself, rather than having a Jovian origin.

If SL9 could say nothing about the water clouds, what about the intermediate cloud layer, composed of ammonium hydrogen sulphide? Initial analysis of Hubble spectra taken shortly after some of the impacts seemed to suggest that this level at least had been affected, and that there were large numbers of sulphur-containing molecules to be seen. But further work on the data showed that this was mistaken: the sulphur detected could also have had a cometary origin. So detailed information about the cloud decks thought to occur on Jupiter has had to wait until the results of the Galileo mission's atmospheric probe.

Many of the questions raised about the comet itself – its size, density and consistency – are still not definitely answered, though some consensus is emerging. The most likely description of the individual fragments is that they were 'rubble piles', conglomerates of stones and rocks held together by their own gravity and measuring a few hundred metres to a kilometre across, with a density about 30 per cent that of ice. The parent comet from which the fragments were torn would probably have been about 2–4 km across. But other descriptions of the fragments, such as the 'Swiss cheese' or 'soufflé' (depending on your preferred cuisine) models, still have their adherents.

One thing SL9 did achieve was to raise the profile of astronomy around the world. For the entire impact week the media were full of the latest details and images. By Christmas 1995 the World Wide Web site set up at JPL had been accessed more than 6 million times. The most powerful collision ever witnessed in our own Solar System certainly had an impact on humanity's collective psyche. While there were some who tried to profit from SL9 as prophets of doom and destruction – comets are renowned for attracting such people – it has raised serious issues about the rôle of cosmic collisions in shaping the environment we live in. And it has perhaps reinforced the notion that the world's peoples will have to pull together, if and when global disaster threatens. If astronomers can do it, why not politicians?

Binocular Variables

TERRY MOSELEY

Variable stars are those that change their brightness (magnitude) for any reason. Over 30,000 are now known, ranging from bright naked-eye stars such as Betelgeuse to faint Cepheids in other galaxies. Some vary because they actually change their light output (intrinsic variables); others because they are binary systems in which one or both stars periodically eclipse the other as seen from the Earth (extrinsic variables).

There are six main classes of variable star, with some 46 types (104, counting sub-types) currently recognized. The first four classes are intrinsic; the other two are extrinsic.

1. **Eruptive variables** A wide variety of stars whose brightness varies because of flares and other processes in their outer atmospheres. Examples: Gamma Cassiopeiæ, T Tauri.
2. **Pulsating variables** These stars, which comprise about two-thirds of all known variables, expand and contract, either regularly or irregularly, causing variations in their light output. Examples: Cepheids, Mira.
3. **Cataclysmic variables** Stars which undergo explosions to a greater or lesser degree; some do so fairly regularly, such as the dwarf novæ (example: U Geminorum); for supernovæ, it is a one-off shattering event radically altering the nature of the star (example: SN 1987A).
4. **X-ray binaries** These are often close binaries, where one member is a compact object such as a white dwarf, or pulsars; they vary in visible light as well as in X-rays. Examples: bursters, polars.
5. **Eclipsing variables** The eclipses may be total or partial, though in a double-eclipsing system there are no known cases of both being total. Examples: Algol, Beta Lyræ.
6. **Rotating variables** The variations are due to the rotation of the star directing brighter or darker sides, or larger or smaller surface areas, towards us; in some cases there may also be some small intrinsic variations. Examples: ellipsoidal variables, pulsars.

Not included in this classification are the so-called 'secular' variables, which may have changed their brightness slowly over a long time; usually the data are insufficient to confirm this. There are other types not properly understood, or yet to be classified.

Nomenclature Some variables have a designation in some other system, such as Delta Cephei. All others later discovered in a particular constellation were given, in order of discovery, English letter designations from R to Z; then RR to RZ, SS to SZ, and so on to ZZ. When these combinations were exceeded, the double letters AA to AZ, BA to BZ, and so on to QZ (omitting J) were assigned. Thus we have as examples R Leonis, SS Cygni, ZZ Ceti and FU Orionis. This system allows for up to 334 variables per constellation. When that number is exceeded, further variables are simply designated V335, V336, and so on, plus the constellation name. An example is Nova Cygni 1975, which is officially called V1500 Cygni. This is a cumbersome system, due to its historical origins, but we are stuck with it. In any case, all *we* need to know is the star's name and its location.

Amplitude The total variation in brightness, from maximum to minimum, is called the amplitude. It may be measured on the photographic magnitude scale, but unless otherwise stated it is in terms of the visual magnitude variation. Sometimes other aspects of the star, such as the spectrum, vary with the brightness, so that the star in effect changes colour slightly. Amplitudes range from about 20 magnitudes (a factor of 100 million!) down to the limit of measurement accuracy, at about 0.001 magnitude. Usually the extreme range is given, but sometimes the star does not always reach these extremes – this is particularly true of the Mira types, irregulars and dwarf novæ. On the other hand, eclipsing variables always have the same range each cycle.

Periods Mean periods, timed from maximum to maximum, range from minutes to many years. Some variables, however, are totally irregular, and no period can be assigned.

Measurements can be made with photoelectric photometers (which can be extremely accurate) or using photographs or CCD images. For our purposes, visual observations with binoculars will suffice; with care and practice they can be accurate to 0.1 magnitude, or a difference in brightness of only 10 per cent. The variable is simply compared with a Sequence – a list of other stars of known, constant magnitude, using special charts prepared by organizations such as the BAA or AAVSO.

Equipment

Binoculars are described concisely by their magnification and aperture: 8 × 40 means a magnification of 8 and front lens diameters of 40 mm. Almost any pair of binoculars can be used for variable-star observation. Larger apertures will show fainter stars, but even the smallest will be better than the unaided eye alone. However, avoid the 'Galilean' or 'opera glass' types, which have no prisms – the image quality and the field of view are poor. Zoom binoculars are generally not ideal for astronomy, and especially not for variables as the field of view is small, but they can be used at a pinch.

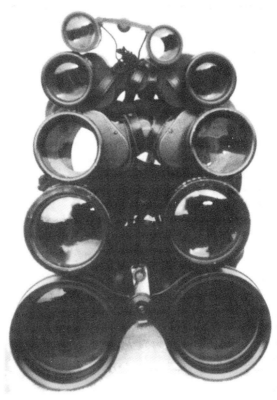

Figure 1. Binoculars for astronomy: Sizes 7 × 25, 8 × 40, 10 × 50, 16 × 60, 30 × 80 (top to bottom). The middle three are the most suitable for observing variables.

Either the conventional porro prism type (sometimes denoted 'ZCF'), with the right-angle bend in the barrels, or the newer and more expensive roof or dach prism type (DCF), with straight barrels, are acceptable. Usually the porro prism types will have a greater aperture for a given price. BAK4 prisms are preferable to BK7 types, which do not transmit as much light; the former will be a bit dearer.

The **exit pupil** is the size of the bundle of light rays emerging from each eyepiece, and is determined by the aperture of the front lenses divided by the magnification, e.g. for 7×50s the exit pupil is $50 \div 7 = 7.1$ mm. It is important that this is no larger than the diameter of the fully expanded (i.e. dark-adapted) pupils of your eyes, or the full amount of light collected by the lenses cannot enter your eyes. The average maximum eye pupil diameter is about 7 mm for children and young adults; by the age of around thirty-five the maximum pupil opening starts to shrink to around 6 mm, and by fifty it may not open any more than 5 mm or so.

Figure 2. Exit pupils: the 10×50s (top) have a 5 mm exit pupil; the 30×80's exit pupil is only 2.7 mm.

Bear this in mind when choosing a pair of binoculars. If you are thirty-five or over, it is unlikely that your eyes will admit all the light gathered by a pair of 7×50s, and the situation is likely to get worse, not better, with time. For those of middle-age or older, a pair with an exit pupil of 5 mm (e.g. 10×50s) is probably better. Remember, with a pair whose exit pupils are exactly the same size as your eye pupils, you will have to get the eyepiece separation exactly right, and keep them perfectly aligned with your own eyes, to admit all the light into your eyes. In practice this is not easy, so choose a pair with slightly smaller exit pupils.

Higher magnifications will darken the sky background, revealing fainter stars, and will also aid identification in crowded starfields. However, any pair with a magnification above $10\times$ really needs to be mounted on a tripod, or some other steady support, to perform at its best, and even $8\times$ and $10\times$ pairs will show fainter stars if mounted. If you have no tripod you can improvise by resting your arms, or the binoculars, on something steady.

Field of view As with telescopes, higher power means smaller field of view, but some (generally, more expensive) designs have wider fields than others for the same magnification. The field of view is quoted either in degrees, or in 'feet at 1000 yards', or 'metres at 1000 metres'. Choose the widest-field pair you can afford, within each size range, so that more comparison stars will be visible in the field. 7×50s should have a field of at least $7°$, or 119 m at 1000 m; 10×50s at least $6°$.

Eye relief is the distance behind the eyepieces at which you place your eyes to get the maximum view: a longer eye relief makes viewing much easier, and prevents the eyepieces from misting up.

Lens coatings Lenses may be described as 'coated', 'multicoated' or 'fully multicoated' (FMC). Such coatings reduce reflections and improve light transmission; look for coloured reflections when you reflect windows or lights in the lenses. Multicoating is a minimum requirement, and 'FMC' is better. Look into the binoculars through the front lenses – the darker the inside, the better.

Choosing a pair
For the beginner, 10×50s are probably the best all-rounders, or 7×50s for younger observers. Cheaper models may not be so pleasant to use, and avoid any pair in which the images provided by the two halves do not precisely coincide, or with which use for more than a few minutes causes eye strain. For a smaller budget, 8×40s

are fine, or even 7 × 35s; anything smaller than these will lack light grasp, although even 5 × 25s *can* be used. If you already have a smallish pair, say 8 × 40s or below, you might think of buying a larger, complementary pair – say 12 × 60s – to extend your observing range, but remember you will also need a tripod. One can often pick up reasonable binoculars and tripods second hand, so they may not cost too much.

Tripod adaptors are available from good photographic stores for about £8 to £10, or you can make your own from scrap metal if you can drill and tap a ¼-inch – 20 (BSW) hole. Some adaptors screw into a socket at the front of the central reinforcing bar; others clamp onto this bar. Some new models do not have any space around the centre bar, so make sure that a tripod adaptor can in fact be fitted before buying any pair with a power above 10×.

Observing methods
There are two main methods of estimating brightness. The simplest and easiest to learn is the **fractional method**. Pick two comparison

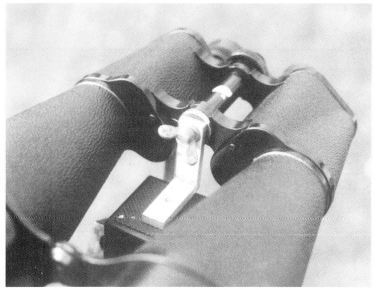

Figure 3. Home-made adaptor: this piece of angle aluminium fits on a tripod and screws into a socket on the centre bar.

Figure 4. Tripod adaptor: this adaptor clamps on to the centre bar of the binoculars, and fits a standard camera tripod.

stars, one brighter and one fainter than the variable. Preferably, they should not differ by more than 0.6 magnitude ($0^m.6$), but sometimes the only ones near enough will differ by more than this. Mentally divide the difference between them into 2, 3, 4 or 5 equal parts, then estimate the brightness of the variable on this scale. For example, if you divide the difference between comparisons 'A' and 'B' into 4 parts, you might estimate the variable as 1 part fainter than A and 3 parts brighter than B. This estimate is then recorded as 'A (1) V (3) B'. Or it might be 2 parts below A and 2 parts brighter than B, which you would record as 'A (2) V (2) B'. If you had used a division of 3 parts, you might record 'A (1) V (2) B' or 'A (2) V (1) B', depending on whether the variable seemed closer in brightness to A or to B. Using an even number of parts allows for the variable being midway in brightness between the two comparison stars. These estimates are later reduced to actual magnitudes from the known brightness of the comparisons. For example, for an estimate 'A (1) V (3) B', where A is $8^m.5$ and B is $8^m.9$, the variable will be $8^m.6$. If the sums don't work out in whole tenths of a magnitude, round to the nearest $0^m.1$, rounding $0^m.05$ to the fainter tenth.

In the **Pogson step method**, the variable is compared with (preferably) at least two comparison stars, one brighter and one fainter, and the difference is estimated directly in tenths of a magnitude. This is a skill which can be acquired with practice, by comparing stars on a few Sequences, and learning what differences of $0^m.1$, $0^m.2$, $0^m.3$, and so on look like. For actual estimates, choose comparisons no more than $0^m.5$ brighter or fainter than the variable, if possible. If there are several comparison stars in the Sequence less than $0^m.5$ brighter or fainter than the variable, make separate estimates for each. This method can show up comparison stars which turn out to be variable themselves. It can also be used when only one comparison star is available, for example when the next comparison star fainter than the variable is too faint to be seen; in such a case comparison(s) from brighter star(s) only can be made, which are better than nothing. Pogson step estimates are recorded as, for example: 'A − 4, = B, C + 1', meaning that the variable is $0^m.4$ fainter than A, equal to B, and $0^m.1$ brighter than C. (Some observers prefer to use the symbols '<' and '>' for 'fainter than' and 'brighter than'; the above estimate would then be written as '$0^m.4 <$ A, = B, $0^m.1 >$ C'.)

Another method, the Argelander step method, is occasionally used, but we can ignore it here.

Negative observations If the variable cannot be seen, record the faintest comparison star certainly visible, thus: 'V < "X"; or V < "Y"'. The importance of a negative observation is that it sets an upper limit to the brightness of the variable at that time.

Sources of error
These are many and varied! The more important ones may be minimized by following these rules:

1. Don't use comparisons too close to the edge of the field of view.
2. Keep the variable and the comparison equidistant from the centre of the field.
3. Avoid twilight, bright moonlight and light-polluted skies where possible.
4. Avoid skies which are hazy or with thin, high (often invisible) cloud. This manifests itself by making all the stars seen vary irregularly in brightness, as it passes over them.
5. Always choose comparison stars which are at nearly the same altitude as the variable, especially if it is low.
6. If possible, avoid making estimates of variables within 15° of the horizon.
7. Make sure you have identified the variable correctly!
8. Avoid bias – do not expect the variable to be a particular brightness because of previous observations.
9. Allow at least 15 minutes for dark-adaptation.
10. Position your head so that the line joining the variable and comparison is parallel to the line of your eyes.
11. Use either direct or averted vision, not a mixture, for each set of comparisons. (In direct vision, the star's image falls on the fovea at the centre of the retina, as in normal daylight viewing; this is where the colour receptors are located. Averted vision means looking slightly to one side of the variable, so that its image falls on the rod cells surrounding the fovea, which are more sensitive to faint light but do not respond to colour. Estimates of red stars are particularly likely to be affected.)

Recording observations
The following information should always be recorded for each observation: Star name; Date; Time (UT or GMT); Instrument used; Sky conditions (e.g. haze, moonlight, light cloud, altitude; on

a scale of 1 to 3, from good to poor); reliability or 'Class' of observation (again, on a scale of 1 to 3, from good to poor – perhaps the variable was at the limit of visibility, or you only got a quick glimpse); and Comparison stars used. Add a column for the derived magnitude, to see the fruits of your labours. If you are using a different observing site, note it under 'Remarks'.

I use the following layout in my log book; you may prefer a variation. Each star has a separate page.

R Coronæ Borealis, 1995

Date	Time	Instru-ment	Sky	Class	Comparison estimates	Magni-tude	Remarks
Oct. 10	20:15	10 × 50	2	2	$0^m.1 < G, 0^m.4 > J$	7.4	Fading
Oct. 15	18:50	10 × 50	1	1	$0^m.1 < L, 0^m.2 > M$	8.7	Fainter
Oct. 17	19:10	30 × 80	1	1	= (Q1)	9.8	Fading fast!

Locating the variable

This can be the hardest part, but you will soon get the hang of it. Find the brightest star on the finder chart, using a good star atlas such as *Norton's 2000.0*. Next, find a recognizable pattern of stars leading from this towards the variable, for example a chain, pair, triangle or quadrilateral. Using such identifiable patterns move across the field until you find the area of the variable. It may be bright and easy to see, or faint or even invisible, depending on its magnitude at the time, the sky conditions and your equipment. For a first attempt, choose a variable which never fades below the limit of your equipment. Ensure that you have identified the variable correctly before making any estimates!

A selection of binocular variables

The following information is given for each star: 'Type; RA & Dec (2000.0); Extreme (and normal) visual amplitude; Mean period in days/years (NB except for Cepheids and Eclipsing types, both amplitude and period may vary from cycle to cycle); Spectrum (K stars are orange, R, M & S stars are reddish); and a range of suitable comparison star magnitudes (information from AAVSO, BAA and Sky Catalog 2000). North is at the top on all charts.

AC Herculis: Type: RV Tauri
RA: 18h 30.3m, Dec +21° 52′
Range: 6.9 to 9.7 (normal range 7.4–9.0)
Period: 75 days
Spectrum: F + K

One of a group of supergiants which pulsate, with alternating primary and secondary minima.

Comparisons:

A = 6.4	F = 8.6
B = 6.5	G = 8.8
C = 7.0	H = 8.9
D = 7.4	J = 9.0
E = 8.1	

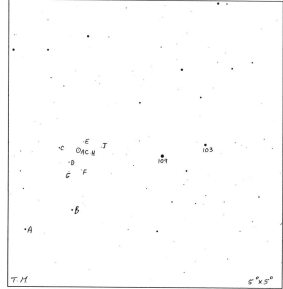

R Hydræ: Type: Mira (long period variable)
RA: 13h 29.7m, Dec −23° 17′
Range: 3.5 to 10.9 (normal range 4.5–9.5)
Period: 390 days (average)
Spectrum: M

A typical Mira type, usually staying within range of good binoculars.

Comparisons:

Gamma (γ) Hya	= 3.0		
Pi (π) Hya*	= 3.3		
Xi (ξ) Hya*	= 3.5		
Alpha (α) Cor*	= 4.0		
Beta (β) Hya*	= 4.3		
Psi (ψ) Hya*	= 4.9		
53 Vir*	= 5.0		
57 Vir*	= 5.2		
63 Vir*	= 5.4		
55 Vir*	= 5.6		
73 Vir*	= 6.0		
M = 6.5		T	= 9.0
P = 7.1		U	= 9.5
Q = 7.6		W	= 9.9
R = 8.0		X	= 10.3
S = 8.5			

* Stars marked thus are not on the chart.

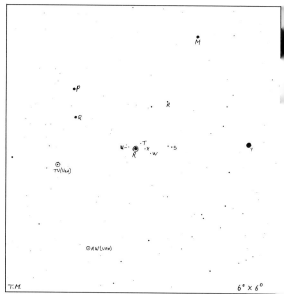

Mu (μ) and Delta (δ) Cephei

Mu (μ): Type: Irregular/Semi-regular
RA: 21h 43.5m, Dec +58° 47′
Range: 3.4 to 5.1 (normally 3.5–4.1)
Period: –
Spectrum: M

Delta (δ): Type: Cepheid
RA: 22h 29.2m, Dec +58° 25′
Range: 3.5 to 4.4
Period: 5.36634 days
Spectrum: F–G

Comparisons:

Zeta (ζ) Cep	= 3.35
Eta (η) Cep	= 3.43
Iota (ι) Cep	= 3.53
Alpha (α) Lac	= 3.77
Epsilon (ε) Cep	= 4.19
Nu (ν) Cep	= 4.29
Beta (β) Lac	= 4.44
4 Lac	= 4.58
π₁ Cyg	= 4.67
9 Cep	= 4.75
Lambda (λ)	= 5.20

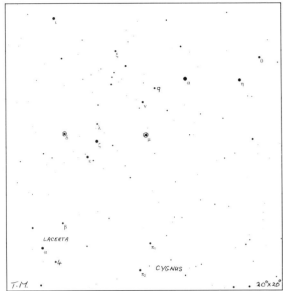

AG Pegasi: Type: Z Andromedæ
(NC? = very slow nova)
RA: 21h 51m, Dec +12° 38′
Range: 6.0 to 9.4
Period: 830 days?
Spectrum: WN + M

One of an odd group of stars, consisting of a cool and a hot star close together, the latter exciting the cool star's outer atmosphere: thought to be similar to very slow novæ.

Comparisons:

A = 5.5		G = 7.6
B = 5.6		H = 7.8
C = 6.1		I = 7.9
D = 6.6		J = 8.0
E = 6.7		K = 8.5
F = 6.8		L = 8.9

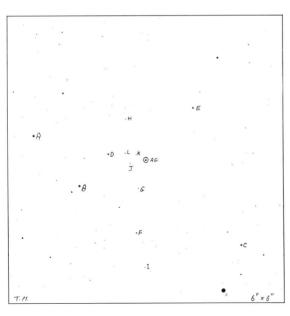

243

UU Aurigae: Type: Semi-regular
RA: 06h 36.5m, Dec +38° 27'
Range: 5.1 to 6.8 (normal range
5.4–6.4)
Period: 234 days (average)
Spectrum: N

A red giant with semi-regular
variations.

Comparisons:

A = 5.3   G = 6.6
B = 5.3   H = 6.7
C = 5.7   J = 6.9
D = 6.2   K = 7.1
E = 6.3   L = 7.2
F = 6.3

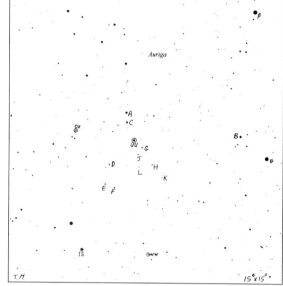

CH Cygni: Type: Z Andromedæ
+ Semi-regular
RA: 19h 24.5m, Dec +50° 14'
Range: 5.6 to 8.7 (normal range
6.4–8.5)
Period: 97 days + Irregular
Spectrum: M + B

An unusual grouping of a
symbiotic star / slow nova, and a
semi-regular variable.

Comparisons:

A = 5.7   F = 8.0
B = 5.8   G = 8.1
C = 6.2   H = 8.5
D = 6.5   I = 8.5
E = 7.4   J = 9.2

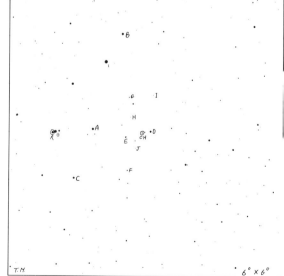

R Scuti and V Aquilæ

R Scuti: Type: RV Tauri
RA: 18h 47.5m, Dec −5° 42′
Range: 4.2 to 8.6 (normally 5–6)
Period: 146 days
Spectrum: G–K

V Aql: Type: Semi-regular
RA: 19h 04.4m, Dec −5° 41′
Range: 6.6 to 8.4
Period: 353 days
Spectrum: N

Comparisons:

Lamdba (λ)	= 3.4	13	= 7.5
C	= 4.1	14	= 7.5
Beta (β)	= 4.4	K	= 7.6
Eta (η)	= 5.0	17	= 7.6
E	= 5.4	18	= 7.7
F	= 6.2	L	= 8.0
G	= 6.5	19	= 8.1
8	= 7.0	20	= 8.3
9	= 7.0	M	= 8.3
H	= 7.1	N	= 8.6
11	= 7.2		

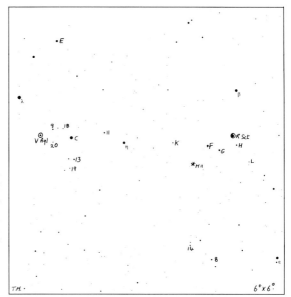

6° × 6°

R Corona Borealis:
Type: RCrB
RA: 15h 48.6m, Dec +28° 09′
Range: 5.7 to 14.8
Period: –
Spectrum: F8

The prototype of the class, this star, which is normally around 6th magnitude, is thought to vary by periodically ejecting clouds of carbon ('soot') from its atmosphere, which obscure its light until they disperse.

Comparisons:

?	= 5.6	E	= 7.9
A	= 6.6	F	= 8.3
B	= 6.7	G	= 8.6
?	= 7.2	H	= 8.9
?	= 7.6	J	= 9.2

8° × 8°

245

Mira; Omicron (o) Ceti:
Type: Mira (Long Period
Variable)
RA: 02h 19.3m, Dec −02° 58.6′
Range: 2.0 to 10.1 (normal range
3.5–9.1)
Period: 332 days (average)
Spectrum: M

The prototype long period
variable; a pulsating red giant
star.

Comparisons:

Alpha (α) = 2.5 (off chart)
Gamma (γ) = 3.5
Delta (δ) = 4.1
Nu   (ν) = 4.9
       N = 5.3
       P = 5.4
       R = 6.0
       S = 6.3
       T = 6.5
       U = 7.2
       V = 7.8
       W = 8.1
       X = 8.4
       Y = 9.0
       Z = 9.3

U Hydræ: Type: Semi-regular
RA: 10h 37.6m, Dec −13° 23′
Range: 4.3 to 6.5 (normal range
4.8–5.8)
Period: 450 days (average)
Spectrum: N

A giant red star with only a very
rough period of about 450 days.

Comparisons:

A = 4.1   G = 5.6
B = 4.7   H = 5.8
C = 5.1   J = 5.9
D = 5.4   K = 5.9
E = 5.4   L = 6.0
F = 5.5   M = 6.2

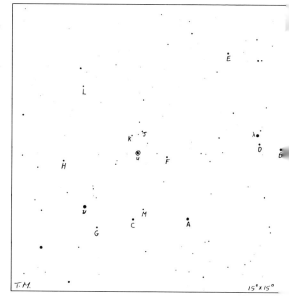

Rho (ρ), and Gamma (γ) Cassiopeia: Types: Semi-regular? and Gamma Cas

ρ: RA: 23ʰ 54.4ᵐ, Dec +57° 30′
Range: 4.2 to 6.2 (normal: 4.5–5.0)
Period: 320 days (average)?
Spectrum: F–K

γ: RA: 0ʰ 56.7ᵐ, Dec +60° 43′
Range: 1.6 to 3.0
Period: Irregular variation over years
Spectrum: B

Comparisons:

Alpha (α) Per* = 1.8
Alpha (α) And* = 2.1
Beta (β) Cas = 2.3
Alpha (α) Cep* = 2.4
Epsilon (ε) Cyg* = 2.5
Delta (δ) Cas = 2.7
Gamma (γ) Per* = 2.9
Epsilon (ε) Cas* = 3.4
Zeta (ζ) Cas = 3.6
Kappa (ϰ) Cas = 4.2
Theta (θ) Cas = 4.3
Lambda (λ) Cas = 4.7
Sigma (σ) Cas = 4.9
I = 5.6
 = 5.7
ϰ = 5.8
 = 6.1
A = 6.3

Stars marked thus are not on the chart, but can be found on any star atlas.

Gamma Cas is a naked-eye star, but is worth watching, and is close to Rho.)

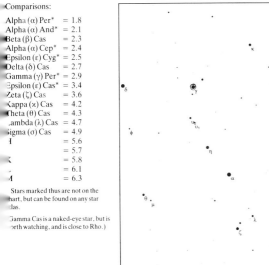

Your results can be of real benefit to astronomical science if you submit them to a society such as the BAA (for the address, see the list at the end of this book) or AAVSO, 25 Birch St, Cambridge, MA 02138, USA.

Bibliography
Webb Society Deep Sky Observers Handbook, *Vol. 8*, *Variable Stars*, John Isles, Enslow, 1990, ISBN 0–89490–208–3.
Observing Variable Stars, David H. Levy, Cambridge University Press, 1989, ISBN 0–89490–208–3.
Burnham's Celestial Handbook, Robert Burnham, Jr, Dover, 1978, ISBN 0–486–24063–0 (3 volumes; details, history and charts for brighter variables).
AAVSO Variable Star Atlas, C. E. Scovil, Sky Publishing Corporation, 1980 (comparisons to magnitude 9 for most bright variables).

The Discovery of Other Planetary Systems

PAUL MURDIN

There have been several searches of nearby stars which ought to have revealed Jupiter-sized planets in orbits around them with periods between 40 days and two decades. Using astrometric data, tracking the flight of stars across the sky, Peter van de Kamp suggested that there were two Jupiters orbiting Barnard's Star with periods of 12 and 26 years. These were not confirmed when later studies were made, and seem to have been due to an instrumental effect. A Canadian survey of 21 stars showed no evidence for Jupiter-sized planets with periods between 40 days and 15 years. An apparently 11 Jupiter-mass object in a highly eccentric orbit around HD 114762 was attributed after further analysis to a brown dwarf of higher mass in a highly inclined orbit. An oscillation of Gamma Cephei with a period of 2.5 years seems to be in synchronism with changes in the star's atmosphere, and is now thought to be due to the star itself, not a companion.

So, up to a few years ago astronomers knew of one planetary system in the Universe – our own Solar System. It was, in fact, becoming worrying that no planets orbiting other stars had been found. After all, numerous philosophers for two and a half thousand years have been convinced on general grounds that there should be other worlds like our own. More specifically, astronomers have recently not only become convinced that planetary systems are necessary for stars to form (they have to get rid of their spin energy into planets), but have also detected protoplanetary disks orbiting young stars, as in the Hubble Space Telescope (HST) images of newly formed stars in the Orion Nebula (Figure 1). The star Beta Pictoris also has such a disk of dust and gas (Figure 2), which the HST has recently imaged to show a warp, attributed by Chris Burrows of the Space Telescope Science Institute to a distortion caused by the presence of a planet in the system.

In 1992 a radio astronomer, A. Wolszczan, timing the rapidly rotating pulsar PSR 1257+12, found oscillations in its period which

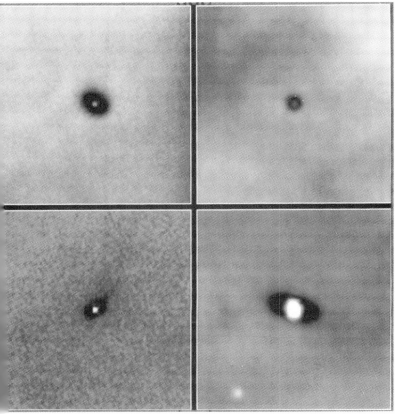

Figure 1. Hubble Space Telescope images of newly discovered protoplanetary disks in the Orion Nebula, 1500 light-years distant, silhouetted against the bright backdrop of hot gas. The circular disks are gas and dust in orbit around a bright, newborn star, each disk tilted at a different angle and thus showing at a different ellipticity. The disks are up to eight times the size of our Solar System; they might evolve to make planets.

indicated that it was orbited by three Earth- and Moon-sized planets. I reported on Wolszczan's discovery in the 1996 *Yearbook*. His system was the second planetary system to be found, but exists in circumstances completely different from our own. Wolszczan's system seems to be the remnants of a supernova explosion in a binary star, a second-generation planetary system, orbiting a star about as unlike the Sun as it is possible to get. Then, in 1995, two

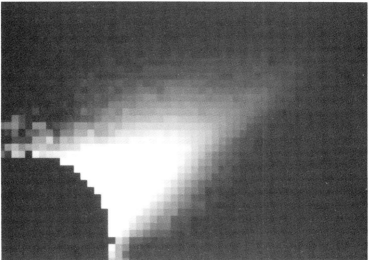

Figure 2. The disk of dust around the star Beta Pictoris (hidden in the lower left corner) is edge-on and shines by reflecting the light of the star. It is analogous to the zodiacal light of our Solar System. The upper image was obtained by the HST; the lower one is a ground-based image. The warp of the disk in the HST image (a subtle effect not readily visible in the raw image) indicates a perturbing effect from a planet in the disk.

teams of astronomers discovered three more planetary systems, each, as currently believed, consisting of a single Jupiter-sized planet orbiting a central star very like our own Sun.

Two Geneva Observatory astronomers, Michel Mayor and Didier Queloz, made the first discovery. They had embarked in April 1994 on a programme to detect any radial velocity variations in a list of 142 nearby Sun-like stars which could be due to the attraction of Jupiters. The idea behind their search was an analogy with our own Solar System. Nearly always, we loosely say that the planets orbit the central Sun – but this is a simplification. In fact, the Sun and the planets orbit around their common centre of mass. Because the Sun is so much more massive than any planets, the centre of mass of the Solar System is below the surface of the Sun, so the Sun scarcely moves in its orbit – though its orbital motion of 13 m/s is somewhat faster than the world's best sprinters can manage, in astronomical terms it is more a slow quiver than an orbit. This delicate motion of the Sun is caused mostly by the effect of the most massive planet of the Solar System, Jupiter, and the main period of the motion is the same as the orbital period of Jupiter, namely about 12 years.

Using the 1.9-m telescope at Haute-Provence Observatory in France, and a specially developed spectrograph which can detect oscillations so small, Mayor and Queloz studied the 142 bright, nearby solar-type stars, hoping eventually to find Jupiters. The stars had been selected as showing, at coarser accuracy, no sign of *large* velocity changes. This meant that they were not members of double-star systems. Astronomers calculate that a planet in a double-star system would loop in complicated orbits among the two stars, and would in a relatively short time be ejected from the system. It seems that planets can survive only in orbit around single stars, showing themselves to be citizens of the Lone Star State.

Mayor and Queloz's programme was a career decision on their part, since they could only be sure that they had found a twin of Jupiter itself by this method by observing at least two periods – 24 years! But after only 18 months, they have established that a number of the stars show radial velocity variations, most of which need additional measurements to reveal any periodicities. They have already discovered a periodic oscillation indicating the existence of a companion planet to the solar-type star 51 Pegasi, 45 light-years distant. Not only was the oscillation many times larger than expected, but its period was very much shorter – a mere 4.2293 days! This discovery was heralded at a European Astronomical Society meeting that I attended in Catania in Italy at the end of September 1995. It was announced by Mayor and Queloz at a meeting on cool stars, held in Florence a week or two later, and published soon after in *Nature*. The planet, designated 51 Peg B, is about Jupiter's mass, with the balance of the evidence pointing to a mass between 0.5 and 2 Jupiter masses. Its orbit is close to circular, and the period of 4 days indicates that it lies much closer to its sun than Jupiter does to our Sun, closer in fact than the distance of any planet in our Solar System from the Sun. The distance of 51 Peg B is one-twentieth of the Earth–Sun distance, just a few tens of star radii, from its parent star.

As news of their discovery spread around the world, the Swiss astronomers' observations were swiftly confirmed, first during a four-day observing run with the 3-m Lick Observatory telescope at San José, California, by Geoffrey Marcy of San Francisco University and Paul Butler of the University of California, and then by a team from the High Altitude Observatory and the Harvard–Smithsonian Center for Astrophysics, who had heard of the discovery. The California team had also been monitoring solar-type stars for radial velocity variations indicating the presence of Jupiters. 51 Pegasi was not on their original observing list because of a mistake in the catalogue from which they compiled their observing programme.

Marcy and Butler went on to announce, at the American Astronomical Society meeting in January 1996 in San Antonio, Texas, the discovery of two more similar cases. 70 Virginis has a Jupiter-sized companion in an eccentric orbit with a period of 116 days; 47 Ursæ Majoris has a similar companion with a period of 1100 days (see the table). The eccentric orbit of 79 Vir B is worrying – some astronomers think this might be a brown dwarf star, rather than a planet.

Star		Planet			
Name	Light distance	Period	Mass (Jupiter = 1)	Distance (AU)	Temperature (°C)
Sun	8 light-minutes	12 years	1	5	−150
51 Peg	45 light-years	4.23 days	0.05–2	0.05	1300
47 UMa	35 light-years	1100 days	2.3	2	−80
70 Vir	35 light-years	117 days	6.6	0.4	variable

The masses and distances of extra-solar planets are subject to uncertainty due to the unknown inclinations of their orbits.

All three of these stars (51 Peg, 47 UMa and 70 Vir) are visible to the naked eye – though you might have to use binoculars if you live in a city area with dirty skies and light pollution. If it is clear tonight, you could get a star chart and try to locate them, imagining their planets in your mind's eye (it sees fainter things than telescopes!). 47 UMa is circumpolar, so it's sure to be above the horizon if you view from Britain. These are relatively bright stars: you need a lot of light to measure accurately the small radial velocity shifts produced by Jupiters. All are relatively near to us – which is why they are bright. Their distances range up to 50 light-years. Because the measurements are so difficult, only the most massive planets can be discovered by means of the equipment presently available – which is why there are no Earth-mass planets yet discovered, though it seems likely they also exist, perhaps in the same planetary systems. And because the time over which the measurements have been made is relatively short, only short-period planets can have been found, at distances from their suns comparable with the Earth–Sun separation or less.

51 Peg's planet is close to its sun, and is therefore quite hot, about 1300°C. It might be argued that any volatile material in the planet, like the gaseous components of our own Jupiter, would have been evaporated long since, or blown away by the solar wind, though this new discovery has already provoked a re-examination of this assertion, with different results – it seems that gaseous planets are more long-lasting than has been commonly supposed, even when roasted like 51 Peg B. 51 Peg B might therefore be a gas giant like Jupiter. It could also be solid; if so, this indicates that when it was formed it would have been up to a hundred times more massive – almost star-sized!

Both the planets around 47 UMa and 70 Vir are cooler, around 0 and 100°C, namely the freezing and boiling points of water. Because of the eccentric orbit, the distance of 70 Vir B from its star is variable, and the temperature varies too. But somewhere on these two planets (or their moons), water is neither ice nor steam but in its liquid phase. This has encouraged everyone to believe that these two planets might sustain life, which can rather simplistically be described as organic chemistry taking place in water solution. However, it is not known whether these planets have a solid surface, or whether they are gas giants like Jupiter, though the analogy with Jupiter suggests the latter.

What astronomers are doing here is providing stages on which the play of life can take place. Biochemists bring together the cast of materials for the play, and biologists write the script, including the natural selection of life forms as they adapt to their environment. For two and a half thousand years, the existence of other planets, apart from the one on which we live, has been a matter of conjecture – for some, almost a matter of faith. It is good to know that there are at least three other stages on which life might possibly evolve.

It is interesting to move from the firm observation of radial velocity variations in three stars, through the scientific deduction of the existence of planets and the calculation of their masses and distances from their stars, to the plausible modelling of the surface conditions on these planets, and further into speculation about what this might all mean about any life on the planets. Waking up one Sunday morning to a phone call, I was provoked by the *Guardian* newspaper's science correspondent into just such speculation on what any life on these planets might look like. I unwisely suggested that because the force of gravity was larger on these planets, life there would be different from life on Earth. Individuals there might be floaters in the gaseous atmosphere, analogous to jellyfish or dandelion seeds. If there is a solid surface to these planets on which life forms dwell, the force of gravity could be a significant factor. 'You, Tim,' I said, 'are tall and thin, because gravity on Earth is relatively weak. Life on these planets might find it difficult to support itself unless it were short and fat. And, in the strong gravity, it might fall over and hurt itself, or something might drop heavily on its head, so it might have armour, like a builder's hard hat. I think of crabs scuttling sideways, not antelopes, gracefully bounding.' This comment, which my friend Tim Radford got illustrated by a newspaper artist, has followed me around for the past few weeks. 'It's life, Jim, but it's short and fat' was one headline.

None of the three recently discovered planets fits well into the picture of the formation of our own Solar System which has been drawn up by astronomers. They are accustomed to thinking of large planets orbiting the colder reaches of a planetary system, like the major planets of our own Solar System, which retain their gases because they are massive and cold. Astronomers had believed that planets as near to their suns as the ones discovered recently would be small terrestrial planets. These new planetary systems, large and close to their star, obviously contradict this notion.

What is next? Confirming these systems and watching their orbits is an obvious step. We have to be sure that the radial velocity variations are truly due to planets rather than some form of pulsations of the stars, as was the case with Gamma Cephei. Planetary orbits are very stable, whereas stellar vibrations are an inaccurate clock. Already the evidence favours the planetary interpretation for 51 Pegasi since so many regular oscillations have been seen.

Eventually small perturbations might turn up, indicating the existence of other planets; this is the convincing evidence in Wolszczan's system, where the mutual gravitational interaction between two of the planets has been detected. There are already indications in the motion of 51 Pegasi that a second planet may exist in the system, another large planet with a period of a few years. Honing the technique to detect smaller planets would be an advance, and would enable us to study the size distribution of planets, with implications for the formation of the Earth.

Other observations might be to look at the stars with accurate photometers to detect the slight diminution of their light at the time each planet passes across its parent sun's disk. These changes, somewhere in effect between a transit of Venus across our Sun and an annular eclipse of the Sun, would clinch the identification of the oscillations as due to planets. They would also confirm the diameter of each planet, so far based on a calculation from the mass and a guess about the density.

Extending the search to other stars is also an obvious move. At first astronomers will carry on looking at solar-type stars, by analogy with our own Solar System which orbits the prototypical solar-type star. Then they will want to see how far from solar a star can be and still have planets – are planetary systems possible around all stars, no matter of what sort?

Direct observation of the planets seems very unlikely with present technology, since the brightness of Jupiter, viewed from a distance well outside the Solar System, is only one-billionth the brightness of the Sun and hidden in its glare. It might be possible eventually to detect extra-solar planets through infrared interferomctry from space, since planets are relatively brighter in the infrared.

What about the detection of life on these planets? It is becoming accepted that molecular oxygen, which is formed in bulk on planets by carbon-based life exhaling, as plants do on the Earth, might be detectable in the spectrum of stars and planets as the signature of life. Both NASA and ESA are actively studying what technical development is needed to make possible the necessary observations from satellites in space.

If in the early part of the next millennium these prospective space missions occur, three of their targets are likely to be 51 Pegasi, 47 Ursæ Majoris and 70 Virginis.

Working through their accumulation of unanalysed data, Marcy and Butler announced in April 1996 the discovery of further planets, both orbiting close to their stars: a 3 jupiter-mass planet orbiting Tau Bootis, and an 0.8 jupiter-mass planet orbiting Rho Cancri. George Gatewood (University of Pittsburgh) reported from astrometry observations in June 1996 a further planet orbiting the red dwarf Lalande 21185 (period 5.8 years, 0.9 jupiter-masses). This star is, at 11 light-years, the fourth nearest to the Sun.

For the latest information, Internet users can consult:

http://www.obspm.fr/departement/darc/planets.

Taxi Ride: The Observatories on La Palma

FRED WATSON

There can be few more spectacular journeys than the drive down from the Observatorio del Roque de los Muchachos to the sea-level airport of Santa Cruz de La Palma. Snaking down the mountainside in an endless sequence of hairpin bends, the road falls 2400 m in 40 km (some 8000 ft in 25 miles). It gives substance to La Palma's reputation as the world's steepest island.

Today, as we leave the mountain top, it is barely dawn. Over to our right, the three domes of the Isaac Newton Group of telescopes are still open as astronomers hurry to complete final calibration exposures on the brightening sky. Nearest is the squat dome of the 2.5-m Isaac Newton Telescope; beyond it, at the very edge of the unseen precipice into the Caldera de Taburiente, is the smaller Jacobus Kapteyn Telescope. And, falling away behind us now, is the giant dome of the 4.2-m William Herschel Telescope that has been my home for the past seven nights. This time yesterday, I was just going to bed at the end of our last night on the telescope; today, after a day's work and a few more restless hours' sleep, I've just got up. As I get older, my biological clocks are less able to cope with such 12-hour phase shifts, and I know that I'll feel decidedly groggy later in the day.

The taxi picks up speed through the curves along the ridge leading to the descent proper. Far below on our left are the still-twinkling lights of the villages along La Palma's northern seaboard. I've never visited them, but I know them well. Many is the time that those miniature, sodium-yellow constellations have provided solace from the isolation of a lengthy observing run, silent reminders of an inhabited world beyond the mountain top. They are old friends.

And then, suddenly, amid the crags on the other side, comes that incredible, breathtaking glimpse into the abyss: the caldera itself, its gaping chasm now carpeted with cloud to the ocean far beyond. Here, for a moment, the ridge is only as wide as the road, the land falling away steeply on either side. In a second, the vision is gone,

Figure 1. Tenerife at dawn (photograph by Fred Watson).

leaving startled newcomers wondering if such a sight could possibly have been real.

But another bend brings another spectacle. Ahead now, to the east, a floor of cloud stretches over the sea to the bright horizon that heralds the sunrise. Emerging from it, etched blue-black against the golden sky, is the magnificent profile of Tenerife, largest of the Canary Islands. From this vantage point, far from the glitz and glitter of the tourist resorts, it presents an image of serene beauty. Its crown is the triangular Pico de Teide (3700 m); its distance of 110 km is diminished almost to nothing by the crystal-clear air.

This morning, Teide is rivalled by an even more distant jewel. High above, Venus shines brilliantly over the scene. And, as if the spectacle were not already stunning enough, one more bend brings one more surprise. Far to the right of Tenerife, down towards the south, another dark profile pierces the cloud deck. It is shy Gomera, an island seldom seen on mornings like this. The vista is breathtaking, and the thought that runs through my mind has been there a hundred times before. 'My God – they actually *pay* me to do this . . .' I wonder what I did to deserve such luck.

*

As we slow to begin our descent into the pine forest, I settle back and reflect on the events of the past seven nights. It's always hard work commissioning a new instrument on the telescope. Commissioning is a species of observing quite different from the normal routine. Instead of trying to discover new things about the Universe, the object is to find out all there is to know about the new piece of equipment. How sensitive is it? How reliable is it? How well does it meet its specification in all its modes of operation? Each and every parameter that future users will need to know for planning and executing their observations has to be determined.

Commissioning is the final proving-ground for all the science and technology that has gone into the instrument's construction. No matter how much laboratory testing has taken place beforehand, it is only when its various systems are integrated with those of the telescope, only when the light from real stars or galaxies traverses the optical path, that its characteristics can be fully determined. To all this investigation, add the inevitable final adjustments and last-minute engineering (occasionally – very occasionally – at the level of trying to get the wretched thing to work at all), and you have a task that takes every waking moment, not merely the hours of darkness.

There is another difference. In conventional observing, the astronomer is (or should be) presented with a telescope and auxiliary instruments that are in peak condition, fully checked out by the observatory staff and all set to go. They are the astronomer's tools, and, if he or she is a good observer, they will be used wisely, with every precious moment of hard-won telescope time properly utilized. Observing will be carried out in the most efficient possible manner to maximize the scientific return from the allocation of time. Alas, it is a fact of life that other things conspire to spoil this ideal. Most often, it is bad weather or poor atmospheric conditions: turbulence, for example, causing the point-like images of stars to inflate into fuzzy balloons (usually known as 'bad seeing'). More rarely, it is a fault with the telescope or auxiliary equipment, bringing the duty technician scurrying out of bed to get the observer back into action and maintain the good reputation of the observatory. Once, I heard of an astronomer who simply didn't turn up for his observing run, but that is another matter altogether. The main purpose is clear: keeping the show on the road is everything while observations are there to be made.

In commissioning, though, the show that has to be kept on the

Figure 2. The dome of the 4.2-m William Herschel Telescope on La Palma (photograph by Fred Watson).

road is the exploration of the new instrument itself. Sometimes, precious minutes tick away while bits of software are frantically rewritten, or eager hands fumble with adjusting screws in the semi-darkness. Occasionally, observing stops altogether for what seems like an eternity while decisions are made about what to do next. Commissioning scientists are usually astronomers themselves, and this kind of inactivity while the stars are shining does not sit well with them. At the back of their mind (and sometimes the front) there is the hope that by the end of the run, they will have become the first to use the new instrument for real astronomy, perhaps making a significant discovery. It's the carrot that leads them to get involved with new instruments in the first place, and it can lead to friction between members of a team.

Often, commissioning runs are scheduled around full Moon, when competition for telescope time is a bit easier and observing can be a little more relaxed. But in the final analysis an instrument that will be used to observe faint objects in the visible region of the spectrum *has* to be commissioned on moonless nights. This has been such a 'dark-time' commissioning run. What time has been lost has been the real thing – premium 4.2-m telescope time – and every now and then the tension has been palpable. Fortunately, such occasions have been few. Our commissioning team has been eight strong, a big group, and we get on extremely well together. But we have all finished the run drained from our efforts.

It would have been worse, but for a tradition we instituted on a previous trip. On one afternoon during the run (usually a Sunday, when there is no day crew around) we always take an hour or so off. We allow ourselves the luxury of a visit to the summit of the mountain, to the 'Rock of the Companions' itself, where giant monoliths huddle together as if deep in ancient conversation, and the view over the island is indescribably beautiful. This little jaunt has come to be known as the 'works trip', and it always astonishes me how refreshing and relaxing it is.

'It's this that makes me glad to be an astronomer,' I had said, when we were at the summit.

'Oh no,' replied one of my colleagues, 'for me, it's the money.' We all laughed.

'And the opportunities for meeting members of the opposite sex,' added another.

'And the job security,' said a third. We fell about with hysterical laughter at three things that definitely do *not* come with a career in

Figure 3. Astronomer Ian Lewis at the 'Rock of the Companions' (photograph by Fred Watson).

astronomy. The relief from the gruelling routine can make even the most banal remarks seem funny.

On this particular works trip, we incorporated a snoop around the construction site for the new 3.5-m Italian National Telescope, named Galileo, just below the summit. Work had progressed well since we had last seen it. Here, I committed an act of petty crime. From the dust outside the locked gate of the site, I picked up a plated, T-headed bolt and pocketed it as a souvenir. My colleagues joked that Galileo will never be finished; somewhere, there will always be a hole whose intended occupant is sitting on a desk in Cambridge . . .

My sleepy thoughts are interrupted as Lionel suddenly brakes hard on the straight between two bends. There's a glimpse of white; the cotton-tail of a rabbit disappears into the pine-litter at the edge of the road. Lionel is evidently a soft-hearted soul, and I have to smile as I think of another astronomical taxi-driver well known to regular users of the Anglo-Australian Telescope in rural New South Wales. Charlie Gale wouldn't have braked. He would have aimed his taxi straight at the unfortunate animal; then, with a 'Jeez, missed the little blighter!', would have returned to whichever yarn from his vast repertoire he was spinning at the time. Like most Australian country-folk, Charlie regards rabbits as dangerous pests. It's a pity he no longer drives taxis; he has retired, gone to better things in Queensland, and the trip to the AAT is far less colourful as a result.

Despite certain similarities (most notably their generous waistlines), Lionel and Charlie are quite different. Lionel is much more reserved. Partly it's because his English isn't very good, though it is still far better than my Spanish. With just the two of us in the taxi, the ride down the mountain is a subdued affair that does not reflect my elation at having the commissioning run out of the way.

Photographs of two smiling, dark-eyed children adorn the Mercedes' dashboard. 'Your grandchildren?' I ask, pointing to them. '*Sí*,' he replies, beaming with pride. He's a nice fellow.

WYFFOS/Autofib-2 is one of the most complex instruments on the entire mountain top. As its double-barrelled name suggests, it has two major components. They are separated by almost the length of the telescope, 20-odd metres, and are connected by 150 strands of delicate optical fibre in armoured cables. They were built at the two extremities of the vales and fens of eastern England: Autofib-2 at the University of Durham, and WYFFOS at the Royal Greenwich Observatory in Cambridge. Together, they form a wide-field multi-object spectroscopy system – an instrument that allows the detailed spectral signature of dozens of objects in the telescope's field of view to be obtained simultaneously. Their task will be to gather data on very large samples of objects so that statistical studies can be carried out. Mapping the three-dimensional structure of the Universe via galaxy redshifts will be one important application.

Autofib-2 is, I suppose, the more spectacular half of the instrument. It boasts a robot, gifted with no mean intelligence, that arranges the ends of the optical fibres on a metal plate 200 mm in diameter in exactly the same geometrical pattern as the target objects in the sky, rather like a rapid, super-accurate weaving loom. (We've all joked that one day, it might knit us an optical pullover that will glow in the dark. Unfortunately, it would mean the end of our fibre-optics system if it did.) When the telescope is pointed at exactly the right bit of sky, the target objects line up with the fibre ends. Their light is captured and transmitted to WYFFOS, whose exquisite optical system turns it into a stack of rainbow spectra revealing the most intimate details of each target. At least, that is what is supposed to happen. Our job, as commissioning scientists,

Figure 4. The 4.2-m William Herschel Telescope, surmounted by Autofib-2. It is connected by optical fibres to WYFFOS, which lives in the enclosed cabin visible on the right in the background. WYFFOS is the unlikely acronym for 'Wide-Field Fibre-Optics Spectrograph' (photograph by Fred Watson).

has been to make it happen. But it has been an uphill task, one whose eventual success has not come easily.

Consider this, for example. The 1° diameter image focused by the WHT's 4.2-m mirror would be a blurred mess were it not for a large system of lenses near the focal plane. This so-called prime-focus corrector sharpens up the image over the 200-mm field of view, but it also introduces a distortion. Stars appear at positions slightly different from where they should be. When Autofib-2 places its fibres on target objects, it has to know about the distortion so it can put them in exactly the right place. While the approximate distortion can be predicted, the only way to determine it accurately is by pointing the telescope at the night sky and making careful measurement of star positions in the field of view. And Autofib-2 is clever enough to be able to do this, in a mode appropriately called MAP.

But – guess what? Autofib-2 has distortions of its own. The fibre gripper moves on an x–y carriage whose axes are not exactly straight, not exactly at right angles to each other, and which change with temperature and tilt. So the place where Autofib-2 thinks it has put down a fibre is not *quite* where it actually is.

We spent a great deal of time before Autofib-2 left Britain

Figure 5. Autofib's metal fibre plate being assembled. All the fibres are in their 'parked' position at the edge of the telescope's field of view. The intelligent robot has not yet been fitted in this picture. In use, it hovers over the fibres, accurately placing them in their required positions before withdrawing to allow starlight to reach the fibres (photograph by Fred Watson).

working on these idiosyncrasies of the robot positioner. The method was to set up a photographic plate containing about a thousand artificial stars with accurately known positions, and let Autofib-2 go and find them. From Autofib's measurements of their positions, we were then able to build a model of the robot's characteristics within its own computer. This also let us deduce the accuracy with which Autofib-2 could send its gripper to any position in the telescope's field. It turned out to be about seven-thousandths of a millimetre, or a little more than 0.1 arc second on the sky. This incredibly small angle is within specification, and we were well pleased.

But things changed when we got to the telescope, and to mapping the distortion of the prime-focus corrector. To do this, we needed the true positions of 50 or so actual stars in the telescope's field of view. These came from measurements with other telescopes, and we knew we had them accurate to about 0.2 arc second. Combining this accuracy with Autofib's intrinsic accuracy of 0.1 arc second led us to expect that we would determine the distortion to a little more than 0.2 arc second. (Errors such as these add quadratically rather than arithmetically; their 'sum' is actually the square root of the sum of the squares.) But when we ran MAP and measured the distortion (many, many times), we found our accuracy was good to only 0.4 arc second – twice as bad as we expected.

In fact, because Autofib-2 currently uses fibres that are 2 arc seconds in diameter (five times the mapping error), this accuracy is just about good enough. It worked fine for the commissioning run, but it would not work for smaller-diameter fibres that are planned in the future. We pondered long and hard over the discrepancy. Was there another source of error we hadn't taken into account? Perhaps Autofib-2 had changed since we had characterized it back in Britain? It seemed unlikely, and to repeat that process would be a long job, not possible within the pressured confines of a commissioning run. It was a mystery that still exercised my mind on the journey down the mountain.

WYFFOS, too, had not been without its problems. This superb instrument, for several years the RGO Technology Division's flagship project, has a novel and complex optical system which brings subtle advantages to its task of dispersing light into the range of electromagnetic vibrations that we perceive as the colours of the spectrum. Each one of the hundred-odd objects fed to WYFFOS by Autofib-2 produces a single spectrum, a line of light varying from

Figure 6. The Autofib-2 fibre assembly and robot atop the William Herschel Telescope (photograph by Fred Watson).

267

blue to red, from short wavelength to long wavelength. Being a multi-object spectrograph, WYFFOS aligns each spectrum beside the next, creating an array of spectra that can be recorded as a single image with a camera. The camera is a masterpiece of optical, mechanical and electronic design – but it is where a freak, unanticipated problem arose.

Although they have a similar basic function, it would be quite wrong to imagine WYFFOS's camera resembling an ordinary pocket camera. In form, it consists of a metal cylinder 345 mm in diameter and 480 mm long (about 13½ by 19 inches) with a thick glass correcting lens at one end, and a steeply curved concave mirror at the other. The mirror forms a compact image of the spectra about two-thirds of the way down the tube, and here is placed that most magical of electronic toys, a CCD detector. This is where the film would have gone if the spectrograph had been designed thirty years ago for photography. The CCD records pictures electronically, with a sensitivity to light twenty times greater than that of photographic film. It is the key to WYFFOS's cherished ability to detect faint, distant galaxies and quasars.

However, the use of a CCD rather than photographic film brings two penalties for spectrograph designers. First, the image surface is curved, and, while film can be bent to match it, a CCD cannot. The solution is reasonably easy: it is to place a convex field-flattening lens immediately in front of the CCD. Second, the CCD has to be operated at a temperature of about $-95°C$ to allow it to build up an image over a period of time. The solution here is to cool it by means of a copper 'cold-finger' connected at one end to the CCD and, at the other, to a four-litre vacuum flask of liquid nitrogen sitting beside the camera body. The cold-finger pulls the heat out of the CCD and cools it. But, in order to prevent serious frosting of the CCD, and conduction of heat into it from the outside world, the entire arrangement has to be free of air; thus, the camera's sealed metal cyclinder must contain a high vacuum (10^{-5} torr, to be exact).

These are routine design considerations, and well understood by spectrograph builders. But this time something went wrong. A matter of hours after the CCD had been cooled to its operating temperature, the field-flattening lens started to fog over. The effect of this phenomenon on the images recorded by the CCD was plain to see: light was being scattered from the bright spectra into the surrounding dark areas. At its worst, a few days after cooling the

Figure 7. The WYFFOS camera on test in Cambridge. The camera itself is the large metal cylinder in the middle of the photograph; its troublesome field-flattening lens is buried deep inside (photograph by Fred Watson).

Figure 8. A bemused project scientist poses with WYFFOS in its enclosure on the telescope (photograph by Ian Lewis).

CCD, scattering was redistributing 50 per cent of the light from each spectrum into its surroundings – a hopeless state of affairs.

We had seen something of this effect before WYFFOS left Britain; indeed, it had been seen in other spectrograph cameras of similar design when they were new. What could be causing it? It was unlikely to be water vapour, for the vacuum pump would have drawn all that out along with the air in the camera. But vacuum vessels like the WYFFOS camera are notorious for 'outgassing' on first being pumped down: all kinds of volatile materials trapped on their internal surfaces start floating off as the pressure falls, and these can re-condense on a cold surface like the field-flattener. The normal remedy for this is to 'cycle' the vessel: that is, to allow it to warm up, pump it down for a lengthy period, then cool it again. In this way, the contaminants can be gradually removed, though sometimes several doses of cycling are required over a period of time.

These procedures had been followed for WYFFOS, and we thought we had everything under control. But when we started looking at spectra during the commissioning run, and saw the scattered light again building up, we realized we had a serious problem. It posed a huge threat to our ability to measure the sensitivity of WYFFOS – the strength of signal that is received from objects of a given brightness in a given time. True, we could estimate the amount of light being scattered, and add that notionally to the measured signal, but that was hardly satisfactory, and depended on us eventually being able to discover just what was forming the mist over the field-flattener and get rid of it permanently – something we were now not altogether convinced of.

After much conferring, we decided that the only thing we could do was abandon our schedule and cycle the camera yet again. It would take an absolute minimum of 30 hours, and would cost us more than a night. Since further tests were required on Autofib-2, our precious telescope time would not be wasted. But it was a hard decision.

It was just after midnight on the fourth night when we finally directed the light from a single star down one fibre into WYFFOS and its recycled camera. Of the scattering there was no sign, and we were able to obtain good measurements of the instrument's sensitivity. They confirmed our expectations: WYFFOS is a first-rate spectrograph. Moreover, we were now at a stage in the commissioning run where some real observations of galaxies could be carried out. Elation lifting our weariness, we crowded around the CCD display in the William Herschel Telescope's control room as the first real scientific results from WYFFOS came in: the spectra of galaxies, dozens at a time, with more than enough signal to determine their redshifts and their distances. Although much remained to be done, here at least were some tangible results, something to prove that WYFFOS/Autofib-2 would be the leading-edge combination we had been promising.

Apparently from nowhere, a bottle of Talisker appeared. Most of us had strong Scottish connections – by birth or education – and a single-malt Scotch whisky was far more appropriate than the champagne traditionally used to celebrate such occasions. Breaking several rules about the presence of drink in the control room, we stood around with a motley collection of mugs, cups and glasses, cheerfully congratulating one another on a job well done as the minutes ticked away on the next exposure. And then, suddenly, we were all very tired.

It was early the following night when the news we had been expecting finally arrived.

'Damn. It's coming back.' Sure enough, tell-tale signs of scattered light were appearing in the dark lanes between the spectra.

Our night with WYFFOS in pristine condition was over, and the rest of the run would consist of routine tests of both halves of the instrument – tests that could be carried out in spite of the gossamer mist now building up again on the field-flattener.

Important questions remained. Would the fogging be cured by further cycling of the camera? All the signs were that it wouldn't. It seemed that this defect might be remedied only by shipping the camera back to Cambridge – a real pain in the neck. Would chemical analysis then be able to identify the nature of the deposit, and would we be able to eliminate it altogether? Questions, questions, still chasing one another around my head as the taxi steadily winds its way down the mountain . . .

Long heralded by a pink tinge to the clouds in the east, the Sun finally rises majestically in a blaze of Canarian glory. We blink like two creatures of the night, caught in the glare of a spotlight. And then, promptly, it sets again behind the same clouds, as we continue our descent through the level of the inversion layer. Through the trees I catch a glimpse of the seaport town of Santa Cruz de La Palma, the island's busy capital, as it wakes to the new day. It is spread beneath us like a map, its hustle and bustle betrayed only by an early-morning ferry shuffling off towards now-invisible Tenerife.

A white car shoots past us, heading back up the mountain. It is an Observatory car, and I recognize the driver as the head of the Isaac Newton Group, the boss himself. An early start to a busy day, no doubt. Such are the penalties of management – but I do envy him his daily trip to work.

And, suddenly, we are in the streets of Santa Cruz, driving along the Avenida Marítima, whose pavements are perpetually washed by spray from the restless Atlantic. The town is bedecked for a festival, and the streets are filled with evidence of last night's revels. Drink-cans, food-wrappings, a few all-night party-goers wandering around like lost souls. It is the most significant fiesta in the island's calendar, the once-in-five-years Bajada de la Virzes – the descent of the Virgin. Pilgrims and tourists flock to La Palma to join the month-long celebration. Our commissioning team must surely be the only visitors on the island to have missed it altogether.

The 10-km stretch from Santa Cruz to the airport always seems to be taken at breakneck speed, even by the wary Lionel. Perhaps it is because it is one of the few straight roads on the island. I hang on to my seat-belt, and wonder vaguely where the traffic police are. But at last we are safely at the airport, and Lionel brings the taxi to a halt. As I get out, I think of things I'd like to say to him. I'd like to tell him that this has been the last of the many enjoyable rides I've had in his car. That he won't see me again for a long time. That I'm going to a new job, an Earth's-diameter away in Australia. But in the end it is merely '*Adiós*,' and the taxi speeds away.

I am early; there's plenty of time for a welcome *café con leche* before my boarding-call. Then, it is on to Binter Canarias flight NT 602 for the short hop to Tenerife; on to Madrid, London, Cambridge. And then – soon – to Sydney, and a new home in little Coonabarabran.

The taxi-ride is over, but the journey is just beginning.

Postscript
The WYFFOS camera did, indeed, have to go back to Cambridge. Analysis revealed that the deposit on the field-flattener was high-vacuum silicone grease that had been used inside the vacuum vessel. It was supposed to be non-volatile at very low pressures, so the misting-up shouldn't have happened – but it did. All traces of the grease have now been removed, and the camera is working perfectly.

Mystery still surrounds the disparity in Autofib's mapping error, however. Further rigorous testing has shown that Autofib-2 itself is not at fault, and the internal computer model of its characteristics is still valid. The spotlight has now been thrown on the accuracy of the test-star positions, and some subtle effects of the telescope's auto-guiding. There are still things to be learned about this wonderful instrument.

Acknowledgements
Part of the purpose of this article is to allow me to pay tribute to the talented people who conceived, designed, built and commissioned WYFFOS/Autofib-2. The many engineers, technicians and scientists involved were universally impressive, and it was a privilege to work with them. My rôle as project scientist for the instrument was a relatively modest one: putting in a few ideas, organizing the testing and commissioning, keeping people in Cambridge, Durham and La Palma talking to one another, and eventually writing about it all.

Contributors to WYFFOS/Autofib-2
University of Durham Shetha Al-Dargazelli, Phil Armstrong, Esperanza Carrasco (INAOE), Andrew Colville, George

Dodsworth, Billy Hogg, Ian Lewis (*Autofib-2 Project Manager*), Steve Lishman, Kevin McGee, Chris Moore, Ken Parkin, Ian Parry (AAO) (*Former Autofib-2 Project Manager*), Ray Sharples, George Teasdale, John Webster, Tim Wilkins.

Isaac Newton Group, La Palma Stuart Barker, Jonathan Burch, Clive Jackman, Chris McCowage, Paul Morrall, Don Polacco, Paul Rees, Nic Walton.

Royal Greenwich Observatory, Cambridge Ron Adams, Bob Argyle, Richard Bingham, Brian Boyle, Terry Bridges, David Carter, Pete Ellis, Nick Ferneyhough, Martin Fisher, David Gellatly (*RGO Project Manager*), Bruce Gentles, Peter Gray (Steward Obs.), Brian Hucklesby, Mike Irwin, David Jackson, Charles Jenkins (*Former RGO Project Scientist*), Mick Johnson, Lewis Jones, Paul Jorden, David King, Robert Laing, Jim Lewis, Paul Martin, Chris Mayer, Paddy Oates, John Pilkington, Janet Sinclair, Howard Stevenson, Philip Taylor, Roberto Terlevich, Percy Terry, Fred Watson (*RGO Project Scientist*), Andy Weise, Sue Worswick.

Some Interesting Variable Stars

JOHN ISLES

The following stars are of interest for many reasons. Of course, the periods and ranges of many variables are not constant from one cycle to another. Finder charts are given on the pages following this list for those stars marked with an asterisk.

Star	RA h	m	Declination °	,	Range	Type	Period days	Spectrum
R Andromedæ	00	24.0	+38	35	5.8–14.9	Mira	409	S
W Andromedæ	02	17.6	+44	18	6.7–14.6	Mira	396	S
U Antliæ	10	35.2	−39	34	5–6	Irregular	–	C
Theta Apodis	14	05.3	−76	48	5–7	Semi-regular	119	M
R Aquarii	23	43.8	−15	17	5.8–12.4	Symbiotic	387	M+Pec
T Aquarii	20	49.9	−05	09	7.2–14.2	Mira	202	M
R Aquilæ	19	06.4	+08	14	5.5–12.0	Mira	284	M
V Aquilæ	19	04.4	−05	41	6.6– 8.4	Semi-regular	353	C
Eta Aquilæ	19	52.5	+01	00	3.5– 4.4	Cepheid	7.2	F–G
U Aræ	17	53.6	−51	41	7.7–14.1	Mira	225	M
R Arietis	02	16.1	+25	03	7.4–13.7	Mira	187	M
U Arietis	03	11.0	+14	48	7.2–15.2	Mira	371	M
R Aurigæ	05	17.3	+53	35	6.7–13.9	Mira	458	M
Epsilon Aurigæ	05	02.0	+43	49	2.9– 3.8	Algol	9892	F+B
R Boötis	14	37.2	+26	44	6.2–13.1	Mira	223	M
W Boötis	14	43.4	+26	32	4.7– 5.4	Semi-regular?	450?	M
X Camelopardalis	04	45.7	+75	06	7.4–14.2	Mira	144	K–M
R Cancri	08	16.6	+11	44	6.1–11.8	Mira	362	M
X Cancri	08	55.4	+17	14	5.6– 7.5	Semi-regular	195?	C
*FW Canis Majoris	07	24.7	−16	12	5.0– 5.5	Gamma Cas	–	–
*R Canis Majoris	07	19.5	−16	24	5.7– 6.3	Algol	1.1	F
S Canis Minoris	07	32.7	+08	19	6.6–13.2	Mira	333	M
*VY Canis Majoris	07	23.0	−25	46	6.5– 9.5	Unique?	–	–
R Canum Ven.	13	49.0	+39	33	6.5–12.9	Mira	329	M
R Carinæ	09	32.2	−62	47	3.9–10.5	Mira	309	M
S Carinæ	10	09.4	−61	33	4.5– 9.9	Mira	149	K–M
l Carinæ	09	45.2	−62	30	3.3– 4.2	Cepheid	35.5	F–K
Eta Carinæ	10	45.1	−59	41	−0.8– 7.9	Irregular	–	Pec
R Cassiopeiæ	23	58.4	+51	24	4.7–13.5	Mira	430	M
S Cassiopeiæ	01	19.7	+72	37	7.9–16.1	Mira	612	S
W Cassiopeiæ	00	54.9	+58	34	7.8–12.5	Mira	406	C
Gamma Cass.	00	56.7	+60	43	1.6– 3.0	Irregular	–	B
Rho Cassiopeiæ	23	54.4	+57	30	4.1– 6.2	Semi-regular	–	F–K
R Centauri	14	16.6	−59	55	5.3–11.8	Mira	546	M
S Centauri	12	24.6	−49	26	7–8	Semi-regular	65	C
T Centauri	13	41.8	−33	36	5.5– 9.0	Semi-regular	90	K–M
S Cephei	21	35.2	+78	37	7.4–12.9	Mira	487	C
T Cephei	21	09.5	+68	29	5.2–11.3	Mira	388	M
Delta Cephei	22	29.2	+58	25	3.5– 4.4	Cepheid	5.4	F–G
Mu Cephei	21	43.5	+58	47	3.4– 5.1	Semi-regular	730	M
U Ceti	02	33.7	−13	09	6.8–13.4	Mira	235	M
W Ceti	00	02.1	−14	41	7.1–14.8	Mira	351	S
*Omicron Ceti	02	19.3	−02	59	2.0–10.1	Mira	332	M

Star	RA h	m	Declination °	,	Range	Type	Period days	Spectrum
R Chamæleontis	08	21.8	−76	21	7.5–14.2	Mira	335	M
T Columbæ	05	19.3	−33	42	6.6–12.7	Mira	226	M
R Comæ Ber.	12	04.3	+18	47	7.1–14.6	Mira	363	M
R Coronæ Bor.	15	48.6	+28	09	5.7–14.8	R Coronæ Bor.	–	C
S Coronæ Bor.	15	21.4	+31	22	5.8–14.1	Mira	360	M
T Coronæ Bor.	15	59.6	+25	55	2.0–10.8	Recurrent nova	–	M+Pec
V Coronæ Bor.	15	49.5	+39	34	6.9–12.6	Mira	358	C
W Coronæ Bor.	16	15.4	+37	48	7.8–14.3	Mira	238	M
R Corvi	12	19.6	−19	15	6.7–14.4	Mira	317	M
R Crucis	12	23.6	−61	38	6.4– 7.2	Cepheid	5.8	F–G
R Cygni	19	36.8	+50	12	6.1–14.4	Mira	426	S
U Cygni	20	19.6	+47	54	5.9–12.1	Mira	463	C
W Cygni	21	36.0	+45	22	5.0– 7.6	Semi-regular	131	M
RT Cygni	19	43.6	+48	47	6.0–13.1	Mira	190	M
SS Cygni	21	42.7	+43	35	7.7–12.4	Dwarf nova	50±	K+Pec
CH Cygni	19	24.5	+50	14	5.6– 9.0	Symbiotic	–	M+B
Chi Cygni	19	50.6	+32	55	3.3–14.2	Mira	408	S
R Delphini	20	14.9	+09	05	7.6–13.8	Mira	285	M
U Delphini	20	45.5	+18	05	5.6– 7.5	Semi-regular	110?	M
EU Delphini	20	37.9	+18	16	5.8– 6.9	Semi-regular	60	M
Beta Doradûs	05	33.6	−62	29	3.5– 4.1	Cepheid	9.8	F–G
R Draconis	16	32.7	+66	45	6.7–13.2	Mira	246	M
T Eridani	03	55.2	−24	02	7.2–13.2	Mira	252	M
R Fornacis	02	29.3	−26	06	7.5–13.0	Mira	389	C
R Geminorum	07	07.4	+22	42	6.0–14.0	Mira	370	S
U Geminorum	07	55.1	+22	00	8.2–14.9	Dwarf nova	105±	Pec+M
*Zeta Geminorum	07	04.1	+20	34	3.6– 4.2	Cepheid	10.2	F–G
*Eta Geminorum	06	14.9	+22	30	3.2– 3.9	Semi-regular	233	M
S Gruis	22	26.1	−48	26	6.0–15.0	Mira	402	M
S Herculis	16	51.9	+14	56	6.4–13.8	Mira	307	M
U Herculis	16	25.8	+18	54	6.4–13.4	Mira	406	M
Alpha Herculis	17	14.6	+14	23	2.7– 4.0	Semi-regular	–	M
68, u Herculis	17	17.3	+33	06	4.7– 5.4	Algol	2.1	B+B
R Horologii	02	53.9	−49	53	4.7–14.3	Mira	408	M
U Horologii	03	52.8	−45	50	6–14	Mira	348	M
R Hydræ	13	29.7	−23	17	3.5–10.9	Mira	389	M
U Hydræ	10	37.6	−13	23	4.3– 6.5	Semi-regular	450?	C
VW Hydri	04	09.1	−71	18	8.4–14.4	Dwarf nova	27±	Pec
R Leonis	09	47.6	+11	26	4.4–11.3	Mira	310	M
R Leonis Minoris	09	45.6	+34	31	6.3–13.2	Mira	372	M
R Leporis	04	59.6	−14	48	5.5–11.7	Mira	427	C
Y Libræ	15	11.7	−06	01	7.6–14.7	Mira	276	M
RS Libræ	15	24.3	−22	55	7.0–13.0	Mira	218	M
Delta Libræ	15	01.0	−08	31	4.9– 5.9	Algol	2.3	A
R Lyncis	07	01.3	+55	20	7.2–14.3	Mira	379	S
R Lyræ	18	55.3	+43	57	3.9– 5.0	Semi-regular	46?	M
RR Lyræ	19	25.5	+42	47	7.1– 8.1	RR Lyræ	0.6	A–F
Beta Lyræ	18	50.1	+33	22	3.3– 4.4	Eclipsing	12.9	B
U Microscopii	20	29.2	−40	25	7.0–14.4	Mira	334	M
*U Monocerotis	07	30.8	−09	47	5.9– 7.8	RV Tauri	91	F–K
V Monocerotis	06	22.7	−02	12	6.0–13.9	Mira	340	M
R Normæ	15	36.0	−49	30	6.5–13.9	Mira	508	M
T Normæ	15	44.1	−54	59	6.2–13.6	Mira	241	M
R Octantis	05	26.1	−86	23	6.3–13.2	Mira	405	M
S Octantis	18	08.7	−86	48	7.2–14.0	Mira	259	M
V Ophiuchi	16	26.7	−12	26	7.3–11.6	Mira	297	C
X Ophiuchi	18	38.3	+08	50	5.9– 9.2	Mira	329	M
RS Ophiuchi	17	50.2	−06	43	4.3–12.5	Recurrent nova	–	OB+M
U Orionis	05	55.8	+20	10	4.8–13.0	Mira	368	M
W Orionis	05	05.4	+01	11	5.9– 7.7	Semi-regular	212	C
Alpha Orionis	05	55.2	+07	24	0.0– 1.3	Semi-regular	2335	M

Star	RA		Declination		Range	Type	Period	Spectrum
	h	m	°	'			days	
S Pavonis	19	55.2	−59	12	6.6–10.4	Semi-regular	381	M
Kappa Pavonis	18	56.9	−67	14	3.9– 4.8	Cepheid	9.1	G
R Pegasi	23	06.8	+10	33	6.9–13.8	Mira	378	M
Beta Pegasi	23	03.8	+28	05	2.3– 2.7	Irregular	−	M
X Persei	03	55.4	+31	03	6.0– 7.0	Gamma Cas	−	O9.5
Beta Persei	03	08.2	+40	57	2.1– 3.4	Algol	2.9	B
Rho Persei	03	05.2	+38	50	3.3– 4.0	Semi-regular	50?	M
Zeta Phœnicis	01	08.4	−55	15	3.9– 4.4	Algol	1.7	B+B
R Pictoris	04	46.2	−49	15	6.4–10.1	Semi-regular	171	M
L² Puppis	07	13.5	−44	39	2.6– 6.2	Semi-regular	141	M
*RS Puppis	08	13.1	−34	35	6.5– 7.7	Cepheid	41.4	G
T Pyxidis	09	04.7	−32	23	6.5–15.3	Recurrent nova	7000±	Pec
U Sagittæ	19	18.8	+19	37	6.5– 9.3	Algol	3.4	B+G
WZ Sagittæ	20	07.6	+17	42	7.0–15.5	Dwarf nova	11900±	A
R Sagittarii	19	16.7	−19	18	6.7–12.8	Mira	270	M
RR Sagittarii	19	55.9	−29	11	5.4–14.0	Mira	336	M
RT Sagittarii	20	17.7	−39	07	6.0–14.1	Mira	306	M
RU Sagittarii	19	58.7	−41	51	6.0–13.8	Mira	240	M
RY Sagittarii	19	16.5	−33	31	5.8–14.0	R Coronæ Bor.	−	G
RR Scorpii	16	56.6	−30	35	5.0–12.4	Mira	281	M
RS Scorpii	16	55.6	−45	06	6.2–13.0	Mira	320	M
RT Scorpii	17	03.5	−36	55	7.0–15.2	Mira	449	S
S Sculptoris	00	15.4	−32	03	5.5–13.6	Mira	363	M
R Scuti	18	47.5	−05	42	4.2– 8.6	RV Tauri	146	G–K
R Serpentis	15	50.7	+15	08	5.2–14.4	Mira	356	M
S Serpentis	15	21.7	+14	19	7.0–14.1	Mira	372	M
T Tauri	04	22.0	+19	32	9.3–13.5	Irregular	−	F–K
SU Tauri	05	49.1	+19	04	9.1–16.9	R Coronæ Bor.	−	G
Lambda Tauri	04	00.7	+12	29	3.4– 3.9	Algol	4.0	B+A
R Trianguli	02	37.0	+34	16	5.4–12.6	Mira	267	M
R Ursæ Majoris	10	44.6	+68	47	6.5–13.7	Mira	302	M
T Ursæ Majoris	12	36.4	+59	29	6.6–13.5	Mira	257	M
U Ursæ Minoris	14	17.3	+66	48	7.1–13.0	Mira	331	M
R Virginis	12	38.5	+06	59	6.1–12.1	Mira	146	M
S Virginis	13	33.0	−07	12	6.3–13.2	Mira	375	M
SS Virginis	12	25.3	+00	48	6.0– 9.6	Semi-regular	364	C
R Vulpeculæ	21	04.4	+23	49	7.0–14.3	Mira	137	M
Z Vulpeculæ	19	21.7	+25	34	7.3– 8.9	Algol	2.5	B+A

R and FW Canis Majoris

Comparison stars:

A = 4.96
B = 5.45
C = 5.46
D = 5.78
E = 6.05
F = 6.09
G = 6.6
H = 6.77

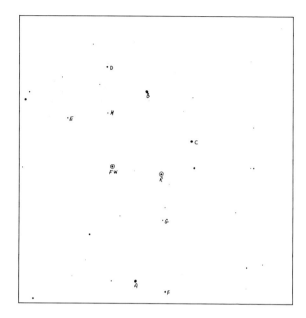

VY Canis Majoris

Comparison stars:

C = 7.0
D = 7.1
E = 8.1
F = 8.4
G = 8.8
H = 9.4

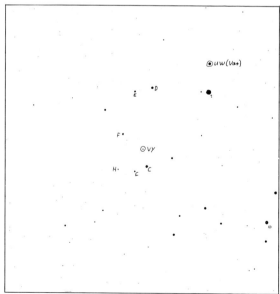

Mira

Comparison stars:

Alpha (α)   = 2.52 (off map)
Gamma (γ) = 3.46
Delta (δ)   = 4.06
Nu (ν)   = 4.87
N   = 5.34
P   = 5.41
R   = 6.00
S   = 6.32
T   = 6.49
U   = 7.19
W   = 8.06
X   = 8.42
y   = 9.00
z   = 9.33

Eta and Zeta Geminorum

Comparison stars:

Epsilon (ε) Gem = 2.98
Zeta (ζ) Tau   = 3.03
Xi (ξ) Gem   = 3.34
Lambda (λ) Gem   = 3.59
Nu (ν) Gem   = 4.14
1 Gem   = 4.15

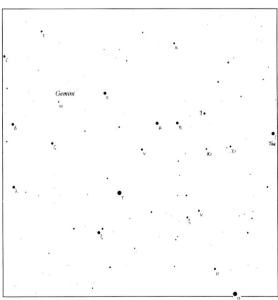

U Monocerotis

Comparison stars:

C = 5.72
D = 5.85
E = 6.00
F = 6.62
G = 6.97
H = 7.51
K = 7.81
L = 8.03

RS Puppis

Comparison stars:

A = 6.4
B = 6.4
C = 7.0
D = 7.4
E = 7.6
F = 8.2
G = 8.3

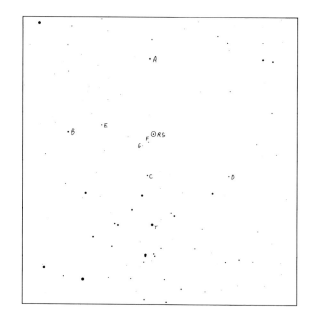

Mira Stars: Maxima, 1997

JOHN ISLES

Below are the predicted dates of maxima for Mira stars that reach magnitude 7.5 or brighter at an average maximum. Individual maxima can in some cases be brighter or fainter than average by a magnitude or more, and all dates are only approximate. The positions, extreme ranges and mean periods of these stars can be found in the preceding list of interesting variable stars.

Star	Mean magnitude at maximum	Dates of maxima
R Andromedæ	6.9	Apr. 17
W Andromedæ	7.4	June 29
R Aquarii	6.5	Apr. 13
R Aquilæ	6.1	Jan. 4, Oct. 15
R Boötis	7.2	Apr. 27, Dec. 7
R Cancri	6.8	Nov. 3
S Canis Minoris	7.5	Apr. 6
R Carinæ	4.6	July 7
S Carinæ	5.7	Feb. 27, July 26, Dec. 23
R Cassiopeiæ	7.0	Mar. 7
R Centauri	5.8	May 11
T Cephei	6.0	Mar. 26
U Ceti	7.5	May 18
Omicron Ceti	3.4	Feb. 15
T Columbæ	7.5	Mar. 12, Oct. 24
S Coronæ Borealis	7.3	Oct. 11
V Coronæ Borealis	7.5	May 12
R Corvi	7.5	Sep. 25
R Cygni	7.5	May. 3
U Cygni	7.2	Apr. 24
RT Cygni	7.3	Feb. 1, Aug. 10
Chi Cygni	5.2	Sep. 26
R Geminorum	7.1	Nov. 1
U Herculis	7.5	Sep. 1
R Horologii	6.0	Nov. 14
U Horologii	7	Feb. 8
R Hydræ	4.5	Apr. 20
R Leonis	5.8	Oct. 14
R Leonis Minoris	7.1	Sep. 5
R Leporis	6.8	Dec. 1

Star	Mean magnitude at maximum	Dates of maxima
RS Libræ	7.5	July 21
V Monocerotis	7.0	Feb. 24
R Normæ	7.2	Nov. 23
T Normæ	7.4	Aug. 6
V Ophiuchi	7.5	Sep. 28
X Ophiuchi	6.8	Oct. 19
U Orionis	6.3	Nov. 4
R Sagittarii	7.3	May 31
RR Sagittarii	6.8	Jan. 16, Dec. 18
RT Sagittarii	7.0	Aug. 19
RU Sagittarii	7.2	Apr. 10, Dec. 7
RR Scorpii	5.9	Sep. 23
RS Scorpii	7.0	Oct. 24
S Sculptoris	6.7	Dec. 10
R Serpentis	6.9	Feb. 15
R Trianguli	6.2	Apr. 21
R Ursæ Majoris	7.5	Sep. 5
R Virginis	6.9	Mar. 18, Aug. 10
S Virginis	7.0	Oct. 14

Some Interesting Double Stars

R. W. ARGYLE

The positions given below correspond to epoch 1997.0.

Star	RA		Decli-nation		Magni-tudes	Separ-ation arc seconds	PA	Cata-logue	Comments
	h	m	°	'			°		
β Tuc	00	31.5	−62	58	4.4, 4.8	27.1	170	L119	Both again difficult doubles.
η Cas	00	49.1	+57	49	3.4, 7.5	12.7	315	Σ60	Easy. Creamy, bluish.
β Phe	01	06.1	−46	43	4.0, 4.2	1.5	324	Slr1	Binary. Yellow. Slowly closing.
ζ Psc	01	13.7	+07	35	5.6, 6.5	22.8	63	Σ100	Yellow, reddish-white.
p Eri	01	39.8	−56	12	5.8, 5.8	11.5	192	Δ5	Period 483 years.
γ Ari	01	53.5	+19	18	4.8, 4.8	7.6	0	Σ180	Very easy. Both white.
α Psc	02	02.0	+02	46	4.2, 5.1	1.8	274	Σ202	Binary, 933 years.
γ And	02	03.9	+42	20	2.3, 5.0	9.4	64	Σ205	Yellow, blue. B is double. Needs 30 cm.
ι Cas AB	02	29.1	+67	24	4.9, 6.9	2.5	231	Σ262	AB is long period binary. Period 840 years.
ι Cas AC					4.9, 8.4	7.2	118		
ω For	02	33.8	−28	14	5.0, 7.7	24.5	109	h3506	Common proper motion.
γ Cet	02	43.3	+03	14	3.5, 7.3	2.9	294	Σ299	Not too easy.
θ Eri	02	58.3	−40	18	3.4, 4.5	8.3	90	Pz 2	Both white.
ε Ari	02	59.2	+21	20	5.2, 5.5	1.5	208	Σ333	Binary. Both white.
Σ331 Per	03	00.9	+47	41	5.3, 6.7	8.5	123	–	Fixed.
α For	03	12.1	−28	59	4.0, 7.0	4.9	299	h3555	Period 314 years. B variable?
f Eri	03	48.6	−37	37	4.8, 5.3	8.2	215	Δ16	Pale yellow. Fixed.
32 Eri	03	54.3	−02	57	4.8, 6.1	6.8	347	Σ470	Fixed.
1 Cam	04	32.0	+53	55	5.7, 6.8	10.3	308	Σ550	Fixed.
ι Pic	04	50.9	−53	28	5.6, 6.4	12.5	58	Δ18	Good object for small apertures. Fixed.
ϰ Lep	05	13.2	−12	56	4.5, 7.4	2.2	356	Σ661	Visible in 7.5 cm.
β Ori	05	14.5	−08	12	0.1, 6.8	9.5	202	Σ668	Companion once thought to be close double.
41 Lep	05	21.8	−24	46	5.4, 6.6	3.5	92	h3752	Deep yellow pair in a rich field.
η Ori	05	24.5	−02	24	3.8, 4.8	1.9	77	Da5	Slow moving binary.
λ Ori	05	35.1	+09	56	3.6, 5.5	4.4	43	Σ738	Fixed.

Star	RA		Decli-nation		Magni-tudes	Separ-ation arc seconds	PA	Cata-logue	Comments
	h	m	°	′			°		
θ Ori AB	05	35.3	−05	23	6.7, 7.9	8.7	32	Σ748	Trapezium in M42.
θ Ori CD					5.1, 6.7	13.4	61		
σ Ori AC	05	38.7	−02	36	4.0, 10.3	11.4	238	Σ762	Quintuple. A is a close double.
σ Ori ED					6.5, 7.5	30.1	231		
ζ Ori	05	40.8	−01	37	1.9, 4.0	2.4	162	Σ774	Can be split in 7.5 cm.
η Gem	06	14.9	+22	30	var., 6.5	1.6	257	β1008	Well seen with 20 cm. Primary orange.
12 Lyn AB	06	46.2	+59	27	5.4, 6.0	1.7	72	Σ948	AB is binary. Period 706 years.
12 Lyn AC					5.4, 7.3	8.6	309		
γ Vol	07	08.8	−70	30	3.9, 5.8	13.8	299	Δ42	Very slow binary.
h3945 CMa	07	16.6	−23	19	4.8, 6.8	26.7	52	–	Contrasting colours.
δ Gem	07	20.1	+21	59	3.5, 8.2	5.8	224	Σ1066	Not too easy. Yellow, pale blue.
α Gem	07	34.6	+31	53	1.9, 2.9	3.6	72	Σ1110	Widening. Easy with 7.5 cm.
ϰ Pup	07	38.8	−26	48	4.5, 4.7	9.8	318	H III 27	Both white.
ζ Cnc AB	08	12.2	+17	39	5.6, 6.0	0.7	103	Σ1196	A is a close double.
ζ Cnc AB-C					5.0, 6.2	6.0	74		
δ Vel	08	44.7	−54	43	2.1, 5.1	2.0	140	I10	Slowly closing. Visible in 10 cm.
ε Hyd	08	46.8	+06	25	3.3, 6.8	2.7	298	Σ1273	PA slowly increasing.
38 Lyn	09	18.8	+36	48	3.9, 6.6	2.6	226	Σ1338	Almost fixed.
ν Car	09	47.1	−65	04	3.1, 6.1	5.0	127	Rmk11	Fixed. Fine in small telescopes.
γ Leo	10	20.0	+19	51	2.2, 3.5	4.4	125	Σ1424	Binary. Period 619 years. Both orange.
s Vel	10	31.9	−45	04	6.2, 6.5	13.5	218	Pz	Fixed.
μ Vel	10	39.3	−55	36	2.7, 6.4	2.6	57	R155	Period 116 years. Widest in 1996.
54 Leo	10	55.6	+24	45	4.5, 6.3	6.5	112	Σ1487	Slowly widening. Pale yellow and white.
ζ UMa	11	18.2	+31	32	4.3, 4.8	1.5	295	Σ1523	Binary, 60 years. Opening. Needs 10 cm.
π Cen	11	21.0	−54	29	4.3, 5.0	0.4	137	I879	Binary, 39.2 years. Very close. Needs 30 cm.
ι Leo	11	23.9	+10	32	4.0, 6.7	1.6	120	Σ1536	Binary, 192 years.
N Hya	11	32.3	−29	16	5.8, 5.9	9.3	210	H III 96	Fixed.
D Cen	12	14.0	−45	43	5.6, 6.8	2.9	244	Rmk14	Orange and white. Closing.
α Cru	12	26.6	−63	06	1.4, 1.9	4.2	114	–	Third star in a low power field.
γ Cen	12	41.5	−48	58	2.9, 2.9	1.2	350	h4539	Period 84 years. Closing. Both yellow.
γ Vir	12	41.7	−01	27	3.5, 3.5	1.9	272	Σ1670	Binary, 168 years.
β Mus	12	46.7	−68	06	3.7, 4.0	1.3	40	R207	Both white. Closing.
μ Cru	12	54.6	−57	11	4.3, 5.3	34.9	17	Δ126	Fixed. Both white.
α CVn	12	56.0	+38	19	2.9, 5.5	19.6	228	Σ1692	Easy. Yellow, bluish.

Star	RA		Decli-nation		Magni-tudes	Separ-ation arc seconds	PA	Cata-logue	Comments
	h	m	°	'			°		
J Cen	13	22.6	−60	59	4.6, 6.5	6.0	343	Δ133	Fixed. A is a close pair.
ζ UMa	13	23.9	+54	56	2.3, 4.0	14.4	151	Σ1744	Very easy. Naked-eye pair with Alcor.
3 Cen	13	51.8	−33	00	4.5, 6.0	7.8	105	H III 101	Both white. Closing slowly.
α Cen	14	39.6	−60	50	0.0, 1.2	16.7	218	Rich	Finest pair in the sky. Period 80 years. Closing.
ζ Boo	14	41.1	+13	44	4.5, 4.6	0.9	301	Σ1865	Both white. Closing, highly inclined orbit.
ε Boo	14	45.0	+27	04	2.5, 4.9	2.8	342	Σ1877	Yellow, blue. Fine pair.
54 Hya	14	46.0	−25	27	5.1, 7.1	8.2	123	H III 97	Closing slowly.
μ Lib	14	49.3	−14	09	5.8, 6.7	2.0	5	β106	Becoming wider. Fine in 7.5 cm.
ξ Boo	14	51.4	+19	06	4.7, 7.0	6.8	320	Σ1888	Fine contrast. Easy.
44 Boo	15	03.8	+47	39	5.3, 6.2	2.1	52	Σ1909	Period 246 years.
π Lup	15	05.1	−47	03	4.6, 4.7	1.7	65	h4728	Widening.
μ Lup	15	18.5	−47	53	5.1, 5.2	24.0	129	Δ180	Almost fixed.
γ Cir	15	23.4	−59	19	5.1, 5.5	0.7	10	h4787	Closing. Needs 20 cm. Long-period binary.
η CrB	15	32.0	+32	17	5.6, 5.9	0.9	49	Σ1937	Both yellow. Period 41 years, near widest separation.
δ Ser	15	34.8	+10	32	4.2, 5.2	4.3	176	Σ1954	Long-period binary.
γ Lup	15	35.1	−41	10	3.5, 3.6	0.7	274	h4786	Binary. 147 years. Needs 20 cm.
ξ Lup	15	56.9	−33	58	5.3, 5.8	13.4	49	Pz	Fixed.
σ CrB	16	14.7	+33	52	5.6, 6.6	7.0	236	Σ2032	Long-period binary. Both white.
α Sco	16	29.4	−26	26	1.2, 5.4	2.7	274	–	Red, green. Difficult from mid-northern latitudes.
λ Oph	16	30.9	+01	59	4.2, 5.2	1.4	27	Σ2055	Period 129 years. Fairly difficult in small apertures.
ζ Her	16	41.3	+31	36	2.9, 5.5	1.4	54	Σ2084	Fine, rapid binary. Period 34 years.
μ Dra	17	05.3	+54	28	5.7, 5.7	2.2	22	Σ2130	Long-period binary. Slowly closing.
α Her	17	14.6	+14	23	var., 5.4	4.6	106	Σ2140	Red, green. Binary.
36 Oph	17	15.3	−26	36	5.1, 5.1	4.9	148	SH243	Period 549 years.
ρ Her	17	23.7	+37	09	4.6, 5.6	4.2	318	Σ2161	Slowly widening.
95 Her	18	01.5	+21	36	5.0, 5.1	6.3	258	Σ2264	Colours thought variable in C19.
70 Oph	18	05.5	+02	30	4.2, 6.0	2.9	159	Σ2272	Opening. Easy in 7.5 cm.
h5014 CrA	18	06.8	−43	25	5.7, 5.7	1.4	5	–	Closing slowly. Orbit poorly known. Needs 10 cm.

Star	RA		Decli-nation		Magni-tudes	Separation arc seconds	PA	Cata-logue	Comments
	h	m	°	′			°		
OΣ358 Her	18	35.9	+16	59	6.8, 7.0	1.4	150	–	Period 292 years.
ε¹ Lyr	18	44.3	+39	40	5.0, 6.1	2.6	351	Σ2382	Quadruple system with ε². Both pairs visible in 7.5 cm.
ε² Lyr	18	44.3	+39	40	5.2, 5.5	2.3	83	Σ2383	
θ Ser	18	56.2	+04	12	4.5, 5.4	22.3	103	Σ2417	Fixed. Very easy.
γ CrA	19	06.4	−37	04	4.8, 5.1	1.3	71	h5084	Beautiful pair. Period 122 years.
β Cyg AB	19	30.7	+27	57	3.1, 5.1	34.1	54	ΣI 43	Glorious. Yellow, blue-greenish. Aa closing.
β Cyg Aa					3.1, 4.0	0.4	135		
δ Cyg	19	45.0	+45	08	2.9, 6.3	2.5	224	Σ2579	Slowly widening.
ε Dra	19	48.2	+70	16	3.8, 7.4	3.2	19	Σ2603	Slow binary.
γ Del	20	46.7	+16	07	4.5, 5.5	9.3	267	Σ2727	Easy. Yellowish.
λ Cyg	20	47.4	+36	29	4.8, 6.1	0.8	8	OΣ413	Difficult binary in small apertures.
ε Equ AB	20	59.1	+04	18	6.0, 6.3	0.9	285	Σ2737	Fine triple. AB is closing.
ε Equ AC					6.0, 7.1	10.0	66		
61 Cyg	21	06.9	+38	45	5.2, 6.0	30.4	149	Σ2758	Nearby binary. Both orange. Period 722 years.
μ Cyg	21	44.1	+28	45	4.8, 6.1	1.9	305	Σ2822	Period 713 years.
θ Ind	21	19.9	−53	27	4.5, 7.0	6.7	266	–	Pale yellow and reddish. Long-period binary.
ξ Cep	22	03.8	+64	38	4.4, 6.5	8.1	276	Σ2863	White and blue.
53 Aqr	22	26.6	−16	45	6.4, 6.6	1.7	357	Sh345	Long-period binary. Closing.
ζ Aqr	22	28.8	−00	01	4.3, 4.5	2.1	193	Σ2909	Slowly widening.
Σ3050 And	23	59.5	+33	43	6.6, 6.6	1.7	331	–	Period 355 years.

Some Interesting Nebulae, Clusters and Galaxies

Object	RA		Declination		Remarks
	h	m	°	′	
M.31 Andromedæ	00	40.7	+41	05	Great Galaxy, visible to naked eye.
H.VIII 78 Cassiopeiæ	00	41.3	+61	36	Fine cluster, between Gamma and Kappa Cassiopeiæ.
M.33 Trianguli	01	31.8	+30	28	Spiral. Difficult with small apertures.
H.VI 33–4 Persei	02	18.3	+56	59	Double cluster; Sword-handle.
△142 Doradus	05	39.1	−69	09	Looped nebula round 30 Doradus. Naked-eye. In Large Magellanic Cloud.
M.1 Tauri	05	32.3	+22	00	Crab Nebula, near Zeta Tauri.
M.42 Orionis	05	33.4	−05	24	Great Nebula. Contains the famous Trapezium, Theta Orionis.
M.35 Geminorum	06	06.5	+24	21	Open cluster near Eta Geminorum.
H.VII 2 Monocerotis	06	30.7	+04	53	Open cluster, just visible to naked eye.
M.41 Canis Majoris	06	45.5	−20	42	Open cluster, just visible to naked eye.
M.47 Puppis	07	34.3	−14	22	Mag. 5.2. Loose cluster.
H.IV 64 Puppis	07	39.6	−18	05	Bright planetary in rich neighbourhood.
M.46 Puppis	07	39.5	−14	42	Open cluster.
M.44 Cancri	08	38	+20	07	Præsepe. Open cluster near Delta Cancri. Visible to naked eye.
M.97 Ursæ Majoris	11	12.6	+55	13	Owl Nebula, diameter 3′. Planetary.
Kappa Crucis	12	50.7	−60	05	'Jewel Box'; open cluster, with stars of contrasting colours.
M.3 Can. Ven.	13	40.6	+28	34	Bright globular.
Omega Centauri	13	23.7	−47	03	Finest of all globulars. Easy with naked eye.
M.80 Scorpii	16	14.9	−22	53	Globular, between Antares and Beta Scorpii.
M.4 Scorpii	16	21.5	−26	26	Open cluster close to Antares.
M.13 Herculis	16	40	+36	31	Globular. Just visible to naked eye.
M.92 Herculis	16	16.1	+43	11	Globular. Between Iota and Eta Herculis.
M.6 Scorpii	17	36.8	−32	11	Open cluster; naked eye.
M.7 Scorpii	17	50.6	−34	48	Very bright open cluster; naked eye.
M.23 Sagittarii	17	54.8	−19	01	Open cluster nearly 50′ in diameter.
H.IV 37 Draconis	17	58.6	+66	38	Bright planetary.
M.8 Sagittarii	18	01.4	−24	23	Lagoon Nebula. Gaseous. Just visible with naked eye.
NGC 6572 Ophiuchi	18	10.9	+06	50	Bright planetary, between Beta Ophiuchi and Zeta Aquilæ.
M.17 Sagittarii	18	18.8	−16	12	Omega Nebula. Gaseous. Large and bright.
M.11 Scuti	18	49.0	−06	19	Wild Duck. Bright open cluster.
M.57 Lyræ	18	52.6	+32	59	Ring Nebula. Brightest of planetaries.
M.27 Vulpeculæ	19	58.1	+22	37	Dumbbell Nebula, near Gamma Sagittæ.
H.IV 1 Aquarii	21	02.1	−11	31	Bright planetary near Nu Aquarii.
M.15 Pegasi	21	28.3	+12	01	Bright globular, near Epsilon Pegasi.
M.39 Cygni	21	31.0	+48	17	Open cluster between Deneb and Alpha Lacertæ. Well seen with low powers.

Our Contributors

Dr John Baruch, of the University of Bradford, is a specialist in automatic and remote-controlled telescopes. He is a strong exponent of working with industry, and has demonstrated how astronomy and its instrumentation have much to offer wealth creation.

Dr Allan Chapman, of Wadham College, Oxford, is probably Britain's leading historian of astronomy. He has published many research papers as well as popular accounts.

Dr Chris Kitchin is Director of the University of Hertfordshire Observatory. He is primarily an astrophysicist and a specialist in designing astronomical equipment.

Dr Ron Maddison is Director of the Observatory at the Astronaut Memorial Planetarium and Observatory in Cocoa, Florida, and President of the International Antique Telescope Society.

Dr John Mason, a graduate from UCL, is a former President of the British Astronomical Association. He specializes in studies of comets and meteors, and is a regular broadcaster on sound and television. He lives at Barnham in Sussex.

Dr Steven Miller lectures in science communication at University College London, where he also carries out research in planetary science. During the collision of Comet Shoemaker–Levy 9 with Jupiter, he led the observing team on the United Kingdom Infrared Telescope in Hawaii, and was a member of the NASA Comet Collision Science Team.

Terry Moseley is by profession a civil servant, but is a well-known amateur astronomer specializing in planetary observation and variable-star work. He is President of the Irish Astronomical Society. He lives in Belfast.

Dr Paul Murdin, OBE, is one of the world's leading astronomers; he has been Director of the Royal Observatory Edinburgh, was for a time in charge of the British telescopes on La Palma, and is now at PPARC. In addition to his technical work, he is well known for his popular books and broadcasts.

Dr Fred Watson is a specialist in fibre optics astronomy. He was for many years at Cambridge University, but is now in charge of the UK Schmidt Telescope at Siding Spring in Australia.

The William Herschel Society maintains the museum established at 19 New King Street, Bath – the only surviving Herschel House. It also undertakes activities of various kinds. New members would be welcome; those interested are asked to contact Dr L. Hilliard at 2 Lambridge, London Road, Bath.

Astronomical Societies in the British Isles

British Astronomical Association
Assistant Secretary: Burlington House, Piccadilly, London W1V 9AG.
Meetings: Lecture Hall of Scientific Societies, Civil Service Commission Building, 23 Savile Row, London W1. Last Wednesday each month (Oct.–June). 5 p.m. and some Saturday afternoons.
Association for Astronomy Education
Secretary: Bob Kibble, 34 Ackland Crescent, Denmark Hill, London SE5 8EQ.
Astronomy Ireland
Secretary: Tony Ryan, PO Box 2888, Dublin 1, Ireland.
Meetings: 2nd and 4th Mondays of each month. Telescope meetings, every clear Saturday.
Federation of Astronomical Societies
Secretary: Mrs Christine Sheldon, Whitehaven, Lower Moor, Pershore, Worcs.
Junior Astronomical Society of Ireland
Secretary: K. Nolan, 5 St Patrick's Crescent, Rathcoole, Co. Dublin.
Meetings: The Royal Dublin Society, Ballsbridge, Dublin 4. Monthly.
Aberdeen and District Astronomical Society
Secretary: Stephen Graham, 25 Davidson Place, Northfield, Aberdeen.
Meetings: Robert Gordon's Institute of Technology, St Andrew's Street, Aberdeen. Friday 7.30 p.m.
Altrincham and District Astronomical Society
Secretary: Colin Henshaw, 10 Delamore Road, Gatley, Cheadle, Cheshire.
Meetings: Public Library, Timperley. 1st Friday of each month, 7.30 p.m.
Astra Astronomy Section
Secretary: Ian Downie, 151 Sword Street, Glasgow G31.
Meetings: Public Library, Airdrie. Weekly.
Aylesbury Astronomical Society
Secretary: Nigel Sheridan, 22 Moor Park, Wendover, Bucks.
Meetings: 1st Monday in month. Details from Secretary.
Bassetlaw Astronomical Society
Secretary: H. Moulson, 5 Magnolia Close, South Anston, South Yorks.
Meetings: Rhodesia Village Hall, Rhodesia, Worksop, Notts. On 2nd and 4th Tuesdays of month at 8 p.m.
Batley & Spenborough Astronomical Society
Secretary: Robert Morton, 22 Links Avenue, Cleckheaton, West Yorks BD19 4EG.
Meetings: Milner K. Ford Observatory, Wilton Park, Batley. Every Thursday, 7.30 p.m.
Bedford Astronomical Society
Secretary: D. Eagle, 24 Copthorne Close, Oakley, Bedford.
Meetings: Bedford School, Burnaby Rd, Bedford. Last Tuesday each month.
Bingham & Brookes Space Organization
Secretary: N. Bingham, 15 Hickmore's Lane, Lindfield, W. Sussex.
Birmingham Astronomical Society
Secretary: J. Spittles, 28 Milverton Road, Knowle, Solihull, West Midlands.
Meetings: Room 146, Aston University, last Tuesday each month, Sept. to June (except Dec., moved to 1st week in Jan.).
Blackpool & District Astronomical Society
Secretary: J. L. Crossley, 24 Fernleigh Close, Bispham, Blackpool, Lancs.
Bolton Astronomical Society
Secretary: Peter Miskiw, 9 Hedley Street, Bolton.
Border Astronomical Society
Secretary: David Pettit, 14 Shap Grove, Carlisle, Cumbria.
Boston Astronomers
Secretary: B. Tongue, South View, Fen Road, Stickford, Boston.
Meetings: Details from the Secretary.
Bradford Astronomical Society
Secretary: John Schofield, Briar Lea, Bromley Road, Bingley, W. Yorks.
Meetings: Eccleshill Library, Bradford 2. Monday fortnightly (with occasional variations).
Braintree, Halstead & District Astronomical Society
Secretary: Heather Reeder, The Knoll, St Peters in the Field, Braintree, Essex.
Meetings: St Peter's Church Hall, St Peter's Road, Braintree, Essex. 3rd Thursday each month, 8 p.m.
Bridgend Astronomical Society
Secretary: Clive Down, 10 Glan y Llyn, Broadlands, North Cornelly, Bridgend.
Meetings: G.P. Room, Recreation Centre, Bridgend, 1st and 3rd Friday monthly, 7.30 p.m.

Bridgwater Astronomical Society
Secretary: W. L. Buckland, 104 Polden Street, Bridgwater, Somerset.
Meetings: Room D10, Bridgwater College, Bath Road Centre, Bridgwater. 2nd Wednesday each month, Sept.–June.
Brighton Astronomical Society
Secretary: Mrs B. C. Smith, Flat 2, 23 Albany Villas, Hove, Sussex BN3 2RS.
Meetings: Preston Tennis Club, Preston Drive, Brighton. Weekly, Tuesdays.
Bristol Astronomical Society
Secretary: Geoff Cane, 9 Sandringham Road, Stoke Gifford, Bristol.
Meetings: Royal Fort (Rm G44), Bristol University. Every Friday each month, Sept.–May. Fortnightly, June–Aug.
Cambridge Astronomical Association
Secretary: R. J. Greening, 20 Cotts Croft, Great Chishill, Royston, Herts.
Meetings: Venues as published in newsletter. 1st and 3rd Friday each month, 8 p.m.
Cardiff Astronomical Society
Secretary: D. W. S. Powell, 1 Tal-y-Bont Road, Ely, Cardiff.
Meetings: Room 230, Dept. Law, University College, Museum Avenue, Cardiff. Alternate Thursdays, 8 p.m.
Castle Point Astronomy Club
Secretary: Miss Zena White, 43 Lambeth Road, Eastwood, Essex.
Meetings: St Michael's Church, Thundersley. Most Wednesdays, 8 p.m.
Chelmsford Astronomers
Secretary: Brendan Clark, 5 Borda Close, Chelmsford, Essex.
Meetings: Once a month.
Chester Astronomical Society
Secretary: Mrs S. Brooks, 39 Halton Road, Great Sutton, South Wirral.
Meetings: Southview Community Centre, Southview Road, Chester. Last Monday each month except Aug. and Dec., 7.30 p.m.
Chester Society of Natural Science Literature and Art
Secretary: Paul Braid, 'White Wing', 38 Bryn Avenue, Old Colwyn, Colwyn Bay, Clwyd.
Meetings: Grosvenor Museum, Chester. Fortnightly.
Chesterfield Astronomical Society
Secretary: P. Lisewski, 148 Old Hall Road, Brampton, Chesterfield.
Meetings: Barnet Observatory, Newbold. Each Friday.
Clacton & District Astronomical Society
Secretary: C. L. Haskell, 105 London Road, Clacton-on-Sea, Essex.
Cleethorpes & District Astronomical Society
Secretary: C. Illingworth, 38 Shaw Drive, Grimsby, S. Humberside.
Meetings: Beacon Hill Observatory, Cleethorpes. 1st Wednesday each month.
Cleveland & Darlington Astronomical Society
Secretary: Neil Haggath, 5 Fountains Crescent, Eston, Middlesbrough, Cleveland.
Meetings: Elmwood Community Centre, Greens Lane, Hartburn, Stockton-on-Tees. Monthly, usually 2nd Friday.
Colchester Amateur Astronomers
Secretary: F. Kelly, 'Middleton', Church Road, Elmstead Market, Colchester, Essex.
Meetings: William Loveless Hall, High Street, Wivenhoe. Friday evenings. Fortnightly.
Cornwall Astronomy Society
Secretary: J. M. Harvey, 2 Helland Gardens, Penryn, Cornwall.
Meetings: Godolphin Club, Wendron Street, Helston, Cornwall. 2nd and 4th Thursday of each month, 7.30 for 8 p.m.
Cotswold Astronomical Society
Secretary: Trevor Talbot, Innisfree, Winchcombe Road, Sedgebarrow, Worcs.
Meetings: Fortnightly in Cheltenham or Gloucester.
Coventry & Warwicks Astronomical Society
Secretary: V. Cooper, 5 Gisburn Close, Woodloes Park, Warwick.
Meetings: Coventry Technical College. 1st Friday each month, Sept.–June.
Crawley Astronomical Society
Secretary: G. Cowley, 67 Climpixy Road, Ifield, Crawley, Sussex.
Meetings: Crawley College of Further Education. Monthly Oct.–June.
Crayford Manor House Astronomical Society
Secretary: R. H. Chambers, Manor House Centre, Crayford, Kent.
Meetings: Manor House Centre, Crayford. Monthly during term-time.
Croydon Astronomical Society
Secretary: John Murrell, 17 Dalmeny Road, Carshalton, Surrey.
Meetings: Lecture Theatre, Royal Russell School, Combe Lane, South Croydon. Alternate Fridays, 7.45 p.m.
Derby & District Astronomical Society
Secretary: Jane D. Kirk, 7 Cromwell Avenue, Findern, Derby.
Meetings: At home of Secretary. 1st and 3rd Friday each month, 7.30 p.m.

Doncaster Astronomical Society
Secretary: J. A. Day, 297 Lonsdale Avenue, Intake, Doncaster.
Meetings: Fridays, weekly.

Dundee Astronomical Society
Secretary: G. Young, 37 Polepark Road, Dundee, Angus.
Meetings: Mills Observatory, Balgay Park, Dundee. 1st Friday each month, 7.30 p.m. Sept.–April.

Easington and District Astronomical Society
Secretary: T. Bradley, 52 Jameson Road, Hartlepool, Co. Durham.
Meetings: Easington Comprehensive School, Easington Colliery. Every 3rd Thursday throughout the year, 7.30 p.m.

Eastbourne Astronomical Society
Secretary: D. C. Gates, Apple Tree Cottage, Stunts Green, Hertsmonceux, East Sussex.
Meetings: St Aiden's Church Hall, 1 Whitley Road, Eastbourne. Monthly (except July and Aug.).

East Lancashire Astronomical Society
Secretary: D. Chadwick, 16 Worston Lane, Great Harwood, Blackburn BB6 7TH.
Meetings: As arranged. Monthly.

Astronomical Society of Edinburgh
Secretary: Graham Rule, 105/19 Causewayside, Edinburgh EH9 1QG.
Meetings: City Observatory, Calton Hill, Edinburgh. Monthly.

Edinburgh University Astronomical Society
Secretary: c/o Dept. of Astronomy, Royal Observatory, Blackford Hill, Edinburgh.

Ewell Astronomical Society
Secretary: Edward Hanna, 91 Tennyson Avenue, Motspur Park, Surrey.
Meetings: 1st Friday of each month.

Exeter Astronomical Society
Secretary: Miss J. Corey, 5 Egham Avenue, Topsham Road, Exeter.
Meetings: The Meeting Room, Wynards, Magdalen Street, Exeter. 1st Thursday of month.

Farnham Astronomical Society
Secretary: Laurence Anslow, 14 Wellington Lane, Farnham, Surrey.
Meetings: Church House, Union Road, Farnham. 2nd Monday each month, 7.45 p.m.

Fitzharry's Astronomical Society (Oxford & District)
Secretary: Mark Harman, 20 Lapwing Lane, Cholsey, Oxon.
Meetings: All Saints Methodist Church, Dorchester Crescent, Abingdon, Oxon.

Furness Astronomical Society
Secretary: A. Thompson, 52 Ocean Road, Walney Island, Barrow-in-Furness, Cumbria.
Meetings: St Mary's Church Centre, Dalton-in-Furness. 2nd Saturday in month, 7.30 p.m. Not Aug.

Fylde Astronomical Society
Secretary: 28 Belvedere Road, Thornton, Lancs.
Meetings: Stanley Hall, Rossendale Avenue South. 1st Wednesday each month.

Astronomical Society of Glasgow
Secretary: Malcolm Kennedy, 32 Cedar Road, Cumbernauld, Glasgow.
Meetings: University of Strathclyde, George St., Glasgow. 3rd Thursday each month, Sept.–April.

Great Ellingham and District Astronomy Club
Secretary: Andrew Briggs, Avondale, Norwich Road, Besthorpe, Norwich.
Meetings: Great Ellingham Recreation Centre, Watton Road, Great Ellingham. 2nd or 3rd Friday each month (check with Secretary), 7.15 p.m.

Greenock Astronomical Society
Secretary: Carl Hempsey, 49 Brisbane Street, Greenock.
Meetings: Greenock Arts Guild, 3 Campbell Street, Greenock.

Grimsby Astronomical Society
Secretary: R. Williams, 14 Richmond Close, Grimsby, South Humberside.
Meetings: Secretary's home. 2nd Thursday each month, 7.30 p.m.

Guernsey: La Société Guernesiaise Astronomy Section
Secretary: G. Falla, Highcliffe, Avenue Beauvais, Ville du Roi, St Peter's Port, Guernsey.
Meetings: The Observatory, St Peter's, Tuesdays, 8 p.m.

Guildford Astronomical Society
Secretary: A. Langmaid, 22 West Mount, Guildford, Surrey.
Meetings: Guildford Institute, Ward Street, Guildford. 1st Thursday each month, except July and Aug., 7.30 p.m.

Gwynedd Astronomical Society
Secretary: P. J. Curtis, Ael-y-bryn, Malltraeth St Newborough, Anglesey, Gwynedd.
Meetings: Physics Lecture Room, Bangor University. 1st Thursday each month, 7.30 p.m.

The Hampshire Astronomical Group
Secretary: R. F. Dodd, 1 Conifer Close, Cowplain, Waterlooville, Hants.
Meetings: Clanfield Observatory. Each Friday, 7.30 p.m.

Astronomical Society of Haringey
Secretary: Wally Baker, 58 Stirling Road, Wood Green, London N22.
Meetings: The Hall of the Good Shepherd, Berwick Road, Wood Green. 3rd Wednesday each month, 8 p.m.

Harrogate Astronomical Society
  Secretary: P. Barton, 31 Gordon Avenue, Harrogate, North Yorkshire.
  Meetings: Harlow Hill Methodist Church Hall, 121 Otley Road, Harrogate. Last Friday each
  month.
Hastings and Battle Astronomical Society
  Secretary: Mrs Karen Pankhurst, 20 High Bank Close, Ore, Hastings, E. Sussex.
  Meetings: Details from Secretary.
Heart of England Astronomical Society
  Secretary: Jean Poyner, 67 Ellerton Road, Kingstanding, Birmingham B44 0QE.
  Meetings: Furnace End Village, every Thursday.
Hebden Bridge Literary & Scientific Society, Astronomical Section
  Secretary: F. Parker, 48 Caldene Avenue, Mytholmroyd, Hebden Bridge, West Yorkshire.
Herschel Astronomy Society
  Secretary: D. R. Whittaker, 149 Farnham Lane, Slough.
  Meetings: Eton College, 2nd Friday each month.
Highlands Astronomical Society
  Secretary: Richard Pearce, 1 Forsyth Street, Hopeman, Elgin.
  Meetings: The Spectrum Centre, Inverness. 1st Tuesday each month, 7.30 p.m.
Horsham Astronomy Group (was Forest Astronomical Society)
  Chairman: Tony Beale, 8 Mill Lane, Lower Beeding, West Sussex.
  Meetings: 1st Wednesday each month. For location contact chairman.
Howards Astronomy Club
  Secretary: H. Ilett, 22 St Georges Avenue, Warblington, Havant, Hants.
  Meetings: To be notified.
Huddersfield Astronomical and Philosophical Society
  Secretary: R. A. Williams, 43 Oaklands Drive, Dalton, Huddersfield.
  Meetings: 4a Railway Street, Huddersfield. Every Friday, 7.30 p.m.
Hull and East Riding Astronomical Society
  Secretary: A. G. Scaife, 19 Beech Road, Elloughton, East Yorks.
  Meetings: Wyke 6th Form College, Bricknell Avenue, Hull. 1st and 3rd Wednesday each month,
  Oct.–Apr., 7.30 p.m.
Ilkeston & District Astronomical Society
  Secretary: Trevor Smith, 129 Heanor Road, Smalley, Derbyshire.
  Meetings: The Friends Meeting Room, Ilkeston Museum, Ilkeston. 2nd Tuesday monthly,
  7.30 p.m.
Ipswich, Orwell Astronomical Society
  Secretary: R. Gooding, 168 Ashcroft Road, Ipswich.
  Meetings: Orwell Park Observatory, Nacton, Ipswich. Wednesdays 8 p.m.
Irish Astronomical Association
  Secretary: Michael Duffy, 26 Ballymurphy Road, Belfast, Northern Ireland.
  Meetings: Room 315, Ashby Institute, Stranmills Road, Belfast. Fortnightly. Wednesdays,
  Sept.–Apr., 7.30 p.m.
Irish Astronomical Society
  Secretary: c/o PO Box 2547, Dublin 15, Ireland.
Isle of Man Astronomical Society
  Secretary: James Martin, Ballaterson Farm, Peel, Isle of Man IM5 3AB.
  Meetings: The Manx Automobile Club, Hill Street, Douglas. 1st Thursday of each month, 8.00 p.m.
Isle of Wight Astronomical Society
  Secretary: J. W. Feakins, 1 Hilltop Cottages, High Street, Freshwater, Isle of Wight.
  Meetings: Unitarian Church Hall, Newport, Isle of Wight. Monthly.
Keele Astronomical Society
  Secretary: Department of Physics, University of Keele, Keele, Staffs.
  Meetings: As arranged during term time.
Kettering and District Astronomical Society
  Asst. Secretary: Steve Williams, 120 Brickhill Road, Wellingborough, Northants.
  Meetings: Quaker Meeting Hall, Northall Street, Kettering, Northants. 1st Tuesday each month.
  7.45 p.m.
King's Lynn Amateur Astronomical Association
  Secretary: P. Twynman, 17 Poplar Avenue, RAF Marham, King's Lynn.
  Meetings: As arranged.
Lancaster and Morecambe Astronomical Society
  Secretary: Miss E. Haygarth, 27 Coulston Road, Bowerham, Lancaster.
  Meetings: Midland Hotel, Morecambe. 1st Wednesday each month except Jan. 7.30 p.m.
Lancaster University Astronomical Society
  Secretary: c/o Students Union, Alexandra Square, University of Lancaster.
  Meetings: As arranged.
Laymans Astronomical Society
  Secretary: John Evans, 10 Arkwright Walk, The Meadows, Nottingham.
  Meetings: The Popular, Bath Street, Ilkeston, Derbyshire. Monthly.

Leeds Astronomical Society
Secretary: A. J. Higgins, 23 Montagu Place, Leeds LS8 2RQ.
Meetings: Lecture Room, City Museum Library, The Headrow, Leeds.
Leicester Astronomical Society
Secretary: Ann Borell, 53 Warden's Walk, Leicester Forest East, Leics.
Meetings: Judgemeadow Community College, Marydene Drive, Evington, Leicester. 2nd and 4th Tuesdays each month, 7.30 p.m.
Letchworth and District Astronomical Society
Secretary: Eric Hutton, 14 Folly Close, Hitchin, Herts.
Meetings: As arranged.
Limerick Astronomy Club
Secretary: Tony O'Hanlon, 26 Ballycannon Heights, Meelick, Co. Clare, Ireland.
Meetings: Limerick Senior College, Limerick, Ireland. Monthly (except June and August), 8 p.m.
Lincoln Astronomical Society
Secretary: G. Winstanley, 36 Cambridge Drive, Washingborough, Lincoln.
Meetings: The Lecture Hall, off Westcliffe Street, Lincoln. 1st Tuesday each month.
Liverpool Astronomical Society
Secretary: David Whittle, 17 Sandy Lane, Tuebrook, Liverpool.
Meetings: City Museum, Liverpool. Wednesdays and Fridays, monthly.
Loughton Astronomical Society
Secretary: Dave Gill, 4 Tower Road, Epping, Essex.
Meetings: Epping Forest College, Borders Lane, Loughton, Essex. Thursdays 8 p.m.
Lowestoft and Great Yarmouth Regional Astronomers (LYRA) Society
Secretary: R. Cheek, 7 The Glades, Lowestoft, Suffolk.
Meetings: Community Wing, Kirkley High School, Kirkley Run, Lowestoft. 3rd Thursday, Sept.–May. Afterwards in School Observatory. 7.15 p.m.
Luton & District Astronomical Society
Secretary: D. Childs, 6 Greenways, Stopsley, Luton.
Meetings: Luton College of Higher Education, Park Square, Luton. Second and last Friday each month, 7.30 p.m.
Lytham St Annes Astronomical Association
Secretary: K. J. Porter, 141 Blackpool Road, Ansdell, Lytham St Annes, Lancs.
Meetings: College of Further Education, Clifton Drive South, Lytham St Annes. 2nd Wednesday monthly Oct.–June.
Macclesfield Astronomical Society
Secretary: Mrs C. Moss, 27 Westminster Road, Macclesfield, Cheshire.
Meetings: The Planetarium, Jodrell Bank, 1st Tuesday each month.
Maidenhead Astronomical Society
Secretary: c/o Chairman, Peter Hunt, Hightrees, Holyport Road, Bray, Berks.
Meetings: Library. Monthly (except July) 1st Friday.
Maidstone Astronomical Society
Secretary: Stephen James, 4 The Cherry Orchard, Haddow, Tonbridge, Kent.
Meetings: Nettlestead Village Hall, 1st Tuesday in month except July and Aug. 7.30 p.m.
Manchester Astronomical Society
Secretary: J. H. Davidson, Godlee Observatory, UMIST, Sackville Street, Manchester 1.
Meetings: At the Observatory, Thursdays, 7.30–9 p.m.
Mansfield and Sutton Astronomical Society
Secretary: G. W. Shepherd, Sherwood Observatory, Coxmoor Road, Sutton-in-Ashfield, Notts.
Meetings: Sherwood Observatory, Coxmoor Road. Last Tuesday each month, 7.45 p.m.
Mexborough and Swinton Astronomical Society
Secretary: Mark R. Benton, 61 The Lea, Swinton, Mexborough, Yorks.
Meetings: Methodist Hall, Piccadilly Road, Swinton, Near Mexborough. Thursdays, 7 p.m.
Mid-Kent Astronomical Society
Secretary: Peter Bassett, 167 Shakespeare Road, Gillingham, Kent.
Meetings: Venue to be arranged. 2nd and last Friday in month.
Milton Keynes Astronomical Society
Secretary: The Secretary, Milton Keynes Astronomical Society, Bradwell Abbey Field Centre, Bradwell, Milton Keynes MK1 39AP.
Meetings: Alternate Tuesdays.
Moray Astronomical Society
Secretary: Richard Pearce, 1 Forsyth Street, Hopeman, Elgin, Moray, Scotland.
Meetings: Village Hall Close, Co. Elgin.
Newbury Amateur Astronomical Society
Secretary: Mrs A. Davies, 11 Sedgfield Road, Greenham, Newbury, Berks.
Meetings: United Reform Church Hall, Cromwell Road, Newbury. Last Friday of month, Aug.–May.
Newcastle-on-Tyne Astronomical Society
Secretary: C. E. Willits, 24 Acomb Avenue, Seaton Delaval, Tyne and Wear.
Meetings: Zoology Lecture Theatre, Newcastle University. Monthly.

North Aston Space & Astronomical Club
Secretary: W. R. Chadburn, 14 Oakdale Road, North Aston, Sheffield.
Meetings: To be notified.
Northamptonshire Natural History Astronomical Society
Secretary: Dr Nick Hewitt, 4 Daimler Close, Northampton.
Meetings: Humphrey Rooms, Castillian Terrace, Northampton. 2nd and last Monday each month.
North Devon Astronomical Society
Secretary: P. G. Vickery, 12 Broad Park Crescent, Ilfracombe, North Devon.
Meetings: Pilton Community College, Chaddiford Lane, Barnstaple. 1st Wednesday each month, Sept.–May.
North Dorset Astronomical Society
Secretary: J. E. M. Coward, The Pharmacy, Stalbridge, Dorset.
Meetings: Charterhay, Stourton, Caundle, Dorset. 2nd Wednesday each month.
North Staffordshire Astronomical Society
Secretary: N. Oldham, 25 Linley Grove, Alsager, Stoke-on-Trent.
Meetings: 1st Wednesday of each month at Cartwright House, Broad Street, Hanley.
North Western Association of Variable Star Observers
Secretary: Jeremy Bullivant, 2 Beaminster Road, Heaton Mersey, Stockport, Cheshire.
Meetings: Four annually.
Norwich Astronomical Society
Secretary: Malcolm Jones, Tabor House, Norwich Road, Malbarton, Norwich.
Meetings: The Observatory, Colney Lane, Colney, Norwich. Every Friday, 7.30 p.m.
Nottingham Astronomical Society
Secretary: C. Brennan, 40 Swindon Close, Giltbrook, Nottingham.
Oldham Astronomical Society
Secretary: P. J. Collins, 25 Park Crescent, Chadderton, Oldham.
Meetings: Werneth Park Study Centre, Frederick Street, Oldham. Fortnightly, Friday.
Open University Astronomical Society
Secretary: Jim Lee, c/o above, Milton Keynes.
Meetings: Open University, Walton Hall, Milton Keynes. As arranged.
Orpington Astronomical Society
Secretary: Dr Ian Carstairs, 38 Brabourne Rise, Beckenham, Kent BR3 2SG.
Meetings: Orpington Parish Church Hall, Bark Hart Road. Thursdays monthly, 7.30 p.m. Sept.–July.
Peterborough Astronomical Society
Secretary: Sheila Thorpe, 6 Cypress Close, Longthorpe, Peterborough.
Meetings: 1st Thursday every month at 7.30 p.m.
Plymouth Astronomical Society
Secretary: Sheila Evans, 40 Billington Close, Eggbuckland, Plymouth.
Meetings: Glynnis Kingdon Centre. 2nd Friday each month.
Port Talbot Astronomical Society (was Astronomical Society of Wales)
Secretary: J. A. Minopoli, 11 Tan Y Bryn Terrace, Penclowdd, Swansea.
Meetings: Port Talbot Arts Centre, 1st Tuesday each month, 7.15 p.m.
Portsmouth Astronomical Society
Secretary: G. B. Bryant, 81 Ringwood Road, Southsea.
Meetings: Monday. Fortnightly.
Preston & District Astronomical Society
Secretary: P. Sloane, 77 Ribby Road, Wrea Green, Kirkham, Preston, Lancs.
Meetings: Moor Park (Jeremiah Horrocks) Observatory, Preston. 2nd Wednesday, last Friday each month. 7.30 p.m.
The Pulsar Group
Secretary: Barry Smith, 157 Reridge Road, Blackburn, Lancs.
Meetings: Amateur Astronomy Centre, Clough Bank, Bacup Road, Todmorden, Lancs. 1st Thursday each month.
Reading Astronomical Society
Secretary: Mrs Muriel Wrigley, 516 Wokingham Road, Earley, Reading.
Meetings: St Peter's Church Hall, Church Road, Earley. Monthly (3rd Saturday), 7 p.m.
Renfrew District Astronomical Society (formerly Paisley A.S.)
Secretary: D. Bankhead, 3c School Wynd, Paisley.
Meetings: Coats Observatory, Oakshaw Street, Paisley. Fridays, 7.30 p.m.
Richmond & Kew Astronomical Society
Secretary: Stewart McLaughlin, 41a Bruce Road, Mitcham, Surrey CR4 2BJ.
Meetings: Richmond Adult College, Parkshot, Richmond, Surrey, and the King's Observatory, Old Deer Park, Richmond, Surrey. Bimonthly.
Rower Astronomical Club
Secretary: Mary Kelly, Knockatore, The Rower, Thomastown, Co. Kilkenny, Ireland.
Salford Astronomical Society
Secretary: J. A. Handford, 45 Burnside Avenue, Salford 6, Lancs.
Meetings: The Observatory, Chaseley Road, Salford.

Salisbury Astronomical Society
Secretary: Mrs R. Collins, Mountains, 3 Fairview Road, Salisbury, Wilts.
Meetings: Salisbury City Library, Market Place, Salisbury.
Sandbach Astronomical Society
Secretary: Phil Benson, 8 Gawsworth Drive, Sandbach, Cheshire.
Meetings: Sandbach School, as arranged.
Scarborough & District Astronomical Society
Secretary: Mrs S. Anderson, Basin House Farm, Sawdon, Scarborough, N. Yorks.
Meetings: Scarborough Public Library. Last Saturday each month, 7–9 p.m.
Scottish Astronomers Group
Secretary: G. Young c/o Mills Observatory, Balgay Park, Ancrum, Dundee.
Meetings: Bimonthly, around the country. Syllabus given on request.
Sheffield Astronomical Society
Secretary: Mrs Lilian M. Keen, 21 Seagrave Drive, Gleadless, Sheffield.
Meetings: City Museum, Weston Park, 3rd Friday each month. 7.30 p.m.
Sidmouth and District Astronomical Society
Secretary: M. Grant, Salters Meadow, Sidmouth, Devon.
Meetings: Norman Lockyer Observatory, Salcombe Hill. 1st Monday in each month.
Society for Popular Astronomy (was Junior Astronomical Society)
Secretary: Guy Fennimore, 36 Fairway, Keyworth, Nottingham.
Meetings: Last Saturday in Jan., Apr., July, Oct., 2.30 p.m. in London.
Solent Amateur Astronomers
Secretary: Ken Medway, 443 Burgess Road, Swaythling, Southampton SO16 3BL.
Meetings: Room 2, Oaklands Community Centre, Fairisle Road, Lordshill, Southampton.
3rd Tuesday.
Southampton Astronomical Society
Secretary: M. R. Hobbs, 124 Winchester Road, Southampton.
Meetings: Room 148, Murray Building, Southampton University, 2nd Thursday each month, 7.30 p.m.
South Downs Astronomical Society
Secretary: J. Green, 46 Central Avenue, Bognor Regis, West Sussex.
Meetings: Assembly Rooms, Chichester. 1st Friday in each month.
South-East Essex Astronomical Society
Secretary: C. Jones, 92 Long Riding, Basildon, Essex.
Meetings: Lecture Theatre, Central Library, Victoria Avenue, Southend-on-Sea. Generally 1st Thursday in month, Sept.–May.
South-East Kent Astronomical Society
Secretary: P. Andrew, 7 Farncombe Way, Whitfield, nr. Dover.
Meetings: Monthly.
South Lincolnshire Astronomical & Geophysical Society
Secretary: Ian Farley, 12 West Road, Bourne, Lincs.
Meetings: South Holland Centre, Spalding. 3rd Thursday each month, Sept.–May. 7.30 p.m.
Southport Astronomical Society
Secretary: R. Rawlinson, 188 Haig Avenue, Southport, Merseyside.
Meetings: Monthly Sept.–May, plus observing sessions.
Southport, Ormskirk and District Astronomical Society
Secretary: J. T. Harrison, 92 Cottage Lane, Ormskirk, Lancs L39 3NJ.
Meetings: Saturday evenings, monthly as arranged.
South Shields Astronomical Society
Secretary: c/o South Tyneside College, St George's Avenue, South Shields.
Meetings: Marine and Technical College. Each Thursday, 7.30 p.m.
South Somerset Astronomical Society
Secretary: G. McNelly, 11 Laxton Close, Taunton, Somerset.
Meetings: Victoria Inn, Skittle Alley, East Reach, Taunton. Last Saturday each month, 7.30 p.m.
South-West Cotswolds Astronomical Society
Secretary: C. R. Wiles, Old Castle House, The Triangle, Malmesbury, Wilts.
Meetings: 2nd Friday each month, 8 p.m. (Sept.–June).
South-West Herts Astronomical Society
Secretary: Frank Phillips, 54 Highfield Way, Rickmansworth, Herts.
Meetings: Rickmansworth. Last Friday each month, Sept.–May.
Stafford and District Astronomical Society
Secretary: Mrs L. Hodkinson, Beecholme, Francis Green Lane, Penkridge, Staffs.
Meetings: Riverside Centre, Stafford. Every 3rd Thursday, Sept.–May, 7.30 p.m.
Stirling Astronomical Society
Secretary: Mrs C. Traynor, 5c St Mary's Wynd, Stirling.
Meetings: Smith Museum & Art Gallery, Dumbarton Road, Stirling. 2nd Friday each month, 7.30 p.m.
Stoke-on-Trent Astronomical Society
Secretary: M. Pace, Sundale, Dunnocksfold Road, Alsager, Stoke-on-Trent.
Meetings: Cartwright House, Broad Street, Hanley. Monthly.

Sussex Astronomical Society
Secretary: Mrs C. G. Sutton, 75 Vale Road, Portslade, Sussex.
Meetings: English Language Centre, Third Avenue, Hove. Every Wednesday, 7.30–9.30 p.m. Sept.–May.

Swansea Astronomical Society
Secretary: D. F. Tovey, 43 Cecil Road, Gowerton, Swansea.
Meetings: Dillwyn Llewellyn School, John Street, Cockett, Swansea. 2nd and 4th Thursday each month at 7.30 p.m.

Tavistock Astronomical Society
Secretary: D. S. Gibbs, Lanherne, Chollacott Lane, Whitchurch, Tavistock, Devon.
Meetings: Science Laboratory, Kelly College, Tavistock. 1st Wednesday in month. 7.30 p.m.

Thames Valley Astronomical Group
Secretary: K. J. Pallet, 82a Tennyson Street, South Lambeth, London SW8 3TH.
Meetings: As arranged.

Thanet Amateur Astronomical Society
Secretary: P. F. Jordan, 85 Crescent Road, Ramsgate.
Meetings: Hilderstone House, Broadstairs, Kent. Monthly.

Torbay Astronomical Society
Secretary: R. Jones, St Helens, Hermose Road, Teignmouth, Devon.
Meetings: Town Hall, Torquay. 3rd Thursday, Oct.–May.

Tullamore Astronomical Society
Secretary: S. McKenna, 145 Arden Vale, Tullamore, Co. Offaly, Ireland.
Meetings: Tullamore Vocational School. Fortnightly, Tuesdays, Oct.–June. 8 p.m.

Tyrone Astronomical Society
Secretary: John Ryan, 105 Coolnafranky Park, Cookstown, Co. Tyrone.
Meetings: Contact Secretary.

Usk Astronomical Society
Secretary: D. J. T. Thomas, 20 Maryport Street, Usk, Gwent.
Meetings: Usk Adult Education Centre, Maryport Street. Weekly, Thursdays (term dates).

Vectis Astronomical Society
Secretary: J. W. Smith, 27 Forest Road, Winford, Sandown, Isle of Wight.
Meetings: 4th Friday each month, except Dec. at Lord Louis Library Meeting Room, Newport, Isle of Wight.

Vigo Astronomical Society
Secretary: Robert Wilson, 43 Admers Wood, Vigo Village, Meopham, Kent DA13 0SP.
Meetings: Vigo Village Hall, as arranged.

Webb Society
Secretary: M. B. Swan, 194 Foundry Lane, Freemantle, Southampton, Hants.
Meetings: As arranged.

Wellingborough District Astronomical Society
Secretary: S. M. Williams, 120 Brickhill Road, Wellingborough, Northants.
Meetings: On 2nd Wednesday. Gloucester Hall, Church Street, Wellingborough, 7.30 p.m.

Wessex Astronomical Society
Secretary: Leslie Fry, 14 Hanhum Road, Corfe Mullen, Dorset.
Meetings: Allendale Centre, Wimborne, Dorset. 1st Tuesday of each month.

West of London Astronomical Society
Secretary: Tom. H. Ella, 25 Boxtree Road, Harrow Weald, Harrow, Middlesex.
Meetings: Monthly, alternately at Hillingdon and North Harrow. 2nd Monday in month, except Aug.

West Midlands Astronomical Association
Secretary: Miss S. Bundy, 93 Greenridge Road, Handsworth Wood, Birmingham.
Meetings: Dr Johnson House, Bull Street, Birmingham. As arranged.

West Yorkshire Astronomical Society
Secretary: K. Willoughby, 11 Hardisty Drive, Pontefract, Yorks.
Meetings: Rosse Observatory, Carleton Community Centre, Carleton Road, Pontefract, each Tuesday, 7.15 to 9 p.m.

Whitby Astronomical Group
Secretary: Mark Dawson, 33 Laburnum Grove, Whitby, North Yorkshire YO21 1HZ.
Meetings: Mission to Seamen, Haggersgate, Whitby. 2nd Tuesday of the month, 7.30 p.m.

Whittington Astronomical Society
Secretary: Peter Williamson, The Observatory, Top Street, Whittington, Shropshire.
Meetings: The Observatory every month.

Wolverhampton Astronomical Society
Secretary: M. Astley, Garwick, 8 Holme Mill, Fordhouses, Wolverhampton.
Meetings: Beckminster Methodist Church Hall, Birches Road, Wolverhampton. Alternate Mondays, Sept.–Apr.

Worcester Astronomical Society
Secretary: Arthur Wilkinson, 179 Henwick Road, St Johns, Worcester.
Meetings: Room 117, Worcester College of Higher Education, Henwick Grove, Worcester. 2nd Thursday each month.

Worthing Astronomical Society

Contact: G. Boots, 101 Ardingly Drive, Worthing, Sussex.

Meetings: Adult Education Centre, Union Place, Worthing, Sussex. 1st Wednesday each month (except Aug.). 7.30 p.m.

Wycombe Astronomical Society

Secretary: P. A. Hodgins, 50 Copners Drive, Holmer Green, High Wycombe, Bucks.

Meetings: 3rd Wednesday each month, 7.45 p.m.

York Astronomical Society

Secretary: Simon Howard, 20 Manor Drive South, Acomb, York.

Meetings: Goddricke College, York University. 1st and 3rd Fridays.

Any society wishing to be included in this list of local societies or to update details is invited to write to the Editor (c/o Macmillan, 25 Eccleston Place, London SW1W 9NF), so that the relevant information may be included in the next edition of the *Yearbook*.